JINGJIAO

JINGJIAO

The Earliest Christian Church in China

Glen L. Thompson

WILLIAM B. EERDMANS PUBLISHING COMPANY

GRAND RAPIDS, MICHIGAN

Wm. B. Eerdmans Publishing Co.
4035 Park East Court SE, Grand Rapids, Michigan 49546
www.eerdmans.com

Book design by Leah Luyk

Printed in the United States of America

30 29 28 27 26 25 24   1 2 3 4 5 6 7

ISBN 978-0-8028-8352-0

Library of Congress Cataloging-in-Publication Data

A catalog record for this book is available from the Library of Congress.

Contents

TABLES

Foreword

Ever since the discovery of the famous "Nestorian Monument" in Xi'an (the site of the ancient Chinese capital city of Chang'an) in 1623, the study of the early diffusion of Christianity in premodern China has been a source of controversy and of fascination. The discovery, made known to the West by Jesuit scholars, was seen by many as too convenient a find for Christian missionaries, then arriving in steady numbers from Europe. The authenticity of the monument (inscribed in AD 781), which gives a unique account of the arrival and diffusion of the "Luminous Religion" (*Jingjiao*) in China, immediately became the subject of a seemingly endless and often circular debate in Western scholarship.

The discovery early in the last century of authentic Jingjiao documents in Chinese, some showing clear traces of Syriac influence, has finally put an end to the debate on authenticity, and scholars are now in a position to study its contents along with the newly discovered documents. The discovery in 2006 of a second Jingjiao inscription (inscribed in AD 814) on a Buddhist-style pillar in Luoyang further adds to the number of authentic Christian documents from the Golden Age of the Silk Road found on Chinese soil.

Moreover, readers of the *Travels* of Marco Polo could have hardly failed to notice the frequent references to "Nestorian" Christians in the service of Kublai Khan in the fourteenth century. Indeed, new discoveries, both textual and archaeological, have added greatly to our knowledge of this second period of diffusion of Christianity in China.

The study of Jingjiao therefore has undergone a major advance in the second half of the last century. This means that earlier standard works on the subject in English by scholars like A. C. Moule and Yoshirō Saeki are now all completely out of date. The need to see Jingjiao as an extension of Central Asian Christianity is now overwhelming, and a new approach is therefore needed. Much of the recent advance in Jingjiao scholarship is published in learned journals and conference proceedings that are relatively inaccessible to undergraduate and theological college students. Fortunately, Dr. Glen Thompson, the author of this volume, has been an integral part of the advance in Jingjiao studies and is uniquely well qualified in the linguistic and historical skills needed for a serious study of Jingjiao. He also has the necessary training as a theologian and historian of mission to assess the relevance of Jingjiao to contemporary efforts to Sinicize Christianity, especially in relation to mainland China.

This well-written and well-researched volume by Dr. Thompson fills a major gap for students of theology, of Eastern church history, and of missiology. I strongly recommend this book to students in these disciplines as well as Christians worldwide who wish to be informed on the fascinating history of Christian mission in China before the age of European colonialism.

SAMUEL N. C. LIEU

Emeritus Professor Samuel N. C. Lieu, FBA, MAE, FRHistS, FSA, FHKAH (Hon.), FRSN, FAHA, is Honorary President International Union of Academies (President, 2017–2021) and Bye Fellow at Robinson College, Cambridge.

ACKNOWLEDGMENTS

It was during a teaching semester in Hong Kong in the fall of 2001 that I first became interested in the Jingjiao. Reports of Martin Palmer's "discovery" of a Tang-era Jingjiao pagoda/church at Louguantai first made me aware of the Jingjiao. His book, *The Jesus Sutras: Rediscovering the Lost Scrolls of Taoist Christianity* (Ballantine Books, 2001), only recently published at the time, was also my initial prod for investigating the Jingjiao story more fully. That fall I was able to travel to mainland China for the first time, see the famous stele in Xi'an, and visit the so-called Da Qin Pagoda at Louguantai.

Although I had learned some Syriac as a student, I knew no Chinese, so my study of the Jingjiao was limited to the studies of Western scholars. I soon heard about a conference on the subject that had been held at the University of Salzburg. Despite my late application, Prof. Peter Hofrichter allowed me to attend the second conference, and I have profited from participation in the five conferences since. The scholarly friendships I developed there have provided me with experts in all aspects of Jingjiao studies of whom I can ask advice and test ideas. I know of no field of study where such collaboration is more needed in order to ensure that one remains on the narrow path. The following pages are heavily indebted to their research.

I owe special thanks to Dr. Lei Shiwei, a specialist in the Northern and Southern Dynasties (one of the eras preceding the Tang period). Dr. Lei selflessly spent many hours reading the text of the stele and other documents with me and teaching me much about the Chinese mind and culture in the process. I have benefited much as well from my colleague on the faculty of Asia Lutheran Seminary, Cheung Kwok Fai, who is himself a budding scholar on the Jingjiao and who has helped me in many ways in the research, writing, and editing phases of the project. A great debt of gratitude is also owed to Starla Siegmann and Jenny Baker, the indefatigable librarians at Wisconsin Lutheran College who continued to locate rare and hard-to-access articles and books that I needed during my research on this project. Special thanks also to President Steve Witte of Asia Lutheran Seminary, who gave me constant encouragement to continue my research interests in this area. I also wish to thank Samuel N. C. Lieu, Matteo Nicolini-Zani, Mark Dickens, David Wilmshurst, and Yvonne Yeung, all of whom read part or all of the manuscript and made suggestions that improved its accuracy in various ways. I owe gratitude also for the careful reading and suggestions provided by editors Tom Raabe and Jenny Hoffman of Eerdmans and my research assistants, Austin Claflin, Robert Read, Josiah Winkel, and Christian Willick.

Finally, this book would never have been written without the generous support and encouragement of Jerry and Kay Fischer and the Fischer Family Foundation. Their financial support allowed me not only to continue but also to significantly increase my research despite my teaching and administrative responsibilities. Their friendship has been an added blessing! It is to them that I dedicate this work.

A Story That Needs Telling—
Correctly

This book tells the story of the first known Christian church movement in China. This church resulted from the work of missionaries from the Syriac tradition who entered China along the famous Silk Road.[1] During the Tang dynasty (618–907), this church referred to itself as the Jingjiao (景教), which can roughly be translated as the "Luminous Teaching." Their buildings were originally known in China as "Persian temples" (波斯寺), but an imperial decree of 745 required them to be called "Da Qin temples" (大秦寺). Da Qin was a designation used to describe the great empires even beyond Persia—that is, Rome, or Byzantium, depending on the time period. As a result, in the church's own surviving documents, the term "Jingjiao" is often preceded by "Da Qin." The new name—Da Qin Jingjiao—clearly indicated that this religion had its origins even farther west than Persia.

We can trace the history of the Jingjiao from its formal arrival in China in 635 until its official suppression by a decree of Emperor Wuzong in 845. Shortly after, a second flowering of the church began in the steppe areas of northwestern China; in the following centuries it spread widely under Mongol rule, peaking in China during the Yuan dynasty (1271–1368). During these later centuries, Chinese sources referred to the Christian church as the Yelikewenjiao (也里可温教). The meaning and significance of this name are still disputed. While our study will concentrate primarily on the Tang period, chapter 7 will give an overview of this later period.

---

1. The Silk Road may better be termed the "silk routes," since it was an interconnected network of roads that ran from the Middle East to China and India. We will use the traditional singular designation for the sake of convenience.

The story that we are about to tell is not well known. Even many with a strong interest in church history have heard little about this manifestation of Christianity. I was among that number until some twenty-five years ago when I was serving as a guest professor in Hong Kong and first heard about the Jingjiao. As I sought to learn more, I discovered that there were few recent books on the subject and that those that did exist in English were either incomplete, outdated, or written from a very slanted perspective.[2] As I delved deeper into the study of the Jingjiao and shared my growing knowledge in the classroom and at conferences, I always had to give a warning about the weaknesses of those existing accounts. This in turn led to friends and students urging me to provide such an account myself. The present volume seeks to do that. Here are some of the reasons that this story needs to be told—correctly.

The Complexities of Asian Mission Work

China holds a unique set of challenges for the spread of the gospel. Fourteen hundred years ago, when the first Jingjiao missionaries arrived, the Chinese could boast a culture whose central elements already went back unbroken for a millennium and a half. This cultural stability had created an ethnocentrism as deeply embedded as that of any other group in the world. At its center were cultural values and a system of writing in which already a large corpus of administrative documents and poetic, philosophical, and religious literature had been preserved. Infused with the indigenous precepts of Confucianism and Daoism, as well as scores of lesser-known schools of thought, Chinese culture considered itself self-sufficient if not yet perfectly developed.

At the heart of the Chinese worldview was also a strong hierarchical feeling that played itself out in strict family and clan structures. A strong central government was also expected; in some periods it took the form of a single power, in others of regional kings or warlords. The central governments were for the most part highly isolationist and often utterly xenophobic. They were expected to exert control over all aspects of daily life that affected the well-being of their people, including religion. This combination of a millennia-old cultural heritage, strong indigenous belief systems, and a strong central government made the successful propagation of nonindigenous religions particularly difficult. In this regard, the Christian Jingjiao, with its claims to be the "only right way," provides an especially

---

2. The best account in English, now almost a century old and therefore very dated, is still that of A. C. Moule, *Christians in China before the Year 1550* (London: SPCK, 1930).

interesting case study for mission historians and theorists. Since modern China maintains many of the same traits and values as it did in previous centuries, our story is of equal interest to those who wish to share the gospel in the Chinese world yet today, whether they themselves are ethnic Chinese or not.

Of particular interest to Christians is the inculturation of theology. As we shall see in the following chapters, the Jingjiao texts that survive make ample use of Confucian, Daoist, and Buddhist terminology and imagery. This fact has led to a variety of competing interpretations. Some have seen Jingjiao spirituality as an attempt to upgrade Christianity by melding it with the best concepts from the other Chinese religions. Others have seen it as an attempt at inculturation that went drastically wrong, leading eventually to the demise of the church in China. Still others have viewed it as a missionary approach that sought to clothe Christian concepts in terms meaningful to the indigenous population.

This leads to a further question: How indigenous did the Jingjiao become? In the margins of the great Xi'an stele text, erected a century and a half after the arrival of the missionaries (see chaps. 2–4), we find not only numerous lines of text in the Syriac language but also the names of dozens of priests and church leaders written in Chinese and Syriac. Did the church in China remain a church of immigrants and foreigners? Did it try and succeed in adding a substantial number of Chinese converts? Did its leadership, language, and message remain essentially "foreign"? Or did its teachings in fact meld with the other local religions?

A millennium later, Jesuit missionaries faced the same problem of indigenizing their mission work. While outwardly quite successful, their methodologies and strategies became highly controversial to rival religious orders within the Roman Catholic Church, and their approach still has many critics today. Others hold up the early Jesuit mission to China as a model of inculturation. The China Inland Mission took a different approach to inculturation in their dress, missionary methodology, and teaching. In our own time, the late bishop K. H. Ting, the longtime head of the governmentally sanctioned Protestant church in China, has called for a Christianity with more "Chinese characteristics." Even more recently, a special committee of the Chinese government issued the "Outline of the Five-Year Working Plan for Promoting the Sinicization of Christianity in Our Country (2018–2022)."[3] The story of the Jingjiao should be of interest to anyone concerned with these issues.

---

3. The lengthy document can be accessed in Chinese at http://www.ccctspm.org/cppcc info/10283. An unofficial English translation can be found at https://www.chinalawtranslate .com/en/outline-of-the-five-year-plan-for-promoting-the-sinification-of-christianity.

From its very beginning, the history of the Jingjiao is also a story of church-state relationships. Upon the arrival of its first official delegation, the church was given formal imperial approval to exist and preach within China. Emperors granted honorary titles to church leaders, asked them to perform rites in their behalf, and provided the church with imperial portraits and calligraphy to be displayed in their buildings. Eventually an imperial decree would outlaw the church. Many parallels have been drawn with Christianity's situation in modern-day China. A thorough study of the Jingjiao is needed to determine whether such parallels are valid and, if so, what can be learned from them.

Finally, the story of the Jingjiao provides one of the few opportunities for mission historians to study the outreach efforts and methodologies of the Church of the East, a church that "almost a millennium ago, extended over a greater part of the globe than did the Roman Church."[4] While the corpus of surviving documents is limited, it still exceeds the corpora of the other Syriac missions both along the Silk Road and in India. A correct telling of the story is also necessary because of lingering claims concerning still-earlier Syriac evangelization work in China—even by the apostle Thomas himself. The relationship between the two sequential Syriac churches in China—the Jingjiao of the Tang period and the Yelikewenjiao of the Song and Yuan dynasties—also deserves more scrutiny than it has received thus far.

Historians of missions might also profit by giving more consideration to the historical, political, and theological parallels between the Jingjiao efforts and the later Catholic and Protestant efforts. The contemporaries of Robert Morrison, the first Protestant missionary to China, and those of the later Hudson Taylor, founder of the China Inland Mission, were aware of the Jingjiao, if only vaguely and inaccurately. They and other missionaries at times adopted, adapted, and avoided strategies on the basis of their understanding of this early "failed" Chinese mission. While such studies are beyond the scope of the current work, a judicious and balanced reexamination of the story of the Jingjiao mission will provide a solid basis for future studies.

A Story for Chinese Christians Today

Finally, this book has been written also for Chinese Christians. In the past several decades contemporary Chinese Protestant Christians have become

4. Christoph Baumer, *The Church of the East: An Illustrated History of Assyrian Christianity*, new ed. (London: I. B. Tauris, 2016), 1.

increasingly aware of the early Syriac Chinese church, and many have taken a keen interest in it. Just knowing that Christianity did exist (legally!) in China almost fourteen hundred years ago has been encouraging to them. If Buddhism arrived about the same time and has been able to have such great influence on their culture, there is hope that Christianity can continue to spread and do the same.

The Jingjiao story is also important from an apologetic viewpoint. The historical record now makes it emphatically clear that Christianity did not first arrive in China with Western colonialists and opium sellers. Even though it literally came from the West, that is, down the Silk Road from Persia, it did not come as a "Western" or an "imperialist" religion. There was a time during China's Golden Age when a whole series of Tang emperors not only allowed Christianity's spread but also gave its leaders honors and its churches gifts. Its members were respected leaders in the government and highly successful generals in the army. Christian soldiers were even instrumental in helping to restore the emperor to his throne after being driven from the capital during the An Lushan rebellion. Many Chinese Christians wish to portray the same to their government and countrymen today: that Christians are good and productive citizens of China.

Today's Chinese Christians will also profit from struggling (along with scholars such as myself) to understand the attempts at inculturation by the Jingjiao. No thinking Christian denies the goal shared by missionaries to China across time and space—that the gospel message and its ritual life should be able to wear Chinese clothes and look and sound authentic to the Chinese mind. The area of disagreement is how this should be done, and to what extent. All human cultures must be "cleansed" by the blood of Christ, including Chinese culture, and so sinful practices and untrue beliefs must be changed as the Christian worldview is embraced. Yet Matteo Ricci, Hudson Taylor, Watchman Nee, and K. Y. Ting all disagreed on how that could best be accomplished and what the results would look like. A study of the Jingjiao can serve as another point of comparison for Chinese Christians as they continue to struggle to be faithful to their religious convictions while remaining loyal to their culture.

Some Chinese Christians have also sought to use the Jingjiao as a rallying point. They have sought to find in their early Jingjiao "roots" a common Christian identity for today's splintered church. While this may be a laudable goal, it faces some major challenges. Most Chinese Christians today do not feel that their greatest need is to define themselves culturally and religiously in opposition to Daoist, Buddhist, or even Confucianist ideals and teaching, as in the days of the Jingjiao. The competition today comes from worldviews that are permeated with capitalism and globalization, and with an increasingly generous addition of postmodernist tenets. Thus, the Jingjiao and its texts may not seem relevant to many of today's problems. On the other hand, the Syriac church has survived over the centuries, and its members both in the Middle East and in its diaspora might argue that point.

A second challenge comes in the realm of church life. The Jingjiao as a faithful branch of its mother Church of the East seems to have remained both highly liturgical and sacramental. Most forms of today's Chinese Protestant church are neither. Thus, a familiarization with the spiritual life of the Jingjiao may not be easy for today's worshipers. Here, however, is an area where significant changes might be discussed. Many of the current Protestant church practices are of rather recent development, and many do not, as sometimes is supposed, go back either to the early church or even to the period of the European Reformation. Rather, they reflect developments growing out of the Second Great Awakening in nineteenth-century America and the twentieth-century evangelical and Pentecostal movements. This discovery has in recent decades been made by various groups within the evangelical church in the West. As a result, some have intentionally returned to more "ancient" liturgical and sacramental observances in an effort to deepen their spiritual lives and broaden their sense of community in space and time, and in so doing reconnect with the ideals of the ancient church. Perhaps a study of the Jingjiao can be an encouragement to Chinese Christians to consider similar changes. Did a highly developed liturgical life and a serious sacramental theology and practice become part of the Jingjiao's "Chinese characteristics"? A thorough and accurate study of the Jingjiao will be of service in all such discussions.

Methodology and Procedures

Chapter 1 will begin our story by providing the historical background to the development of the Jingjiao's mother church. The development of Syriac-speaking Christianity in the Middle East, its relationship to the Greek church, its important doctrinal and practical developments, and its mission work will all be covered in preparation for studying its great mission along the Silk Road. The most famous and important artifact of the Jingjiao, the large stele found four hundred years ago in Chang'an (modern Xi'an), will serve as the centerpiece for chapters 2–3. Chapter 2 will detail the discovery of the stone, its contents, and the complexities involved in properly interpreting its message. Chapter 3 will then sketch the historical background of Tang China into which the Syriac church came, and then use the historical portions of the stele text to describe the first 150 years of the Jingjiao presence in China, from its initial entry in 635 until the stele text was composed and erected in 781.

Chapter 4 will move to a discussion of the other surviving Jingjiao documents—the Dunhuang texts and the newly discovered Luoyang pillar. Having discussed the main sources of our knowledge of the Jingjiao, chapter 5 will summarize the religious situation in China at the time of the Tang dynasty, then illustrate the new Christian teaching that was proclaimed in the Jingjiao documents. Chapter 6 will describe the organization and later history of the Jingjiao, its ongoing relationship with the mother church in Persia, and its eventual suppression. Chapter 7 will provide a brief overview of the Yelikewenjiao, the revival of Syriac Christianity under the late Song and Yuan dynasties. The epilogue will attempt to give a balanced account of what can and cannot be said about the Syriac churches in China, and their relevance for today. Appendix 1 provides the Chinese and Syriac texts of the Chang'an stele together with a new English translation.

I have sought to make the story of the Jingjiao relevant to those Chinese who can read in English. At the same time, I have attempted to make the narrative accessible to all interested readers, even those who have little background in Chinese history and culture. For the latter, it may help if I offer a few words of explanation about the Chinese language. Classical Chinese words most often consist of one or two characters. Other characters contain no translatable meaning but are instead used as grammatical or syntactical markers, or, in poetry, simply as fillers to preserve the rhythm and formal structure of the poem. Because some of the argumentation in this study is based on such characters, I will normally refer to *characters* (rather than *words*) when discussing usage in particular passages. In all important situations I will include the actual character, the official alphabetic transliteration (pinyin), and the English equivalent. The pinyin is provided for those readers who know no Chinese but would like to have an approximation of its pronunciation. Citations from Chinese sources are normally given in translation, with references to the original text (and English editions, where they exist) provided in the footnotes. Other footnotes provide explanatory comments or bibliographic references for those who wish to read further. When discussing Syriac words, they will be provided in transliteration.[5] Thus, the hope is that the general reader can enjoy the full story without consulting the footnotes, yet those who have a deeper

---

5. I have followed the transliteration system found in *The SBL Handbook of Style*, 2nd ed. (Atlanta: SBL Press, 2014), 62–63.

interest will be provided with the necessary tools for further study as well as the rationale or scholarly support for my arguments.

Except for a few well-known cities and people, the official Chinese pinyin system will be used for transliterating names from Chinese into English. The names of people will normally be given according to the Chinese custom, with the last, or family, name first (always one character), then the given name of one or two characters. Thus the family name of the Christian scholar Li Zhizao (李之藻), mentioned in chapter 2, is Li, and his given name is Zhizao. Also, Chinese emperors are best known today by the temple names they received after their deaths. For the convenience of our readers, we will use those names even when speaking of the emperor while he was still living. A few recent changes have been made to the pinyin system that may not be reflected in my usage. However, the modern pronunciation often is considerably different from that used at the time of the documents we will be studying. Therefore, scholars must use reconstructed pronunciations from the Tang period to help explain the way people at that time transliterated biblical names and the like.[6]

Finally, the Syriac-speaking church that brought the gospel to Tang-dynasty China, and the churches it founded, such as the Jingjiao, have traditionally been referred to as "Nestorian" by scholars and nonscholars alike. During the past quarter-century, however, there has been a growing scholarly consensus that such a label is misleading.[7] The Syriac-speaking church in question has traditionally called itself the Church of the East, and its daughter church in China was called the Jingjiao. I have tried wherever possible to limit myself to that usage. This issue will be discussed more fully in several chapters.

6. The accepted system is elaborated by Edwin Pulleyblank in his *Middle Chinese: A Study in Historical Phonology* (Vancouver: University of British Columbia Press, 1984).

7. The reasoning is expressed eloquently in the article by Sebastian P. Brock, "The 'Nestorian' Church: A Lamentable Misnomer," *Bulletin of the John Rylands Library* 78, no. 3 (Autumn 1996): 23–35. Reprinted with original pagination as chapter 1 in S. Brock, *Fire from Heaven: Studies in Syriac Theology and Liturgy*, Variorum Collected Studies Series (Aldershot, UK: Ashgate, 2006).

Chapter 1

THE SYRIAC CHURCH
AND ITS EASTWARD MISSION

During the nineteenth and twentieth centuries, Christianity truly became a global religion. Yet today, much of the world still views it as a "Western" religion, even though no one questions that its birthplace was the Middle East. In its earliest years, the Christian movement consisted mostly of Jews either inside Palestine or in the Jewish diaspora communities scattered around the Mediterranean and the Middle East. But in reality, the church was bicultural from the very beginning. When the Spirit descended on that first Pentecost day, all the church's holy texts and its theology were thoroughly "Eastern," products of the Semitic heritage of the Jewish people. Yet, from that day on, almost all the new texts it produced over the next two centuries were written in Greek, the foundational language and culture of "Western" civilization. The combination of these two, what is often called the Judeo-Christian tradition, created a monotheistic worldview and morality, even though in many respects the Middle Eastern heritage of the church was seemingly overwhelmed first by Greek, then by Latin, components.

Already by the end of the first century, the church had become increasingly "Hellenized"; that is, it took on the Greek language and addressed itself increasingly to Greco-Roman culture. With the destruction of Jerusalem and its population during the Jewish revolts in the years surrounding AD 70 and 135, the connection with the Holy Land was further reduced. By the fourth century, when in Palestine bishop Eusebius of Caesarea wrote the first surviving history of the church, it was for the most part a history of the church in the eastern or Greek-speaking half of the Roman Empire. Over the following centuries, the focus would shift westward, with the Greek heritage of the church being absorbed by the Latin-speaking church of western Europe. The Roman Catholic Church and the Protestant churches that came out of it during and after the Reformation remained the focus of most written histories of the church right up to our own time. Church history in most seminaries still consists overwhelmingly of a study of fifteen centuries of the European church followed by a history of the Protestant Reformation and the churches and missions that emanated from it. The term "Eastern church" usually refers to the Greek and other Orthodox churches of the eastern Mediterranean or eastern Europe.

The *Real* Eastern Church

Yet, although church history was increasingly viewed from a Western viewpoint, the church had actually spread eastward from Palestine just as rapidly and effectively as it had spread to the west. Here it was the Jewish heritage as much as the Greek that was preserved, at least in its language. As the gospel moved eastward out of the Roman Empire, it spread into new eastern realms in dialects that were very similar to the Aramaic spoken in first-century Palestine. One of the main dialects is known to us as Syriac. Although its script was different from that of Aramaic texts and its pronunciation varied from region to region, its vocabulary and grammar were essentially the same as that spoken by Jesus and his apostles.

While the Acts of the Apostles and the letters of Saint Paul give us an outline of Christianity's early spread to the west, we have no similar account for the east. Therefore, we cannot trace in detail how the gospel took root in the various areas of the Middle East. The Christian congregation in Syria's metropolis, Antioch on the Orontes, clearly played a leading role. That city had been founded to serve as the royal city for one of the Macedonian generals who succeeded Alexander the Great in the late fourth century BC. Soon it became the economic and cultural center for the northeastern corner of the Mediterranean. Several centuries later, it also became the early Christian center in the region. The Acts of the Apostles tells of the growing congregation there, one in which the Jews reached out to the Greek-speaking population and eventually sent off Paul and Barnabas on the so-called First Missionary Journey (Acts 13). It was also at Antioch where the followers of Jesus of Nazareth were first given the name "Christians" (Acts 11:26). This city would remain one of the chief cities of Greek Christendom until the Muslim conquests in the seventh century. But Antioch was also from its foundation a city that looked eastward as much as it did westward. It was from Antioch that the great trading caravans began their journey across the Syrian Desert to the great Mesopotamian rivers, the Tigris and Euphrates. The routes continued from there—some by sea via the

Gulf of Arabia to India, others overland—to the many emporia along the silk roads of Central Asia.

Although the details are no longer known, the mission zeal of the Antioch congregation had a great impact also in this easterly direction. In the centuries that followed, various stories circulated crediting the apostles Matthew, Thomas, and Thaddeus with evangelistic work in this area. Thaddeus, supposedly one of the seventy-two disciples sent on a brief mission trip by Jesus (Luke 10:1–24), came to be known as Addai in the Syriac church, which remembered him as the great apostle to eastern Syria and, in particular, to the city of Edessa.[1] It is just as likely that Christianity spread more organically through the witness of lay merchants and travelers, as was the case in so many other areas. We are specifically told that "Parthians, Medes and Elamites, and residents of Mesopotamia"[2] were among the Jews present for Peter's Pentecost sermon (Acts 2:9), and these converts likely formed the first wave of missionaries as they took the gospel home with them. In any case, by the end of the first century there were Christian groups in numerous Syrian and Mesopotamian cities, and most of these groups used dialects of Aramaic, like Syriac, as their main language of worship. By the end of the second century, Syriac translations of the New Testament Scriptures were being made and circulated, and hymns and liturgical compositions such as the Odes of Solomon were in use. Already in the mid-second century, a Christian from this area named Tatian compressed the four New Testament Gospels in Greek into one continuous narrative in Syriac. His *Diatessaron* (meaning "through the four") became a tool used throughout the Syriac-speaking church for centuries to come.

Saint Thomas in China?

Among Jesus's twelve apostles, Thomas has traditionally been connected with the spread of the Syriac-speaking church to even more distant lands. The Acts of Thomas, written about AD 200, portrays Jesus's apostles casting lots to determine on which region each was to focus his mission outreach. In this way Thomas was assigned India. The apostle still showed his "doubting" character, however, as the text records that it was only with reluctance that he finally

---

1. See Eusebius, *Church History* 1.13, where the apostle Thomas is said to have sent Thaddeus/Addai to Edessa to heal and convert its king, Abgar. Eusebius writes that the documents that he adduces to support the story were translated from Syriac.

2. Biblical translations in the book are the author's.

left and successfully planted churches on the subcontinent. Writing about the same time, Clement of Alexandria seems to disagree, recording that Thomas's main work was in Parthia, a view confirmed shortly afterward by Origen. Yet the Syriac-speaking church, as seen in works such as the third-century *Didascalia Apostolorum* and several fourth-century hymns of Ephrem of Nisibis, became firm in its conviction that Thomas was the great apostle to India. Today's Mar Thoma Church in India still reiterates that claim. It is clear from a variety of evidence that the Syriac-speaking church did evangelize on the subcontinent and did plant a church body in the Malabar region, where it has remained until this day. Yet scholars remain divided on the question of dating it to the first-century work of Thomas.[3]

Recent publications and Internet articles have asserted that Thomas not only evangelized in India but also traveled farther to ancient China. These claims cite a prayer found in a Syro-Malabar liturgy that remembers Thomas, by whose work "the Chinese and the Ethiopians were converted to the truth." During the past several centuries, a few Christian authors have picked up on this notice and made it part of their arguments for an early Christian presence in China. The two most recent proponents of Thomas visiting India are a Chinese seminary professor, Wang Weifan, and a Catholic layman from France, Pierre Perrier. The latter has gone so far as to give a precise chronology of Thomas's visits to India and China. According to him, Thomas went first to Nineveh and Parthia (AD 42–48) before going to the Indus Valley (49–51); then he evangelized along the Malabar coast (52–54), the Ganges and Indonesia (54), and returned to Malabar (55–58), settling in the southwestern city of Meilapouram (62–64). From there he sailed to China in 64, traveling up the Yellow River from Lianyungang via Xuzhou and Kaifeng to Luoyang, where he founded a church in 68. After returning to India via Japan, he was martyred there in 72.[4]

In reality, we have no evidence whatsoever for such claims. The above-mentioned authors base their theory on the following evidence: (1) rock carv-

---

3. On the early stories about Thomas's ministry, see the chapter on Thomas in W. Brian Shelton, *Quest for the Historical Apostles: Tracing Their Lives and Legacies* (Grand Rapids: Baker Books, 2018), esp. 178–83. The conviction that the current Mar Thoma Church was founded by Thomas is evident from the recent book of essays by scholars from that church. K. S. Mathew, J. C. Chennattuserry, and A. Bungalowparambil, eds., *St. Thomas and India: Recent Researches* (Minneapolis: Fortress, 2020).

4. See Pierre Perrier and Xavier Walter, *Thomas Fonde l'Église en Chine (65–68 Ap J.-C.)* (Paris: Jubilé, 2008). Wang Weifan's claims were picked up by Ted Olson in *Christianity Today*'s blog: https://www.christianitytoday.com/ct/2002/october7/19.14.html.

ings on Kongwangshan in Lianyungang, which they date to the first century and interpret as images of Thomas, the Virgin Mary, and the Chi-Rho symbol; (2) Han-dynasty tomb carvings in Xuzhou that purportedly show biblical stories as well as a Passover lamb and the Christian fish symbol; (3) a claim that the medieval Jewish community in Kaifeng actually goes back to the New Testament era; and (4) a reinterpretation of the history and foundation legends surrounding the White Horse Monastery in Luoyang (an early Buddhist structure) to indicate that it was originally a Christian church established by Thomas.

When these claims are examined more closely, they are seen to have no basis in fact but are rather the product of wishful thinking. The Lianyungang carvings might have been made in the first century, but there is nothing to indicate that they are anything other than Chinese figures, and there is no sign anywhere of a Chi-Rho—a Greek abbreviation that would have been meaningless to Syriac-speakers and therefore was never used in the Syriac church! The Han-era tombs of Xuzhou have typical Chinese decorations of the period with nothing to indicate Christian influence. The once substantial Jewish community in Kaifeng has now all but disappeared, but the steles, manuscripts, and oral traditions it has left behind all point to the tenth or eleventh century AD as the date of the community's founding. And, finally, there is no evidence that the White Horse Monastery in Luoyang was ever anything other than a Buddhist temple.[5] The truth is that we have no evidence of a Christian mission to China in the earliest centuries.

Trade had existed between China and the West since Roman times. Hellenistic Greek sailors first discovered how to use the monsoon winds to sail to India, but not until centuries after the Arabs and Indians had mastered their use. About the time of Christ's birth, Roman ships began more regular trips down the African coast or along the coast of Arabia and as far as the west coast of India. There they took on loads of exotic animals, spices, and other luxury goods—including Chinese silk. Recent studies have indicated that even high-quality Chinese steel was increasingly valued in the West during the early imperial period of Rome. Yet this maritime version of the Silk Road was one of segmented trade. Romans and Arabs traded as far as India; Indians or Malaysians took the goods from there inland, or farther across the Bay of Bengal

---

5. See Glen L. Thompson, "Did Christianity (or St. Thomas) Come to First-Century China?" in *Byzantium to China: Religion, History, and Culture on the Silk Roads; Studies in Honour of Samuel N. C. Lieu*, ed. K. Parry and G. Mikkelsen, Texts and Studies in Eastern Christianity (Leiden: Brill, 2022), 519–45.

to Malaysia; Malay or Chinese traders then took the products still farther to the ports along the South China Sea, and then inland. The overland route was just as compartmentalized and segmented. Chinese goods were passed on to Kushans (in modern Afghanistan and its surrounding areas), who sold them to Parthians and Arabs, who in turn passed them on to merchants from the Roman Empire. How many such exchanges took place on a given route varied considerably, but the one constant was that there were, as far as we know, virtually no traders who went from one end to the other.[6]

We must rid ourselves of the later stereotypes of the long-distance commercial trips of Marco Polo and of the long missionary voyages of Hudson Taylor and David Livingstone. What is more likely is that early Christians spread the gospel more slowly from region to region. Individual Christians may have penetrated China from time to time, but there is no evidence of a Christian church sprouting there in the first five centuries AD, nor is there evidence that Christians from India played a role. Rather, Christianity's entrance into China was an extension of the larger picture of Christianity's slow permeation of Mesopotamia and Persia via the areas along the Silk Road.

The Mesopotamian Church Develops

During the second century, two cities in particular became Christian centers in Mesopotamia. Edessa, located 175 miles northeast of Antioch at the junction of two trade routes, was capital of the kingdom of Osroene, sandwiched between the Roman and Parthian Empires. A series of Nabatean kings, many called by the dynastic name of Abgar, ruled for several centuries before and after Christ, usually owing fealty to one of their two giant neighbors. A Christian community was thriving in Osroene by the early third century, and the king himself may have been a convert to the faith.

Five hundred miles to the east was the city of Arbela (modern Erbil in Iraq), capital of the kingdom of Adiabene. This area lay more firmly within the Parthian sphere of influence. About the same time that Saint Paul was becoming a Christian on the road to Damascus, Adiabene's royal family was converting

---

6. The case is laid out in detail in Thompson, "Did Christianity (or St. Thomas) Come to First-Century China?" On Greco-Roman trade with India, see most recently David Graf, "The Silk Road between Syria and China," in *Trade, Commerce, and the State in the Roman World*, ed. Andrew Wilson and Alan Bowman (Oxford: Oxford University Press, 2018), 443–530.

to Judaism, and this indirectly prepared the way for Christian evangelism there. During the second century, Arbela became a second center of Syriac-speaking Christianity. The city of Nisibis, midway between Edessa and Arbela, would in the third and fourth centuries become a third center of the church in northern Mesopotamia.

From cities such as these the gospel spread throughout Mesopotamia in the second and third centuries. During this entire period the new believers experienced very little persecution. Only for brief periods, usually when an area came under control of the Romans, did organized persecution take place. But in the vast areas controlled by the Parthians, the church benefited from the regime's attitude of toleration toward the many religions in its realm.[7]

A drastic change took place, however, when the Parthians, rulers of Mesopotamia and Persia for half a millennium (227 BC–AD 224), were overthrown by the Sasanian military machine. Although the capital remained at Seleucia-Ctesiphon in central Mesopotamia, the new dynasty originated from a different Iranian tribe. Their rule would last until it was overwhelmed by Islamic armies in the mid-seventh century. The Sasanid kings worked to restore the ancient dualistic Persian religion of Zoroastrianism to prominence, purity, and unity. Their priests (known in the West as magi) worshiped Ahura Mazda in his fire temples, and they became key players in state policy decisions. Eventually the Zoroastrian high priest became second only to the king in power, and the Sasanian kingdom became a semitheocracy.

In the mid-third century, a second development further complicated the religious picture in Persia. A charismatic ascetic preacher named Mani appeared there and openly attacked the current practices of traditional Persian religions, including those of Zoroaster. Mani called on the people to follow his new teaching, which melded his own insights with terminology and teachings from a multitude of religions, including Christianity.[8] Mani's radical ideas led to his imprisonment, torture, and death, followed by a crackdown on his adherents. Christians were at first merely caught in the crossfire of this battle between the traditionalist Zoroastrian government and the Manichaeans (Mani's fol-

---

7. For the complicated debates surrounding the nature of early Syrian Christianity, see Paul McKechnie, "How Far Is It from Antioch to Edessa?" in *Aspects of the Roman East*, vol. 2, *Papers in Honour of Professor Sir Fergus Millar FBA*, ed. Samuel N. C. Lieu and Paul McKechnie (Turnhout: Brepols, 2015), 192–211.

8. On the development and early history of Manichaeism, see the early chapters in Samuel N. C. Lieu, *Manichaeism in the Later Roman Empire and Medieval China: A Historical Survey*, 2nd ed., Wissenschaftliche Untersuchungen zum Neuen Testament 63 (Tübingen: Mohr Siebeck, 1992). Lieu argues that Manichaeism began as a Christian sect.

lowers). Yet by the fourth century, the growing Christian community became itself a target of the magi and their government backers. This was intensified by the ongoing conflicts between the Sasanian Empire and the eastern Roman or Byzantine Empire. Once Christianity became a religion favored by Roman emperors in the fourth century, the Sasanians began viewing the Christians inside their own territory as possible fifth columnists. While organized opposition was still sporadic, hundreds of martyrdoms did occur, especially during the reigns of Shapur II (AD 309–379) and Yazdegerd II (438–457).

In the meantime, however, Christianity had continued to spread and flourish in the East. The later third and early fourth centuries saw two important developments within Syriac Christianity. One was the gradual formalization of church organization under the local bishops. The idea of one bishop overseeing the Christians of a city or rural district had established itself quite widely in the eastern Mediterranean Greek-speaking church in the second century. The surviving letters of Ignatius of Antioch (d. ca. AD 116) show this development already in the early decades of that century. However, the Syriac-speaking churches were much slower to adopt this type of monarchic bishopric. This did happen, however, in the third century, although it is only in the early fourth century that our surviving sources first begin naming bishops, such as Bishop Qona of Edessa and Jacob of Nisibis. Similarly, the use of church synods or councils—gatherings of bishops and church leaders to discuss common issues of doctrine and practice—started much later in Mesopotamia than in the Greco-Roman church. The first one mentioned in the Syriac sources was held in 314–315 in Seleucia-Ctesiphon. The reasons behind this seeming lack of interest in wider church cooperation and organization are hard to determine, but they may well have included cultural issues (the more clan-oriented attitudes of Semitic patterns of authority and decision making) and environmental factors (the possibility of a more organized church being viewed by the government as a politically dangerous entity).[9]

The second important development in the early Syriac church was the growth of asceticism. While the early monastic impulse in the church is often thought of as an Egyptian development, by the late second century Christian hermits were already to be found in Syria and, soon after, in Persia as well. These men were not only known for their austere lives of prayer and self-denial but were also important players in the church's spread. Referred to

9. McKechnie notes that at the AD 325 Council of Nicaea, there were five bishops from Syria Phoenice, twenty-three from Syria, and nine from Mesopotamia ("How Far Is It?," 193). These men would have traveled some 450–900 miles to attend.

by the fourth century as "sons and daughters of the covenant," they became respected fixtures in the life of the Syriac church and often played roles in the controversies that arose over proper Christian life and doctrine. Even more than in the Greek and Latin churches, monks did not remain isolated from mainstream church affairs but could play instrumental roles in the structure and hierarchy of the wider Syriac-speaking church. Two figures from the early fourth century serve as examples. Jacob of Nisibis not only was famous for his strict devotion to the ascetic life but also was a representative of the Syriac church at the Council of Nicaea in 325. Slightly later, the learned Persian monk Aphrahat lived some type of monastic life. Twenty-three of his sermon-like *Demonstrationes* have survived, and he may even have served as a local bishop. He was an early example of the overlap of the monastic calling with service to and engagement in the larger church, a trend that would become common-place in the Syriac tradition.[10]

Independence and Controversy

The fifth century saw additional momentous changes in the church of Mesopo-tamia and Persia. The periodic wars between the Sasanian and Byzantine em-perors continued to bring with them bouts of persecution, but the growth of the church continued unabated. Early in the century we hear of several church councils in Seleucia that firmed up the organization of the eastern church as a separate entity. The synod of AD 410 brought together forty bishops from across Mesopotamia. The council unanimously elected Bishop Isaac of Se-leucia not only to chair the meeting but also to continue to head the church after its conclusion. From that point forward, whoever was elected bishop of Seleucia-Ctesiphon was considered the "catholicos and chief bishop of the east." The head bishop oversaw the church in both the city of Ctesiphon, the old Persian city on the east bank of the Tigris River, and the Hellenistic city of Seleucia across from it on the west bank of the river.

The council selected five other bishops as metropolitans with administra-tive authority over their respective geographical areas (called provinces). They

---

10. The best short studies of this development of the Church of the East are the first chap-ter of Wilhelm Baum and Dietmar W. Winkler, *The Church of the East: A Concise History* (London: Routledge Curzon, 2003), 7–41, and chap. 1 of David Wilmshurst, *The Martyred Church: A History of the Church of the East* (London: East & West Publishing, 2011), 1–50. On Aphrahat, see Wilmshurst, 46–47.

served in much the same capacity as archbishops in the Latin church. The Syriac leaders further showed their solidarity with the Greco-Roman "catholic" church by confirming adherence to the decisions or canons of the Council of Nicaea and to the teachings of its creed. On the other hand, it is clear from the accounts of this council and the two synods that followed in the next fourteen years that the Persian church, while still respectful of its western brothers, increasingly saw itself as independent in all matters of administration. Appeals to the bishop of Antioch or other Western bishops were prohibited. The Church of the East, the name by which it came to refer to itself, wished to stand on its own. The proceedings of these early councils may have been circulated and preserved, at least in part, to reassure the Sasanian government that it was not dependent on, nor owed any allegiance to, anyone in the Byzantine Empire.[11]

While the fifth century was a period of unification within the Persian church, the western Roman Empire was disintegrating politically under constant pressure from barbarian tribes, and the church of the eastern Roman Empire was experiencing major fragmentation. The latter was caused by different hermeneutical and doctrinal emphases, exacerbated by rivalries over honor and prestige among the top church leaders. The bishop or patriarch of Constantinople, the "New Rome," was becoming increasingly arrogant in his attitude toward the other, more ancient Christian centers of the East, Antioch and Alexandria in particular. At the same time, these latter two cities were becoming increasingly confrontational toward each other in their approaches to interpreting the Bible. Antiochene scholars practiced a more literal approach to Scripture, as seen in the extensive commentaries of its master exegetes, Diodore of Tarsus (d. 392) and Theodore of Mopsuestia (d. 428). The Alexandrian leaders in Egypt, on the other hand, had since the days of Origen (d. 254) given more stress to spiritual and allegorical methods of interpretation. In the first half of the fifth century, these differences in approach came to a head in the debate over the most proper way to describe the relationship between the two natures of Christ. The Antiochenes thought Christ's natures were more loosely connected and stressed his humanity; the Egyptians emphasized the absolute unity of the natures and the divinity of Christ.

The end result was a three-way split in the eastern church. Nestorius, the bishop of Constantinople who led a mostly Syrian faction, was said to teach that Christ had two separate natures, so at the Council of Ephesus in 431 he was excommunicated together with his followers (the Dyophysites, more com-

---

11. On the development of the Church of the East's administration and structure, see Wilmshurst, *The Martyred Church*, 32–40.

monly referred to in the West as "Nestorians"). Soon after, major sections of the Egyptian (Coptic) and Syrian churches who seemed to support a single nature in Christ (the Monophysites, or, more accurately, Miaphysites) were excommunicated by the remainder of the Byzantine church at the Council of Chalcedon in 451.[12] Although there would be some continuing debates, the remainder of the Greek-speaking church, together with the Latin-speaking western church, developed a centrist position that held that Christ's two natures were united, but without a confusion of the two. Christ was both true God and true man, and these natures were united intimately in what came to be called the *hypostatic union*. This essentially mystical (that is, irrational and unexplainable) position is still held by Eastern Orthodox, Roman Catholics, and Protestants.

The intense vitriolic and political infighting that marred these theological disputes splintered the Middle Eastern church, and it remains shattered yet today. The Miaphysite groups eventually continued to function as two regional church bodies—the Coptic church of Egypt (and Ethiopia) and the Miaphysite church of Syria (later called Jacobite, and today's Syrian/Syriac Orthodox). The Byzantine emperors tried to suppress both Miaphysite and Nestorian teachings, so many of their leaders and adherents fled eastward across the border into Sasanid territory.

The Persian church seemed untouched by this doctrinal controversy for some time, but this could not last. In 486, a Persian synod rejected both the Miaphysite position and the Byzantine position as it had been spelled out at the Council of Chalcedon in 451. This reaction came when Theodore of Mopsuestia, Theodoret of Cyrrhus, and Ibas of Edessa, men whom the Persian church embraced as orthodox, were increasingly vilified as heretics by the Latin and Greek bishops. Edessa and its important theological training school also became strongly Dyophysite in the mid-fifth century. Although by this period it was firmly on the Roman side of the border, it had continued to train large numbers of clergy for the church in Persia. However, because it was rumored to be a hotbed of "Nestorianism," the Greek emperor Zeno ordered the school of Edessa closed in 489. Students and faculty were encouraged by leaders of the Persian church to reopen the school across the border in Nisibis, and there it did in fact become a center of Dyophysite teaching.[13]

---

12. The 431 and 451 councils are commonly numbered today as the Third and Fourth Ecumenical Councils. On Miaphysite as a more accurate term, see S. Brock, "Miaphysite, Not Monophysite!" *Cristianesimo nella storia* 37 (2016): 45–52.

13. For a vivid description of student life at the school, see Wilmshurst, *The Martyred Church*, 58–59.

Despite these controversies, the Mesopotamian church sought to maintain its own middle path, declaring its theological independence while still seeing itself as united with other parts of the church that held to its position. When Persian church leaders would visit Antioch or Constantinople in the coming centuries, they regularly communed with the Byzantine church. While the Persian church remembered Nestorius with honor for his courageous stand and heroic exile, it was not the more radical Christology attributed to Nestorius that was taught but instead the more traditional Dyophysite theology of Theodore that had predated the entire controversy. The Byzantine and Latin churches, however, did not see this distinction, and so the Persian Church of the East was soon referred to regularly by the western churches as the "Nestorian church."[14]

Solidification and Expansion

During the fifth and sixth centuries, the Church of the East led an uneasy existence. Although outright persecution took place only periodically, the church still lived under constant threat. Its outreach was also constantly under attack, for a Persian could be executed for converting from Zoroastrianism to Christianity. The patriarch, or catholicos, of the church, based in the capital of Seleucia-Ctesiphon, sought to keep on good terms with the Sasanian ruler and often could only be appointed with his approval. Besides these outside threats, there were periodic power struggles within the Persian church, usually created by weak or sycophantic patriarchs, or by ongoing tensions between factions within the church. Sometimes this took the form of disputes between monastic leaders and other church leaders. At other times it was caused by continuing friction between the two major Syriac-speaking churches, which were both found throughout Mesopotamia—the Dyophysite Church of the East and the Miaphysite "Jacobite" church. In the previous century, after one of the wars against Byzantium, Shapur II had transplanted thousands of captured Greek Christians to central Persia. This group continued to worship in their own Greek traditions, and for several centuries this complicated the picture even further and served as yet another source of tension in some areas.

14. For a good summary of the Church of the East's theological position, see Sebastian Brock, "The Christology of the Church of the East," in *Traditions and Heritage of the Christian East*, ed. D. Afinogenov and A. Muraviev (Moscow: Izdatelstvo "Indrik," 1966), 159–79. Reprinted with original pagination as chap. 3 in Brock, *Fire from Heaven: Studies in Syriac Theology and Liturgy*, Variorum Collected Studies Series (Aldershot, UK: Ashgate, 2006).

Despite these problems, Christianity continued to deepen its roots and spread into new areas of the East. The heartland of the Persian church remained Mesopotamia, and especially the more northerly area of modern Iraq and eastern Syria. But the church also continued to spread into the surrounding regions of Arabia and what is now Iran and Afghanistan. By the end of the fourth century, Christian churches and monasteries existed on both the eastern and western coasts of the Arabian Peninsula and on several islands in the Persian Gulf. While these were planted in a variety of ways and consisted of Christians of various traditions, most Arab Christians became part of the Church of the East.

In many regions of what is now Iran, Christians remained a small minority, but the gospel found more fertile soil in Elam (the northern and eastern coasts of the Persian Gulf) and the province of Fars immediately to its east, as well as in the areas along the southern coast of the Caspian Sea. Fars was one of the areas where Greek captives had been settled, and this may have been the impetus for the spread in that region. But this area was also part of the Zoroastrian heartland, and that served as an ongoing obstacle to mission work. While it is hard to gauge from our limited source material the overall spread within the Sasanian realm, the records of synods give us some assistance.

As mentioned earlier, the synod of 410 was attended by forty bishops, five of whom had been designated as metropolitans under the oversight of the patriarch of Seleucia. The placement of these metropolitans indicates the areas of Christian density within Mesopotamia—Nisibis and Erbil in the north, Kirkuk and Seleucia-Ctesiphon in the center, and Beth Lapat (Gundeshapur) and Basra in the south near the Persian Gulf (see map 1). The synodal records also mention attendance by representatives from "distant lands," including bishops from Fars, the islands of the Persian Gulf, Beth Madaye (Hamadan) in central Iran, Beth Riqaye (Rai), and from the lands of Abrasahar (Nishapur in northeastern Persia). They also resolved to establish new bishoprics in other distant areas.[15] Just ten years later, the synod of 420 included bishops from Armenia and Azerbaijan, and in 424 bishops attended from the eastern coast of the Persian Gulf at Rev Ardashir, as well as from Isfahan and Merv at the northeast extremity of Persia (in modern Turkmenistan). By the mid-sixth century, the bishops of Merv and Rev Ardashir had been elevated to metro-

---

15. See M. J. Birnie's English translation of the surviving record from the synod of 410 at "The Council of Mar 'Ishaq (AD 410)," accessed April 4, 2023, https://www.fourthcentury .com/the-council-of-mar-ishaq-ad-410/. On the identification of the bishoprics, see Wilmshurst, *The Martyred Church*, 34–40.

politans. And by the time of the Arab conquest in the mid-seventh century, the Church of the East could boast of having nine metropolitans overseeing at least ninety-six other bishops.[16]

Christianity along the Silk Road

To the east and northeast of the Persian heartland, nomadic peoples and urban centers stretched across the land north of the Hindu Kush Mountains, the countries today called Turkmenistan, Afghanistan, Uzbekistan, Tajikistan, Kyrgyzstan, and Kazakhstan, as far as the western reaches of China. It was across this often bleak and hostile terrain that the camel caravans carried their precious cargo of silk from east to west and other commodities in the opposite direction. In antiquity, the political and military control of this area was often as complicated as it is today, with many smaller peoples and tribes seeking control over parts of the area and its trade. Church of the East bishops had existed in the cities of Nishapur, Merv, and Herat already by 424 (see map 2).

Northeast of Merv (near modern-day Mary in Turkmenistan), the main artery of the Silk Road split. One road headed southeast along the Oxus River before veering off through Balkh and then crossing the western Hindu Kush to Kabul and on to Taxila in the Punjab area of the subcontinent; the other ran northeast across the mountains through Bukhara and Samarkand to Kashgar (today in the westernmost Chinese province of Xinjiang). Between the two routes was a circular plain known in antiquity as Bactria. It lies like an inlet jutting into the area south of the Pamir Mountains and north of the Hindu Kush. After being conquered by Alexander the Great, it became the center of a Hellenistic kingdom for several centuries. It was then under the control of the Kushan Empire until the Sasanians made the area into one of their vassal states. For centuries the Bactrian merchants of this area played an important role in trade between China, India, and the West.

In the fifth century, a federation of steppe tribes known as the Hephthalites or White Huns descended upon Persia, taking over Bactria and parts of Persia and northwest India until the mid-sixth century. Between 450 and 550, there were frequent contacts and struggles between the Hephthalites and the Sasanians. As part of this process, there was an influx of Christians into the area—soldiers, traders, and "Nestorian" priests, many of whom shared their

---

16. On these early bishoprics and metropolitans, see Erica C. D. Hunter, "The Church of the East in Central Asia," *Bulletin of the John Rylands Library* 78, no. 3 (1996): 133–34.

faith. About 550, a Hephthalite Christian priest was sent by the Hephthalite king to Khosrow I asking that Patriarch Mar Aba I ordain him and send him back to be bishop for the Hephthalites. A bishop of the Hephthalites was in attendance at the Church of the East synod in Mesopotamia in 585.[17]

The more northerly arm of the Silk Road ran from Merv north to the Pamir Mountains, crossed the Oxus River to Bukhara, and then continued on to Samarkand. This area, bounded by the Caspian Sea to the west and the Aral Sea to the northwest, was the home of the Sogdian peoples. Once controlled by Persia, its inhabitants were principally of Iranian descent. While this area also fell under Hephthalite control in the fifth and sixth centuries, Sogdian merchants continued to dominate the Silk Road trading economy. Porcelain statuettes of these Sogdian traders became commonplace in Tang China, their large beards, prominent noses, and bulging eyes clearly distinct from sculptural depictions of the local Chinese. The Sogdian language became the *lingua franca* of the silk routes in this period. The northwestern quadrant of the area, known as Khwarazm, was normally part of the Sasanid realm. Christianity seems to have been a bit slower to spread to this area, the first evidence being grave objects decorated with crosses from the late seventh century and a few late seventh- and early eighth-century coins depicting rulers of Khwarazm with crosses on their crowns. By that time the Sogdian language was being written in a script based on Aramaic.

The heart of Sogdiana, however, was the area of Samarkand (in modern Uzbekistan). When UNESCO (United Nations Educational, Scientific, and Cultural Organization) declared Samarkand a World Heritage Site in 2001, they called it the "crossroads of culture," a name that would have fit the city at almost any period of its 2,700-year history. Although we have few details, Samarkand also became a regional center for the Church of the East, and the city seems to have become the seat of a metropolitan bishop by the late sixth century.[18]

The faith spread farther eastward from Samarkand across the Jaxartes River to Tashkent (the capital of modern Uzbekistan), and on to Kashgar and its oases, today the most westerly city in China (2,500 miles west of Beijing!). Just to the west of Kashgar, the northern "highway" that came across the mountains from Bactria was rejoined by the mountain road from Balkh. At Kashgar the

17. See Mark Dickens, "Syriac Christianity in Central Asia," in *The Syriac World*, ed. Daniel King (London: Routledge, 2019), 583–624, esp. 585.

18. For details, see Dickens, "Syriac Christianity in Central Asia," 583–624; also Wilmshurst, *The Martyred Church*, 118–21.

road to the east again split, one fork going north and the other south, both following the edges of the Taklamakan Desert (a part of the larger Tarim Basin). These areas were part of the Göktürk or Blue Turk (突厥) Empire until it fell in the seventh century. Because of its position along the Silk Road, it is probable that Christianity was present in the region of Kashgar already in the sixth century, but archaeological evidence for this comes only from a later period. After the creation of the new Sui Empire in China (582–618) and the Tang dynasty that followed it (618–907), China increasingly supported Turkic tribes such as the Tiele (ancestors of the Uyghur people) against their Turkic rivals. Chinese sources document the frequent diplomatic and military contacts that connected these Turkish peoples with the Byzantines and the Chinese during the late sixth and seventh centuries. They also describe the resettlement in Chinese territory of tens of thousands of captured Turks.

Two incidents that found their way into ancient sources remind us that we lack detailed knowledge of the spread of Christianity into this region. The first took place in 591 and was recorded by the Byzantine historian Theophylact Simocatta, writing about 630. A Sasanid general named Bahram had usurped the throne and forced Emperor Khosrow II to seek help from his foe, Byzantium. With the latter's aid, Khosrow defeated Bahram and regained his throne. According to Theophylact, Byzantine advisors were present at the victory and noticed something strange about some of Bahram's captured soldiers—they had crosses tattooed on their foreheads. It turned out that these men were Turkic soldiers who had joined Bahram after the defeat of their own army. When questioned, the soldiers explained that they had been tattooed by their mothers to protect them during an epidemic, in imitation of local Christian mothers who had used this technique to protect their own babies.[19]

The second incident dates to about 644 and is contained in the *Khuzistan Chronicle*, written in Syriac about 670 and edited by Ignatius Guidi as the *Chronicon Anonymum*.[20] It involves Elias (or Eliya), the metropolitan of Merv (d. ca. 660), and an unspecified Turkic king. During a chance meeting near Merv, the bishop pleaded with the king not to lead his army to further war. Elias then won a power encounter with the local heathen priests by calming a demon-induced storm by making the sign of the cross. As a result the king

19. For an English translation of this passage, see Michael Whitby and Mary Whitby, *The History of Theophylact Simocatta* (Oxford: Clarendon, 1986), 146–47.

20. Pierre Nautin argues that the Chronicle was authored by Elias of Merv himself, and the story of his conversion of the Turkic king was added later as an appendix. See his "L'Auteur de la 'Chronique Anonyme de Guidi': Élie de Merew," *Revue de l'histoire des religions* 199, no. 3 (1982): 303–14.

and his army were baptized before Elias returned home.[21] These almost randomly preserved incidents remind us of how little we actually know about the extent of Christianity's spread in Central Asia, and that our lack of knowledge should not be equated with the lack of a Christian presence in these areas. In 651 Patriarch Isho'yahb III could write of "more than twenty bishops and two metropolitans in the East."[22]

Seismic Changes

The Syriac Church of the East went through a series of peaks and valleys in the late sixth and early seventh centuries. In the mid-sixth century, word came that the Western council held at Constantinople in 553 (known in the West as the Fifth Ecumenical Council) had posthumously condemned the long-dead Theodore of Mopsuestia and his writings, the most respected theologian and exegete of the Church of the East. This embittered many Persian Christians and soured relations with the Greek church for centuries to come. In addition, by 600, the great theological School of Nisibis, the source of training for so many church leaders, waned in size and importance. Following the discrediting of its leader, many students and faculty packed their bags and went elsewhere, leaving a psychological and educational void in the church.[23] To make matters even worse, during parts of the long reign of Khosrow I (d. 579), in many respects a good and fair monarch, the patriarch of the Church of the East (a convert from Zoroastrianism) was imprisoned. The quality of succeeding patriarchs was inadequate for the challenges of the period. This was topped off with a twenty-year vacancy (608–628), during which the Sasanian ruler refused to allow the election of a new patriarch. This deprived the Christian community of its most important voice not just spiritually but politically. According to Sasanid law, the Christians were a recognized minority community, and the patriarch was to function as their legal spokesperson and advocate.[24]

---

21. A translation of the passage is found on 305–6 of Alphonse Mingana, "The Early Spread of Christianity in Central Asia and the Far East: A New Document," *Bulletin of the John Rylands Library* 9, no. 2 (1925): 297–371. Guidi's Latin translation of the story can be found in *Chronica Minora: Chronicon anonymum de ultimis regibus Persarum*, Corpus Scriptorum Christanorum Orientalium 2, Scriptores Syri 2 (Paris: Typographeo Reipublicae, 1903), 28–29.

22. Cited by Dickens, *Syriac Christianity in Central Asia*, 587.

23. See the description in Wilmshurst, *The Martyred Church*, 61.

24. Some have used the word *melet* or *millet* to describe these minority communities, but that is an anachronistic use of Ottoman terminology.

The late sixth century also saw increased competition from the Miaphysite Christians in Persia. During that century, the able Miaphysite priest Jacob Baradaeus (d. 578) not only preached but organized and spread his Miaphysite Christology with great success throughout Mesopotamia. About 558 the Miaphysites were able to appoint their own metropolitan in Tekrit, a sign of their strength and standing. Jacob's name would literally live on, for soon after this is when the Syriac Miaphysites began to be labeled by others as "Jacobites" (although not a name they used of themselves). Yet despite their growing size and influence, the government continued to view all types of Christians as part of the one Christian community, and the patriarch of the Church of the East continued to be its spokesman. The Miaphysite challenge was in part met by the larger Church of the East with new customs designed to distinguish its own clergy from that of its opponents. In the late fifth century, they took the surprising step of abolishing clerical celibacy for priests and also created a distinctive form of tonsure for their clergy. The rivalry between the two Christian groups, however, seemed to distract both sides to some degree from their larger mission of converting non-Christians.

Even so, the beginning of the seventh century saw a resurgence in the Church of the East. Its members continued to play prominent roles in society, such as serving as important court physicians for the Sasanian royal families. The most memorable of these was the devout Christian queen Shirin, the favorite wife of Khosrow II (r. 589–628).[25] A monastic revival also began under Abraham of Kashkar (d. 586). It continued well into the next century, resulting in a renewed commitment to the spirituality and discipline of the ascetic life.

But then disaster struck. War between the Byzantine and Sasanid Empires again broke out in 602. By 618 the Sasanian forces had swept all opposition before them, taking Jerusalem, Egypt, and Asia Minor, until they were within view of Constantinople itself. The pendulum then reversed just as suddenly; by 627, the Sasanid strongholds in Mesopotamia were being surrounded by Greek armies. Peace came only when both sides had exhausted themselves, leaving the door open for a new power broker in the region. Little did anyone suspect that within only a few years' time, Arab raiders would sweep out of the southern desert to end Sasanian rule and permanently annex much of Byzantium's territory.

25. On the queen Shirin, see Wilhelm Baum, *Shirin: Christian—Queen—Myth of Love; A Woman of Late Antiquity—Historical Reality and Literary Effect* (Piscataway, NJ: Gorgias, 2004).

As previously noted, the church of Persia suffered during these times of political turmoil with Byzantium, the "Christian West." And yet its spiritual and missionary impulses continued to thrive and grow. As the home church in Persia struggled on in the aftermath of the great wars of the early seventh century, and as the first forebodings were arriving from Arabia, the Church of the East approved what was perhaps their most ambitious undertaking yet—sending a delegation over four thousand miles eastward along the Silk Road to the court of the great Chinese emperor in the hopes of establishing a Chinese Christian church.

Chapter 2

THE STELE FROM CHANG'AN

On a hot day in 1623 in the heartland of ancient China, a group of laborers worked at digging out the foundation of a building. They were in a village some thirty miles southwest of Xi'an, a city that had served as a capital of China on and off for the previous 2,500 years. Already in the time of Israel's king David, it had been the capital of the Western Zhao dynasty (1046–771 BC); it was known at that time as Fenghao. By the time of Christ, it was serving as the capital of the Han dynasty (206 BC–AD 220), which had changed the city's name to Chang'an—perpetual peace. It was again the capital under the Sui (AD 581–618) and Tang (618–907) dynasties. But by the seventeenth century, it was only a shadow of its former self. The sixteen-mile-long city wall, built in 200 BC to enclose fourteen square miles of city, had been replaced in the Ming dynasty (1364–1644) with one less than half as long, and the new royal capital of Beijing was now 550 miles to the northeast.

The glory of the ancient capital was probably far from the mind of those laborers when their shovels struck a large, hard object. We can only imagine their surprise as they slowly uncovered a large limestone stele that had been carefully buried long before. They soon recognized the nature of the object. Similar stones could be seen in temples and public areas across China bearing the sayings of Confucius, lists of successful graduates of the imperial examinations, and imperial edicts. When they had uncovered the entire stone, it stood nearly ten feet in height, three feet wide, and a foot thick, dimensions fairly typical for an official stele. The front was inscribed with thirty-two vertical columns of wonderfully preserved writing containing more than 1,750 beautiful Chinese characters (see figure 1).[1]

1. The text of the stele with an English translation and some commentary by Samuel N. C. Lieu and Lance Eccles can be found online at http://www.unionacademique.org

But the workmen soon noticed two things that were different about this particular stone tablet. The first was the unusual decoration at the very top. Between the usual mythological creatures, they saw an object that resembled the Chinese character for *ten* rising out of a lotus blossom; it consisted of a horizontal bar bisecting a vertical bar. It was almost certainly the first time the workmen had set eyes upon a Christian cross. Second, beneath the main text on the front and along the two sides, there was a second form of writing, unlike anything they had ever seen. The laborers had no way of knowing that the strange script originated far to the west in the Middle East, and that it contained writing in the Syriac language, the language that had been used in Christian churches from Mesopotamia all the way to China. If any of those workmen could read Chinese, however, they might have noted that the final line said that the stone had been erected nine hundred years earlier during the great Tang dynasty. And they could only wonder at the meaning of the large nine-character heading between the cross and the body: *Monument of the Spread of the Da Qin Luminous Teaching in China.*[2]

The workmen notified their supervisor as soon as they realized that this was not just another stone that needed to be moved. Word then spread up the chain of authority to the provincial prefect in Chang'an. He arranged for the stone to be moved into the city. There it quickly caught the attention of a scholar named Zhang Gengyu. Zhang was himself a Roman Catholic Christian, having been baptized in 1621 into the "Heavenly Studies" by a Jesuit missionary. A small group of Jesuits had found a way to enter xenophobic China several decades earlier, and by then they had a few hundred converts. Part of their evangelistic strategy had been to foster relationships with the Chinese scholars (often referred to as *mandarins*) who held most of the important positions in

---

/content/files/10362790247079243.pdf. See also the recently published English translation and commentary of Matteo Nicolini-Zani, *The Luminous Way to the East: Texts and History of the First Encounter of Christianity with China* (Oxford: Oxford University Press, 2022), 197–221. A comparison of these two very competent and up-to-date translations will show the English reader how the ambiguity of classical Chinese leaves much to the interpreter. In the following pages I for the most part give my own translation of passages after consulting not only these two but also numerous other translations.

2. For a complete study of the stele, see Paul Pelliot, *L'inscription Nestorienne de Si-Ngan-Fou*, ed. Antonino Forte (Kyoto: Scuola di studi sull'Asia orientale; Paris: Collège de France Institut des Hautes Etudes Chinoises, 1996). Michael Keevak provides an interesting history and interpretation of the stele since its rediscovery in *The Story of a Stele: China's Nestorian Monument and Its Reception in the West, 1625–1916* (Hong Kong: Hong Kong University Press, 2008).

the government bureaucracy, and Zhang was one of these scholars. Zhang had years of practice in reading ancient texts, and so he had no trouble reading the stele's message. Yet he had never before seen a text like this one, nor had he heard of the Jingjiao, the Luminous Teaching mentioned in the heading. Yet soon Zhang began to suspect that this Da Qin Luminous Teaching was in some way related to the Christian faith he had adopted. As he read further, his excitement increased, for the text convinced him that his own new faith had been preached in China nearly a thousand years earlier with the approval of several Tang emperors! Taking ink and rice paper, he made a rubbing of the stone, the time-honored way of copying ancient texts, then sent it off to his old friend, fellow scholar, and fellow Christian Li Zhizao (1565–1630).

A decade or so earlier, Li, later known to the Jesuit missionaries as Dr. Leo, had become friends with some of the Jesuits—those strange new foreign teachers who dressed like Confucian scholars, learned the Chinese language, and could discuss the Confucian classics. After being nursed back to health in 1610 by the Jesuit Matteo Ricci, Li had been baptized. Although he had held some of the highest positions in the imperial government, he soon retired to devote his remaining years to translating Western books into Chinese and to composing his own works about his new faith. He too became ecstatic when he saw Zhang's rubbing and read its text. In 1625, Li published the complete Chinese text of the stele, together with a brief accompanying essay entitled "After Reading the Stele Inscription of the Luminous Teaching." In it, he described how he received the ink rubbing of the text from Zhang together with an explanatory letter in which Zhang asked surprisedly, "Is this not the same teaching as the Heavenly Studies transmitted by Mr. Li Xitai [the Chinese name of Matteo Ricci]?" Zhang then continued, "I read it, and found this was indeed the case."[3]

An Object of Study and Controversy

Knowing the importance of the discovery, Li had immediately alerted the Jesuit missionaries about the find. It was exactly the discovery for which they

---

3. A translation of Li Zhizao's original work is now available for the first time as appendix 1 in Matteo Nicolini-Zani, *The Interpretation of Tang Christianity in the Late Ming China Mission: Manuel Dias Jr.'s Correct Explanation of the Tang "Stele Eulogy on the Luminous Teaching" (1644)* (Leiden: Brill, 2023), 275–81. Chinese scholars of the Ming period who had converted to Christianity gave their new religion the name "Heavenly Studies" (天學, *tian xue*).

had been hoping and praying. One of the biggest obstacles their message faced in China was that it was considered "new." In a civilization that was millennia old and built on stability and tradition, new teachings were generally despised. A later Chinese emperor was said to have asked one of the Jesuits why God had kept the Chinese in ignorance for so long if God truly desired the salvation of all men and if a knowledge of Jesus was necessary for salvation. It would strengthen their missionary arguments considerably if they were now able to show their Chinese hearers that the Christian message was not new to China but had been there long before.

As a result, the veteran Jesuit missionary Nicolas Trigault was sent to Chang'an to see the inscription firsthand. Soon after, the Jesuit procurator of all China and Japan, Alvaro Semedo, went to inspect it as well. Both men joyfully concurred that the monument firmly established that Christianity had been in China a millennium earlier. The Jesuits had met with much resistance when they had tried to enter China, and at the time of the stele's discovery it was still uncertain how long they would be allowed to remain. But now, if the Jesuit presence was questioned in the future, they could show proof that they were only continuing the Christian work begun in China long before—work that had received imperial approval from the great Tang emperors!

Trigault made a Latin translation of the stele, and a French translation was published in France in 1628. The following year, the Syriac portion of the text was translated, although it remained unpublished until 1902. Knowing that remnants of the Syriac church were still present in South India, Semedo, while on a return trip to Europe, stopped to consult the bishop of Cranganore about the text. Cranganore was in the Kerala district of southwest India, an area where the Syriac-speaking church had existed since the earliest centuries and where the Jesuits had also established a base of operations in the late sixteenth century.

The Jesuits had earlier learned that Christians had once existed in China from the accounts of medieval Western travelers like Marco Polo. Those travelers had immediately identified the Chinese Christians as "Nestorians," as was the practice among Western Christians. The Jesuits, however, now conveniently ignored this identification since they wished to use the stone to prove the existence of an early Christian presence in China that was typical of their own beliefs. When the original Chinese and Syriac texts of the inscription were published together by Athanasius Kircher in his *China Illustrata* (Amsterdam, 1667), the author commented, "The translation of this Sino-Syrian monument will force the heretics to admit that ten centuries ago preachers of the Divine Word taught sound doctrine that conforms to modern orthodoxy, and that the doctrine which spread in China by evangelical preaching was the same which the universal Roman Catholic Church today holds up to be believed." The publication of the stele's long text in Chinese characters, together with an attempt to render it phonetically using the Latin alphabet, actually sparked the first major European interest in the study of the Chinese language.[4]

Kircher's book was soon joined by numerous others, for the story of an early Christian presence in China captured the imagination of European scholars. Enlightenment skeptics such as Voltaire, as well as numerous Protestant scholars, saw the discovery as "too convenient" and quickly labeled it a Jesuit forgery.[5] However, soon the Syriac text was also being studied by other European linguists. In 1718, Eusèbe Renaudot argued convincingly for the monument's authenticity and its association with the mission work of the Syriac church.[6] During the two centuries that followed, a steady stream of books and pamphlets on the stele and the "Nestorian" church in China was published. Although a few inscribed crosses and Christian tombstones came to light in the intervening years, right up to the twentieth century the Chang'an inscription remained the single greatest proof and the only substantial testimony to an early church in China.

The Danish aristocrat and adventurer Fritz Holm heard the story of the stele while in China in 1901 and later concocted a plan to purchase it for the British Museum. Holm traveled again to China in 1907, during the tumultuous final days of the Qing Empire. After seeing the stone standing unprotected near the Chongren Temple (as in figure 1), he resolved for "scientific purposes" to save the immense stele by transporting it out of China. When he failed to obtain permission to purchase it, he briefly laid plans to steal it. Even with his resources, however, he would never have been able to smuggle the two-ton stone over 350 miles of rough terrain to the nearest railway line! Eventually, the resourceful Dane hired local workmen to make an exact full-size replica,

---

4. The quote comes from the abridged English translation of Kircher's work: *China Illustrata* (Bloomington: Indiana University Research Institute for Inner Asian Studies, 1987), 1.

5. See the relevant excerpts from Voltaire's *An Essay on Universal History: The Manners and Spirit of Nations*, cited in G. Thompson, "France and the Study of China and Its Religions," in *French Perceptions of Religious and Philosophical Thought in Qing China*, ed. Florian Knothe (Hong Kong: Hong Kong University Press, forthcoming).

6. Eusebius Renaudot, *Ancient Accounts of India and China by Two Mohammedan Travellers Who Went to Those Parts in the 9th Century* (London: Samuel Harding, 1733; reprint, New Delhi: Asian Educational Services, 1995).

which he succeeded in taking to America. It remained on display in New York's Metropolitan Museum for eight years. Eventually the copy ended up in Rome, but a dozen plaster casts were made and put on display in various European museums. The monumental stele continues to arouse occasional scholarly and popular interest, and it remains to this day the most well-known testimony to an early Christian presence in China.[7]

The Beautiful Stone

The stele was moved in 1907 and now occupies a prominent place in the Stele Forest (Beilin, 碑林) Museum in Xi'an. As the name suggests, the museum in the old capital city consists almost entirely of a forest of tall steles like the one discovered in 1623. That stately stele, covered by protective glass, is seen by thousands of local visitors and tourists each year. It consists of a single piece of black limestone that was carefully cut and shaped. It is almost one meter wide and more than twenty-five centimeters thick. The main rectangular part of the stele measures almost two meters in height, but the body is surmounted by a semicircular top that extends the height an additional eighty centimeters. In the center of this extension is a rectangular space for the heading, which consists of nine Chinese characters divided into three rows (see figure 2).[8]

In the triangular area above the nine characters is a small cross, eight centimeters high and six centimeters wide. It is depicted rising from a lotus from which clouds also emanate to surround the base. A flower fills each of the two bottom corners of the triangular space.[9] The cross itself has flared ends with three circular "pearls" at all four of its extremities, and a larger circle (surrounded by four smaller circles) where the arms intersect. Charles A. Stewart has argued that this form of the cross, referred to either as the *crux Vaticana* or *crux gemmata*, originated in a reliquary cross that contained (in its cir-

---

7. Holm actually published a version of his shenanigans in *My Nestorian Adventure in China: A Popular Account of the Holm-Nestorian Expedition to Sian-Fu and Its Results* (New York: Revell, 1923).

8. Because of the stele's positioning within the museum and its glass covering, it is impossible to take a clear photograph of the text. For that reason we will reproduce photos of the author's purchased ink rubbings.

9. The lotus and clouds are similar to the lotus throne on which Buddhas sit and the clouds often seen in Daoist imagery. See Nicolini-Zani, *The Luminous Way*, 121–26.

cular center) a part of the True Cross. The cross was discovered in Palestine by Constantine the Great's mother, Helena, about 326. In Stewart's view, a reliquary presented by Emperor Justin II to Pope John II about 568 and still in the Vatican today, with a circular center and pearled extensions, preserves for us an image of the original (now lost) Jerusalem reliquary. That original True Cross reliquary was captured by the Sasanids in 614 and entrusted to the Church of the East in Seleucia for nearly fifteen years until it was recaptured by the Byzantines and returned to Palestine. From then on, however, its iconic form was repeatedly used by the Church of the East in Central Asia, explaining its depiction on the stele.[10]

Two winged dragons, one on each side of the heading, combine their efforts to support a pearl above the cross. This part of the top section (minus the cross and pearl) was a standard iconographic pattern used on such steles, and thus probably came from the workshop with the dragons and pearl already carved and ready to have the heading and the text inscribed according to the instructions of the purchaser. The triangular area with the flowers and cross seems to be the work of a different hand. Perhaps it was a Jingjiao craftsman who made use of the small blank space above the heading to alert those passing by that this normal-looking stele, surmounted by mythological creatures, was not what it seemed to be at first glance.

While the nine-character heading is easily translated, it does pose some interesting questions. As with all parts of the stele, the reader must begin in the top right and read vertically.[11] A loose translation is: "Stele concerning the Luminous Teaching from Da Qin Spreading in China." The character *jing* clearly means "luminous," yet its form here and in all the other Jingjiao texts we will discuss in chapter 4 is a unique variation from the normal form 景. Normally a rectangle with a line dividing it in two (日, *ri*, meaning "sun") is on top, and a simple rectangle (口, *kou*, "mouth") is below the line in the middle of the character. These two are reversed in the Jingjiao version of the character. Samuel Lieu has suggested that this was a purposeful change that became in effect a distinctive logo for the religion, and that this would give

---

10. Charles A. Stewart, "Iconography of Syriac Gravestones in Kyrgyzstan and Kazakhstan," in *Silk Road Traces*, ed. Li Tang and Dietmar W. Winkler, Orientalia-Patristica-Oecumenica 21 (Vienna: LIT Verlag, 2022), 166, 180, fig. 11p, and 181, fig. 13a. Note that the *crux Vaticana* also has curled objects around its base similar in appearance to the clouds at the base of the Jingjiao stele.

11. For a more detailed description of the stele itself, its importance, and debates surrounding it over the years, see Nicolini-Zani, *The Luminous Way*, 117–36.

it an "auspicious and radiant" name.[12] Lieu further argues that designating China in the heading with the uncommon term "Middle Kingdom" (中國, Zhongguo) was also a well-thought-out decision, as it did not limit itself to a single dynastic name. It was also a suitable parallel to the other geographical term, "Da Qin" (or Great Chin), a name that evoked some powerful kingdom far to the west. Thus both terms were "timeless" and had an equal "claim to mythological greatness."[13]

The main area on the front of the tablet is filled with thirty-two vertical columns of text with places for sixty-two characters in each column. Column 1 consists of ten characters announcing the subject of the stele. After repeating the seven characters of the heading, it adds "poem with commentary" (頌並序). Column 2 begins halfway down the stele and says that the author of the text was a certain Jingjing (景淨). After a space comes the first Syriac writing. It gives the author's Syriac name as Adam (ʾdʾm) and describes him as a priest, *chorepiscopus* (qwrʾpysqwpʾ, country bishop), and pʾpšhy of China.[14]

Column 3 begins the main body of the inscription, which then continues uninterrupted through column 30. There are a number of blank spaces in the body of the text—twenty-two in all. In some places there is a single blank space, in others two spaces. The Western observer might deduce that these mark ends of sentences or sections. In fact, they are honorific in nature and are a traditional method to indicate that the characters that immediately follow the space denote an important person, usually the name of an emperor. On the Jingjiao stele, however, such blank spaces also precede the name of the Christian God. The first three spaces on the tablet, in columns 3, 6, and 7, are all followed closely by the characters 三一 (*san yi*), "three one." Preceding

12. See figure 2 for the distinctive *jing* character. It is not among the standard Unicode fonts, so we must print the normal form. Samuel N. C. Lieu, "The 'Romanitas' of the Xi'an Inscription," in *From the Oxus River to the Chinese Shores*, ed. Li Tang and Dietmar W. Winkler, Orientalia-Patristica-Oecumenica 5 (Vienna: LIT Verlag, 2013), 135–37. Various theories about the name choice and meaning of Jingjiao are reviewed in Zhang Xiaogui, "Why Did Chinese Christians Name Their Religion Jingjiao," in *Winds of Jingjiao*, ed. Dietmar Winkler and Li Tang, Orientalia-Patristica-Oecumenica 9 (Vienna: LIT Verlag, 2016), 283–309.

13. See Lieu's extensive discussion in "Persons, Titles, and Places in the Xi'an Monument," in *Artifact, Text, Context*, ed. Li Tang and Dietmar W. Winkler, Orientalia-Patristica-Oecumenica 17 (Vienna: LIT, 2020), 64–69, quote on 69. Lieu revisited the subject in his article "From Rome (Da Qin 大秦) to China (Zhongguo 中國): The Xi'an 西安 (Nestorian) Monument as a Bilingual and Transcultural Document," in *The Church of the East in Central Asia and China*, ed. Samuel N. C. Lieu and Glen L. Thompson, China and the Mediterranean World 1 (Turnhout: Brepols, 2020), 126–29 on Da Qin, and 131–33 on Zhongguo.

14. On the term pʾpšhy see below, 44.

the "three one" in the first two of these examples is the character for the first-person personal pronoun ("I," "my," "we," or "our"). In this way the author makes it clear from the outset that he is giving the highest possible honor not only to the Tang emperors but also to "our Three-One" God.

The text closes with two additional columns of supplementary material. Column 31 dates the erection of the stele to Sunday, the seventh day of the first month of the second year of the Jianzhong era. This was the period of Emperor Dezong's rule, which extended from 780 to 783. Thus, the stele was erected on Sunday, February 4, 781. It further names Mar Hananisho as the one in charge of the entire Church of the East at that time. To honor the patriarch, an honorary space is left before his name as well. Actually, Hananisho II had died the preceding year (AD 780) and been succeeded by Timothy I in May of 780. That news, however, had apparently not yet crossed the 3,600 miles from Persia to Chang'an when the stone was being carved.[15] Column 31 ends with the repetition of the name and title of the patriarch in Syriac. Column 32 then provides the name of the man responsible for the beautiful calligraphy on the tablet: "Lu Xiuyan, minister and councilor of the court, formerly military commander for Tai Zhou district." (See figure 3.)

At the very bottom of the stele, in the twenty centimeters beneath the main text, are an additional twenty-three short lines of vertical text, mostly in Syriac. After repeating the date, the text along the bottom mentions five members of the Jingjiao clergy that played key roles in the erection of the tablet. Since the stele is nearly a foot thick, there are twenty-five centimeters of width on each of the stone's two sides available for additional writing. On the left side is a list of forty-one Jingjiao clergy, arranged in four groups. Each line gives one Syriac name written vertically, usually followed by the person's Chinese name written just beneath. Unfortunately, some of the writing is illegible because a Chinese tourist visiting the site in 1895 inscribed an ostentatious remembrance of his visit over much of this side of the stele. The right side contains a similar list of twenty-nine clergy in Syriac; all but three are followed by Chinese names. An early twentieth-century Chinese inscription was added to this side, but fortunately the characters are of smaller size and were placed below the ancient

---

15. Only nine months separated the erection of the stele from Timothy's consecration, and the inscription would have been completed some time before the dedication ceremony. Hence there is no need for Max Deeg's alternative political explanation for the use of Hananisho's name ("An Anachronism in the Stele of Xi'an—Why Haenanisho?" in Winkler and Tang, *Winds of Jingjiao*, 243–51).

text. It has been assumed that the clergy names on the sides were inscribed at the same time as the texts on the stele's front. In any case, the names are a valuable resource for any attempt to understand the nature of the Jingjiao's organization and makeup. (See figure 4.)

Referencing the Text

On the front of the stele, two introductory columns and two columns of conclusory material frame the twenty-eight vertical columns that contain the 1,697 characters of the body of the text. This is usually described as consisting of three distinct sections—a theological prologue (columns 3–10), a historical section (10–26), and a concluding poem (26–30). However, there has been little study of the text's structure, partly because of the lack of a good reference system.[16] As a result, no uniform way to refer to individual passages within the text has developed. As was usual in ancient texts, there are no punctuation marks or other visual clues to indicate divisions within the text. Some scholars have divided the text into anywhere from five to ninety-four sections, while others have left it without divisions. In an attempt to be less subjective, I have broken the text into its smallest sense-units, with each displayed and numbered as a separate line (see appendix 1). This allows the reader to visually see the microstructure of the text. These units are then identified first by the column number (1–32) and then by the sense-unit within the column, separated by a period (or full stop). Thus, the first two characters of column 3 are identified as 3.1, the next four characters of the column as 3.2, etc. In this way a simple system has been constructed that (1) allows the reader to quickly find passages in the photographs and rubbings, and (2) serves as a logical notational system for referencing passages. In addition, when the text is printed by sense-units, the reader can easily see the rhythm and parallelisms of the text, for these short, multicharacter lines are the building blocks of classical Chinese prose and poetry, both structurally and grammatically. As an example, column 3 is made up of eleven and a half units, 3.1 to 3.12. (When a unit runs from the end of one line to the beginning of the next, it is numbered with the line in which it begins.) The reader will benefit from the

---

16. For a fuller discussion of earlier methods of referencing the stele and views of its structure, see Glen L. Thompson, "The Structure of the Stele," in Tang and Winkler, *Artifact, Text, Context*, 161–93. The text with the author's reference system is provided in appendix 1.

value of the system throughout the remainder of this book, as it is used for all citations of the stele.

Formal Chinese prose and poetry put much of the responsibility for communication on the reader. Words normally consist of one or two syllables, each character being one syllable; this makes short lines possible. On the other hand, most notional or content words (实字, *shizi*) are flexible in that they are not limited to one grammatical function. Many content words can be used as nouns, verbs, and adjectives, depending on the context. This makes interpretation more challenging. Other Chinese characters are known as function words (虚字, *xuzi*). These are often untranslatable but serve in various grammatical functions as conjunctions, prepositions, intensifiers, aspect and discourse markers, or even just to fill out a line to its proper poetical length. In classical Chinese, however, these function words are kept to a minimum, and this adds still more to the ambiguity of both the grammar and the syntax. The result is that the interpreter needs all the help he or she can get. A comparison of any two translations for even a short section of the stele text will quickly illustrate this point. As we shall see, however, printing the text in a way that visually allows the reader to see parallelisms in vocabulary and structure can be an important aid in interpretation.

The Macrostructure of the Text: *Song Bing Xu* (頌並序)

As mentioned earlier, the main text of the stele is usually described as consisting of three distinct sections—a theological prologue (3.1–10.9), a historical overview (10.10–26.7), and a concluding poem (26.8–30.11). All three sections also end with several lines of thanksgiving. Yet it has often been overlooked that the key to the macrostructure of the text is clearly indicated in the first column of the stele, which begins with the title—the same last seven characters of the stele's heading (lacking only the opening *Da Qin*). This title in the first column, however, then adds a three-character description of the text—*song bing xu* (頌並序). The middle character, 並, *bing*, serves as a preposition or conjunction to connect the words before and after it. Thus, it is at times translated as "equal to; side by side with; and; also; what is more; both," or simply "with." The entire phrase has been variously translated as "eulogy . . . with an orderly account" (Moule), "eulogy . . . with a preface" (Saeki), "eulogy with an introduction" (Pelliot), or "eulogy with preface" (Lieu/Eccles). Thus the stele text describes itself as a "*song* with *xu*."

The first character, 頌, *song*, is consistently translated as "eulogy." It can be used as a general word for poetry, but also has the more restricted meaning of an ancient poem of praise—an ode or eulogy. For example, one of the foundational *Five Classics* of Chinese literature and culture is the *Classic of Poetry*. Each of the final forty poems in it is a *song*, with the most recent ones dating to 700 BC. These are panegyrics that were used in imperial and religious rituals and were normally sung to the accompaniment of bells, chimes, and drums. Each line was composed of four characters and included internal and ending rhymes. Zhi Yu (摯虞), writing circa AD 300, in his *Discourse on Literary Compositions Divided by Genre*, lists the 頌, *song*, among the "six modes of poetry," saying that they are considered

> the most excellent examples of poetry. In antiquity when wise emperors and enlightened kings accomplished their deeds and established order, then the sound of lauds [*song*] arose. Thereupon, scribes recorded these pieces and musicians set to music these compositions in order to present them in the ancestral temples and announce them to the ghosts and spirits. Thus, what the lauds [*song*] praise is the virtue of wise kings.[17]

The *song* on the Jingjiao stele is the concluding section of the text (26.8–30.11). It is introduced with a two-character marker (26.8), which could be paraphrased as "the formal composition reads as follows." Then follow fifty-eight lines of four characters each, ending with four seven-character lines. The poem opens with an ode to the true God, and then continues with praises for each of six Tang emperors. Thus, it is very similar to the *song* described by Zhi Yu several centuries earlier.

Although appearing at the end of the stele text, this is the central element of the honorary stele, and it was most likely the first part of the text to be composed. The *xu* (序)—usually translated as "prologue" or "introduction"—referred to what preceded the *song*. This introduction is some six times as long as the text it is introducing. Thus, it would be appropriate to call it a commentary. Indeed, table 1 makes it clear that each part of the concluding poetic ode or eulogy has a corresponding and usually much longer equivalent in the previous sections. The only anomaly is the three-column reference to the Christian general and benefactor Yisi, who is not mentioned in the eulogy/poem.

17. The translation is that of Wendy Swartz in *Early Medieval China: A Sourcebook*, ed. Wendy Swartz et al. (New York: Columbia University Press, 2014), 277.

Table 1. The Chang'an stele text as commentary and poetic eulogy

COMMENTARY (3.1–26.7)	EULOGY/POEM (26.8–30.11)
3.2–10.9 The eternal God and his church	26.9–27.1 The Lord without origin
10.10–15.6 Taizong and Alopen's arrival	27.2–27.11 Taizong
15.7–16.15 Gaozong	27.12–28.4 Gaozong
17.1–19.11 Xuanzong	28.5–28.12 Xuanzong
19.12–20.4 Suzong	28.13–29.6 Suzong
20.5–21.3 Daizong	29.7–29.14 Daizong
21.4–22.12 Dezong's Jianzhong period	29.15–30.7 Dezong's Jianzhong period
22.13–26.3 General Yisi	
26.4–26.7 Thanksgiving to the Lord	30.8–30.11 Thanksgiving to the Three-One

The historical section of the 序 (*xu*) runs from 10.10 to 26.7 and serves as a commentary on the next six sections of the poem that eulogize six Tang emperors. The commentary sections not only follow the same chronological order as the poem sections but mirror and expand on them in numerous ways. For example, the lines of the poem praising Taizong (emperor from AD 626 to 649) tell how during his reign "the pure, bright Luminous Teaching was introduced to our Tang kingdom. Its scriptures were translated and temples built" (27.6–27.8). The commentary (10.10–14.2) clarifies that it was Alopen who first introduced the faith by bringing the Christian Scriptures to the Tang court (10.13–11.4) and also further explains that the Scriptures were translated and examined thoroughly by the royal bureaucracy (11.5–11.8). The same word used in the poem for the Jingjiao holy books (*jing*, 27.8) is used in this section of the commentary three times to refer to the Jingjiao sacred texts (11.1, 11.5, and 12.6). The building of Christian temples in 27.8 is fleshed out as well with the description of the temple built in the Yining district of the capital (13.3–13.5). In fact, the commentary quotes the edict of Taizong in which the Jingjiao's path to imperial approval is recounted, ending with the pronouncement that "it is appropriate that it [the Jingjiao teaching] be propagated [*xing*, as in the stele heading and 1.1] everywhere beneath heaven [i.e., throughout the empire]" (13.1–13.2).

Similarly, in the eulogy's lines on Xuanzong (28.5–28.12), the ambiguous comment that he cultivated "true rule" (真正) is followed by three parallel lines:

> His imperial tablets were radiant;
> his celestial writings were resplendent.
> The imperial portraits glittered like gems.

The commentary (17.1–19.11) explains that the emperor sent portraits of five emperors as a gift for display in the Jingjiao church (17.6). Later, when Bishop Jihe, a metropolitan bishop newly arrived from Da Qin, paid his respects at the court, Xuanzong presented him with some of his own imperial calligraphy to adorn his church (18.12–19.5). These details make the otherwise vague references in the eulogy perfectly meaningful. Thus, the historical section does indeed serve as a commentary on the shorter, more formulaic, and at times even cryptic poem.[18]

But where does the commentary begin? One would not naturally expect a traditional tripartite structure from the stele's description of itself as "eulogy with commentary." One would expect to see the opening theological section, although it spans eight columns of text, as the commentary on the opening section of the poem (see table 2). The material in those columns follows a natural progression logically and theologically—creation, fall, incarnation, salvation, proclamation. Yet it is at least suggestive that a number of the same themes and vocabulary are found in the introductory eight lines of the poem in roughly the same order (26.9–27.1). A closer examination of the details and vocabulary makes such a reading even more plausible. The line "The True Lord is without beginning" (26.9) is repeated in the commentary with the two parts simply reversed (3.9). It is then given more specificity by the proper name Aluohe (3.10), which follows it. The "profound stillness" (寂) and "unchanging" (常) of 26.10 are both used in 3.2 of the commentary. Line 26.13 is especially telling. It states that "dividing his being he came to earth."

---

18. In many of the quotations from the stele that appear in this and the subsequent chapters, I will insert "Com." (for "commentary") or "Poem" before giving the column and sense-unit numbers; this will remind the reader that the information is coming from one or the other of the two parts of the stele.

Line 6.4–6.7 expands on that with "our Three-One divided being [分身], the luminous and honorable Messiah, concealing his true majesty, appeared as a human being." The mention of the sun dispelling darkness in 26.15 is reprised in a fuller if still somewhat cryptic expression that may refer to the crucifixion of Christ: "The Luminous Sun was hung up to dispel the darkness" (7.8). Examples could be multiplied.

Table 2. The opening section of the poem compared to the theological commentary

EULOGY/POEM	COMMENTARY
26.9 The True Lord without beginning	3.2–10 the still and unchanging
26.10 still and unchanging	Three-One God
26.11 with power and capacity to create	3.11–4.10 his creative work
26.12 establishing earth and heavens	4.11–6.3 Satan and his work
26.13 dividing his being he came to earth	6.4–6.11 the incarnation
26.14 to save everyone	6.12–8.3 the Messiah's life and work
26.15 dispelling darkness	8.4–10.1 the church and its life
27.1 all this proves the true and deep	10.2–10.9 This Luminous Teaching is a mystery

Thus, the entire theological section (3.2–10.9) does serve as a commentary on 26.9–27.1, producing the bipartite "ode with commentary" as promised in column 1. One final structural argument confirms this reading. Both the commentary and ode begin with two-character markers that serve to alert the reader to the beginning of a major section—粵若 in 3.1 and 詞曰 in 26.8. There is no such marker at the beginning of the historical section (before 10.10). The two blank spaces found there are merely the usual marker of the impending name of Emperor Taizong. Thus, there is a strong case for understanding the 頌並序 (*song bing xu*) as indicating that textual structure is only twofold.

This pattern of a prose introduction to a poem appears frequently in Chinese literature. A recent volume of translated texts, *Early Medieval China: A Sourcebook* (2014), edited by Wendy Swartz and others, gives two examples from circa

AD 400, both from the section on inscriptions about "Buddha's shadow."[19] The monk Shi Huiyuan of Jin provided a prose description of the cave where the shadow was to be found and the monk's association with it before presenting a sixty-eight-line poem; his text then concludes with a final, shorter prose description of the setting up of the inscription, just as we have in columns 31–32 of the Chang'an stele. A second inscription gives a shorter prose introduction by Xie Lingyun followed by his seventy-six-line poem, all in four-character lines on the same topic. According to Swartz's translation, the title of Xie's work was "Inscription on Buddha's Shadow (with Preface) 佛影銘 (並序)"—ending with the same *bing xu* as in column 1 of our stele. Thus we can see that the bipartite structure of the stele was a traditional option for a Chinese writer, yet it allowed the author some flexibility in its execution.

Composition and Production

First, we review the process that began with an idea for a memorial monument and ended in a text displayed for the public. Multiple steps and numerous people were involved. It was also a cross-cultural endeavor, as the bilingual texts of the bottom and sides of the stone make clear. Government and ecclesiastical red tape was involved. Since the stele would be displayed publicly, it had to have the approval of government authorities; and since it would be perhaps the most public statement of the Jingjiao's history and theology anywhere in China, church authorities would also have to preapprove its content as well as its "presentation." The complexity of the process is borne out by the stele itself, which credits a number of people responsible for seeing the project through to completion.

Column 2 consists in two short statements—the first one in Chinese, the second in Syriac.[20] The Chinese reads: "Composed by the monk Jingjing of the Da Qin Monastery." After a space, the Syriac says: "Adam, priest and chorepiscopus and *p'pšy* of China." It thus appears that the author had the Syriac name Adam and the Chinese name Jingjing, and that he was a monk who not

---

19. Swartz et al., *Early Medieval China*, 415–21.

20. All references to the Syriac portions of the stele are identified by the Syriac line or section number as assigned in the Eccles and Lieu text and translation. These are also used by Nicolini-Zani in his translation (see n. 1 above for both of these). We also will refer to Chinese sections at the bottom and two sides of the stele using numbers 33–100 as assigned by Eccles and Lieu.

only served as a priest but also had the higher rank of chorepiscopus (literally "rural bishop").

There has been significant debate on the meaning of the Syriac word *p'pšy* (or *p'pš'* as some read the text on the stele), used only here in all our surviving Jingjiao documents. One theory held that it was an adaptation of the Syriac *papas*, a designation for metropolitan bishop. The metropolitan was virtually equivalent to an archbishop in the Latin church—a bishop who oversaw other bishops in the region. Due to the great distances involved, metropolitans who served outside of the Persian heartland were granted the authority to ordain bishops themselves, a privilege otherwise reserved for the patriarch-catholicos himself. Jingjing might have been accurately called *p'pšy of China* as the most senior cleric in the country during the late eighth century. Samuel Lieu, an earlier supporter of this theory, has now abandoned it, however, interpreting the term as a phonetic transcription of a Chinese term for priest, *fashi*. It was, he argues, a term "already well used in Central Asia as a title for a priest, similar to *monsignor* in the Catholic Church."[21] However, because it is here part of the phrase "*p'pšy* of China" and Adam had several words earlier been described as a "priest and *chorepiscopus*," it must have some other special meaning here. The primary audience for the Syriac text on the stele would have been the local clergy and perhaps other leaders of the immigrant community. Therefore, it is most likely that the expression was to denote an administrative position over the church in the entire country, perhaps equivalent to a metropolitan. Having said that, we will leave the term untranslated.

But what precisely was Adam's role in the creation of the stele? The verb used is 述, *shu*, which normally means to narrate, state, or relate something. A more specific word for writing or composing (such as 纂, *zuan*) was not used. Yet the implication is clear that this high-ranking cleric composed the text, both the ode and the commentary. Further, by giving his name and church rank in Chinese, the reader would normally infer that Jingjing had composed the text in Chinese.

If Jingjing was the metropolitan, the highest-ranking cleric in the Jingjiao church, there would have been no need for him to gain approval for his text from others within the church. What assistance he did seek during the composition or the editing process is unknown. However, a note in Syriac at the

---

21. Lieu, "From Rome (Da Qin 大秦) to China (Zhongguo 中國)," 134–38, and "Persons, Titles, and Places in the Xi'an Monument," in Tang and Winkler, *Artifact, Text, Context*, 72–77. Nicolini-Zani agrees with this interpretation (*The Luminous Way*, 198n5).

bottom of the stele by another high church official, seemingly the chorepiscopus of the capital city Chang'an, indicates that the text had received church
approval for its accuracy: "The things written on it [are] the teaching of our
Savior and the preaching of our fathers to the emperors of China" (S10–13).

It is probable that already at an early stage Jingjing/Adam had submitted the text for official government approval. Indeed, the commentary text
describes how, when the first delegation arrived in Chang'an, their religious
texts had to be examined and approved by the imperial officials before the
clergy were allowed to spread their teachings and establish congregations
(11.5–11.8). Although the Jingjiao now had a nearly 150-year history in the
country, this new stele took the form of an official document. It would be displayed in public and be purported to accurately describe not only approved
religious teachings but also Chinese history and the church's relationships
with numerous emperors. Jingjing was well aware as he composed the text
that it would have to be vetted by the imperial bureaucracy. This must be
remembered when the reader studies what is said, what is not said, and how
everything is said on the stele.

In the last column of the stele, column 32, we learn that "The calligraphy
is that of Lu Xiuyan, minister and councilor of the court, formerly military
commander for Tai Zhou district." The word at the end of this column is 書,
shu. It is the character still used today for a book and often refers to the actual
writing in a book, that is, the calligraphy itself. A more precise translation,
then, might be: "Lu Xiuyan . . . did the calligraphy." Unfortunately, Chinese
records never mention Lu Xiuyan in any other context, although the calligraphy of the stele has often been praised as a masterpiece of the period. Since
no reference to a Christian office or Syriac name is given in column 32, we
can assume that Lu was not a Christian but was chosen and hired for his exceptional calligraphic skills.

Whether the calligrapher or the stonecutter transferred the text onto the
stone, it was the latter who incised the characters so beautifully into the limestone. The text does not provide the name of the stone carver, for he was
considered just a craftsman, yet his skill is obvious even to Westerners who
know no Chinese. Some Chinese stone carvers were able to inscribe Sanskrit
and Sogdian letters as well as the characters of their own language. However,
we cannot be sure whether the Syriac on the stele is the work of a second
craftsman or the same one who did the Chinese.

The stele does mention several other men involved in the stele project. The
first Syriac text at the bottom of the tablet face (S3–13) reads:

In the year One Thousand and Ninety and Two of the Greeks Mar Yazdbuzid, priest and Chorepiscopus of Kumdān [Chang'an] the capital city, son
of the late Milis priest, from Balkh a city of Tokharistan [northern Afghan-
istan], erected this stone tablet. The things written on it [are] the teaching
of our Savior and the preaching of our fathers to the emperors of China.

[Chinese] monk Ling Bao (33) [Syriac] Adam deacon son of the chorepiscopus Yazdbuzid.

Yazdbozid was the Syriac name for Yisi, the church benefactor praised in
22.13–26.3. Now quite aged and likely retired from active military duty, he was
not only a priest but also had the title of chorepiscopus of Chang'an, serving
under Adam/Jingjing, the apparent metropolitan bishop. Yazdbozid is also
credited here with "setting up this stone," no doubt by providing some of the
considerable funding necessary to complete the project. The three generations
of a single ecclesiastical family mentioned here—his father, Milis, originally a
priest in Balkh, and his son the deacon Adam—remind us that celibacy was
not a requirement for clergy in the Church of the East.[22]

After a reference in the bottom center to the priest and chorepiscopus Mar
Sargis (S16–17), two other men are mentioned in the final eight lines on the
right side of the stele's bottom. There a mixed Chinese and Syriac text reads:

[Chinese] Supervisor of the erection of the stele: the monk Xingtong (34–
35); [Syriac] the priest Sabranisho (S18).

[Syriac] Gabriel priest and archdeacon and head of the church of Kumdān
[Chang'an] and of Sarag [Luoyang] (S19–21).

[Chinese] Assistant Supervisor [of the stele's erection]: the Master of Imperial Rites, recipient of the Imperially conferred Purple Gown, the Chief
Monk Yeli (36–38).

As with Lingbao/Adam, it is difficult to know whether these names refer to
two men (each with a Syriac and a Chinese name) or four different men. They
are all mentioned, it seems, because of their involvement in the erection of
the tablet. Yeli was not only the abbot of a Jingjiao monastery but also had an

---

22. Although the monk Lingbao may have been a separate person, it could also be the
Chinese name for the deacon Adam. This would explain the strange insertion of a Chinese
name in this otherwise all-Syriac section.

important position within the imperial department of sacred rites. Perhaps he was commissioned to ensure that the project received government approval at its various stages, including the dedication ceremony. Church members like these, who were also important government officials, could use their *guanxi*, the social credits they had amassed in the complex web of interpersonal relationships within the government bureaucracy, to benefit the church at times like these.

In summary, the beautiful stele that is so important to our knowledge of early Christianity in China was the result of a complicated project. Adam, together with Yazdbozid, most likely first conceived the idea and did the initial planning. After it was written, the "ode with commentary" was sent to the appropriate government offices for approval, which perhaps involved Yeli, the "master of the imperial rites." Funding would also have to be raised, either from within the church coffers or from benefactors such as Yisi. After obtaining government approval and funding, Lu Xiuyan was hired to do the calligraphy and the stone was purchased. A stone carver was then hired to incise Lu Xiuyan's beautiful characters onto the stone. Finally, Yazdbozid saw to its transportation and erection, assisted by the priests Yeli and Sabranisho. Finally, on Sunday, February 4, 781, a dedication service was held to celebrate the completed project and to thank God for nearly 150 years of blessings upon the Jingjiao church in China. How surprised Adam, Yazdbozid, and the others involved would have been to know that twelve centuries later their project would still be admired for its beauty and that the text would still be studied by scholars seeking to understand them and their church.

One Stele, Two Messages

It is absolutely essential to keep in mind this complicated process as we interpret the message of the stele. Too often those who have translated and studied the text have forgotten that it was a public document, not a devotional tract, a creedal statement, or a catechism for new converts.[23] It publicly attested to everyone who read it that the imperial authorities had given their blessing to the spread

---

23. Forgetting the public nature and purpose of the inscription led Charles Stang to make some unwarranted conclusions in his article "The 'Nestorian' (Jingjiao) Monument and Its Theology of the Cross," in *Syriac in Its Multi-Cultural Context*, ed. Herman G. B. Tuele (Leuven: Peeters, 2017), 107–18. See the discussion in Glen L. Thompson, "The Cross and Jingjiao Theology," in Tang and Winkler, *Silk Road Traces*, 355–74.

of this religion that had come from outside China. The nine huge characters of the heading proclaimed loudly and clearly: The emperors have approved "THE SPREAD IN CHINA OF THE LUMINOUS RELIGION FROM DA QIN"! Even the illiterate could see from the monumental size of the tablet that this could not be the work of some persecuted or marginalized group. Whatever organization used an ornamental version of the *ten* character (the cross) as its symbol, it had financial resources and governmental connections.

Unfortunately, we don't know exactly where the stele was erected. Most likely it stood in a courtyard outside a church and facing the street. But clearly Adam knew that it would have two very different sets of readers. The first were the Christian faithful who would pass it on their way to and from church. They would read with pride and assurance the account of their church's teaching and its history in China. The second were the non-Christian readers—government officials approving the text, passersby who would stop to admire and read it, and perhaps even some "seekers" who would read the text as they encountered the stele outside the church.

This dual audience is what made the composition of the text a difficult assignment for Jingjing, and today it still makes interpreting the stele text a complicated hermeneutical exercise for its modern readers. Christian interpreters of the past several centuries have often criticized the text for its use of Confucian and Daoist terminology, and because its review of Christian teaching lacks specific references to Christ's suffering, death, and resurrection. Martin Palmer, on the other hand, viewed the text as "a kind of Taoist Christian Rosetta stone of the spiritual imagination." Paul Pelliot, Max Deeg, and others have shone a spotlight on its use of Buddhist and Daoist terms. None of these observations can be put into proper perspective, however, until the dual nature of the audience is recognized. Adam wrote the text with the understanding that a Confucian scholar in the government bureaucracy would have to read and understand it as an acceptable explanation of the Jingjiao's religious and ethical teaching. But he would also be making sure that it was not seen as subversive or offensive to the Chinese government, its people, and its other religious traditions. Its description of Chinese history had to give appropriate honor and "face" to the imperial family. This is not to say that such bureaucrats, or the patrons of Buddhism and Daoism that read the stele, would totally understand and agree with all of the Jingjiao teaching and its implications. But the message had to be couched in terms that could generally be understood as being neither treasonable nor threatening to the imperial regime, nor would it inflame China's other constituent religious and philosophical groups.

On the other hand, Jingjing's text had to proclaim the Christian message and describe church practice in a way that was acceptable to and understood by its own adherents. Obviously choices had to be made about which teachings to include and which practices to highlight. Similarly, the history of the church in China had to be told in a way that would emphasize the imperial favors the church had received while at the same time remaining vague about the periods when tensions and outright persecution had arisen. It was key to a successful narrative, therefore, that Jingjing not only find the right vocabulary to use but also make judicious decisions on what to include, what to emphasize, and what to pass over in silence. The text of the stele was not to be a primer in Christian teaching and practice, yet it had to be true to the fundamental teachings of Christianity and not distort them. Did Adam's text achieve this? That it was allowed to be erected tells us that it did receive state approval. The contemporary verdict of the Jingjiao priest and chorepiscopus Yazdbozid inscribed in Syriac at the bottom of the stele tells us it also satisfied church officials: "The things written on it [are] the teaching of our Savior and the preaching of our fathers to the emperors of China" (S10–13). Since this latter testimonial was given only in Syriac on the stele, we can conclude that it was meant as an "imprimatur" and as a reassurance to the Christian readers within the church.

Thus, the stele's Chinese text has two messages for two distinct audiences. This explains why it has been so difficult for scholars to successfully write a single commentary on the stele. Every section can and ought to be read both from a Christian perspective and from the viewpoint of a Chinese non-Christian. For example, the commentary opens with a description of God's creative work: He created the cross character to establish the four corners of the world (3.11). 十 (*shi*) is the character for the number ten, but it can also refer to the four cardinal directions (north, south, east, west). The second-century Chinese dictionary entitled *Explaining Language and Analyzing Characters* (說文解字) says, "Ten is the number of completeness. The horizontal stroke denotes east and west; the vertical stroke north and south, so the four directions and the center are in agreement." Thus, non-Christian readers could understand the stele's opening words as describing how the deity established the four corners of the world (with China, the Middle Kingdom, at its center). Christian readers could equally read it as a poetic picture of how God not only created the world but how the cross of Christ overshadows history from its very beginning and would be planted throughout the world (cf. 1 Pet. 1:19–20). It is thus untrue, as has been suggested, that this indicates that the Chinese church had changed the meaning of the cross. Rather, since the significance of the cross as a method of capital punishment was completely foreign to Chinese culture, the use of the cross as a public symbol was reinterpreted for unbelievers while its original meaning could still have been taught in catechetical settings.[24]

The second line of the couplet says: "He stirred up the original wind and brought to life the two forces" (3.12). On the one hand, a Christian reader would immediately see the first half of the line as a reflection of Genesis 1:2, the Spirit of God hovering over the waters, and the "two forces" as referring to the creation of light and darkness in Genesis 1:4. A non-Christian Chinese reader would likely be struck by the expression "two forces" in the second half of the sentence and connect it with the ideas of yin and yang in Chinese creation stories, a usage already centuries old at the time the stele text was composed. The next couplet says: "The dark and void were changed, and heaven and earth came into being; sun and moon began to move and day and night commenced" (4.1–4.2). While not reproducing the precise details of either the biblical account or any of the Chinese creation stories, the wording of the poem would have raised no eyebrows among either audience.

The text then continues with two couplets of four-character lines:

> He created 10,000 creatures,
> and then he created the first man.
> He bestowed goodness and harmony on him,
> and commanded him to govern land and sea. (4.3–4.6)

In these lines man's position as the crown and overseer of creation clearly echoes Genesis 1:27–28. A Christian might think further of Paul's words in the New Testament, that man was "created to be like God in true righteousness and holiness" (Eph. 4:24). A non-Christian Chinese reader, however, would have read the third line completely differently. For the "goodness" mentioned here would have conjured up thoughts of the "goodness of heart" spoken of by the famous philosopher Mencius (d. 289 BC) and in an early Daoist text; and "harmony" was the deeply seated ideal for man and society in the teaching of Confucius and in nearly every other Chinese worldview. Interestingly, the "harmony" character, 和, can also be read as "companion." Thus, a Christian might see this line as a reference to the creation of woman as man's mate, and that God was "bestowing a good companion on him." For the Christian, 4.6 is clearly a reflection of Genesis 1:26 and 28 where man is commanded to subdue and rule over the rest of creation. A Buddhist reading the final two characters (化海) could associate it with the entire "ocean" or "extent" (海) of the present

24. See previous note.

"changing world" (化), which man must try to transcend. Lines 4.7–4.10 further describe the original state of man, speaking of it as empty, colorless, and with an absence of desire. This would resonate with Daoist and Buddhist alike who sought to empty their hearts and minds of worldly matters. Christians would think of Adam and Eve's original absence of evil desires, and of the sin that filled humankind after the Fall.

One final example: 4.11–5.1 speaks of Satan (transliterating his name from Syriac) and how he deludes and deceives from the inside. While evil gods do not play a large role in Chinese and Daoist traditions, shamans have always played a role in Chinese culture and still do, especially in rural areas. And this account would have raised no eyebrows among Buddhists either. Even though it is often not overtly acknowledged, the Chinese have a deep-seated conviction that evil does exist and does trouble the world, bringing sinful chaos of all kinds. Its various manifestations are described extensively in the next thirteen lines (5.2–6.3)—a subject that would have resonated in any culture. In a similar way, the author of the Jingjiao stele continued to craft his text carefully throughout, writing in a way that would positively engage both Christian and non-Christian Chinese readers.

The importance of this great monument—and the complexity of interpreting it—should now be apparent. In chapter 5 we will return to the theological content of the stele and mine its text for information on the teaching of the Jingjiao church. However, this text also remains our most complete source of information on the history of the Jingjiao and of its clergy (some seventy are named on the stele). In the next chapter we will use the historical sections of the stele to trace the history of the Jingjiao church in China from its very beginning in 635 until the stele's erection in 781.

Chapter 3

THE JINGJIAO IS PLANTED AND GROWS

Many of the main elements of Chinese civilization have evolved continuously over more than three thousand years. The current writing system was developing well before 1000 BC, as the many surviving examples of the so-called oracle bones demonstrate. Thousands of characters were in use already in the first half of the first millennium before Christ. During the second half of that millennium, a system of Chinese cultural values and worldview took shape, much of which has remained highly influential right up until the twentieth century. Prominent among these were the philosophical ideas of Confucius (ca. 551–479 BC) and his contemporaries.

It was not until the Qin dynasty had overcome its regional rivals, however, that political unity was established for the first time in much of what we now consider China. By 220 BC the Qin emperor had unified the Chinese heartland between the Yangtse and Yellow Rivers. The tremendous power of this short-lived dynasty can still be felt by the modern tourist who visits Xi'an to view the terra-cotta funerary army of the dynasty's first emperor, known as Qin Shi Huang. Rejecting the traditional title of "king" (*wang*), he invented a new title for himself, *Huangdi* (皇帝). Until that time, the character 帝, *di*, was used only of the legendary Five Emperors from the third millennium BC or of deities—either the highest god in the religion of the earlier Shang dynasty (ca. 1600–1041 BC) or a god associated with one of China's five sacred mountains. In this way, a name was created that has ever since meant "emperor" in China, the same way the name Caesar became a term used of all Roman emperors. The new emperor also built hundreds of miles of roads and canals and linked numerous earlier defensive walls to form the earliest version of the Great Wall.

The brief Qin reign was followed by the longer Han period (206 BC–AD 220), a time of prosperity and cultural solidification. During this period, Chinese influence expanded westward, and China's silk and other goods became valued commodities in India, the Middle East, and the Mediterranean. Another period of disintegration followed, with northern states warring against those in the south until the Sui dynasty reunited the heartland about AD 580. This aristocratic family was one of many from northwest China that had intermarried with leading families of the "barbarian" nomads in that area. This provided them with a base for future conquests in that direction.

As the Sui took control, they reigned through local militias, introduced a unified legal code, and doled out farmland to the peasants. Yet within a quarter century of their rise, all of their achievements were jeopardized by their leaders' decision to invade Korea. By 614, when a fourth attempt ended in complete failure, many Chinese were convinced that the dynasty had lost the "mandate of heaven," the divine favor and sanction necessary for them to rule. Heaven had turned against the rulers due to their pride and lack of concern for the welfare of their own country and its people. The dynasty's collapse was swift. Yet their successors would usher in what is still often considered the greatest age of Chinese civilization.[1]

The Rise of the Tang

In 617, a long-standing and high-ranking military commander named Li Yuan led a revolt against the Sui emperor. By the following year he was in control of the capital. It took his fledgling dynasty another ten years, however, to solidify control over the rest of China. Gaozu, the temple name that Li Yuan was given after his death and by which he is most commonly known, also came from a northern clan. He and his successors put much time and effort into becoming steeped in Chinese culture and tradition and in patronizing the traditional arts. They kept most of the Sui administrative structures and economic reforms intact. They also supported a resurgence of Confucian values while portraying themselves as pious descendants of the Daoist sage Laozi. These steps were a sort of "make China great again" campaign by which they sought to nurture widespread support for their new dynasty from both major moral traditions. An edict of 624 boasted: "Since the degenerate age of decline, the elegant Dao has sunk into oblivion. For endless years the Confucian breeze has not been fanned. . . . Cherished words and books are all ashes. . . . The customs of the schools have been destroyed. . . . But now, since China has been purified

---

1. On the Sui, see the still useful overview of Arthur F. Wright, *The Sui Dynasty* (New York: Knopf, 1978).

and shields and weapons are gradually being put away, the profession of civil officials can again flourish."[2]

However, in one important way, the new Tang ruler did not follow in the footsteps of his Sui predecessors.[3] The second Sui emperor, Yangdi (r. 605–616), had become a Buddhist. Already during the later Han dynasty, that religion had begun spreading from India into China and had increasingly become an important cultural and religious influence. But only in the seventh century did Buddhism become truly Chinese, in part due to the new version called Tiantai that began receiving imperial support under Yangdi. By the 620s there were more than one hundred Buddhist temples in the Sui/Tang capital city of Chang'an alone! When the Tang ruler Gaozu took control, however, he quickly moved to limit the influence of the Buddhists, ordering the closure of all but three of those temples. He also closed two-thirds of the Daoist temples. But these actions were a major miscalculation on his part. Within three months of his edicts and with the backing of Buddhist and Daoist leaders, the aging emperor was sent into retirement and replaced by one of his sons. That son was Li Shimin, but he is better known by his temple name Taizong.

The Xi'an stele tells us that it was during the reign of Taizong that a delegation of Christians arrived in the Chinese capital with a request to be allowed to begin operation. The text also traces the results of that mission over the century and a half that followed, and it is still our best glimpse into the Jingjiao and its development. In the following pages we will trace that history, citing both the stele's poetic elegy (labeled as "poem") and the commentary wherever applicable.

China at the Time of Taizong (626–649)

The stele text really gives very little detail about the actual reign of Taizong. Here are the brief statements it provides:

> The most illustrious emperor's way surpassed that of previous rulers. He assumed control and dispelled chaos; the empire increased and flourished. (Poem 27.2–27.5)

2. Collection of Tang Imperial Edicts (*Tang da zhaoling ji*, 唐大诏令集) 35 (Beijing: Commercial Press, 1959), 105.6a–7a.

3. For the Tang, see Mark Edward Lewis, *China's Cosmopolitan Empire: The Tang Dynasty*, History of Imperial China 3 (Cambridge, MA: Belknap Press of Harvard University Press, 2009).

Taizong, a cultured emperor, shone brightly and created new fortune, a brilliant sage governing his people. (Com. 10.10–10.12)

The text about his years as emperor concentrates instead on the arrival of the Christian missionaries and the resulting imperial edict. This may partly be a result of the 150-year gap between Taizong's rule and the composition of the stele text. The chaos the emperor is said to have ended in the first of the two above quotations may be the power struggle and discord that surrounded his father's attempted suppression of the Buddhist and Daoist segments of the population; yet it could equally be a more general reference to his solidification of power for the new dynasty. Looking back, Jingjing could say with little exaggeration that Taizong's achievements surpassed those of his predecessors and that he took China to new economic and political heights, as well as enlarged the empire. Today he is still remembered as one of the giants of Chinese imperial history.

While not especially innovative, Taizong capably consolidated the administrative system established by the previous Sui dynasty and furthered the development of governmental institutions such as the examination system, which chose bureaucrats for local and national appointments on the basis of a thorough knowledge of Confucian precepts. That system was slowly refined over the centuries that followed and continued in use until 1905! The strength and stability of the new dynasty, together with its establishment of protectorates among the oasis kingdoms of the far northwest, allowed the commercial land routes between China and the Middle East to thrive as never before. The interconnecting trade routes that developed are today referred to as the Silk Road. This trade had already begun under the Han dynasty, but since the distances were so great, commerce could flourish along its paths only in times when both Persia and China had strong central governments.

Although Silk Road trade was not a major factor in the prosperity of China as a whole, the intercultural openness that it fostered was instrumental in shaping the image and the legacy of the Tang. The beautiful three-color (*sancai*) glazed figurines of foreign horses, camels, traders, dancers, and courtiers that were placed in tombs of the period are still admired in museums around the world today. The cultural confidence created by the country's prosperity, combined with the influences of the new foreign contacts, resulted in great achievements in other arts as well, notably calligraphy, painting, and poetry. Thus, under the Tang, China experienced one of its rare periods of openness to the outside world in contrast to its normally xenophobic and isolationist policies. This golden age was still in its early stages when the first known Christian missionaries arrived at the capital Chang'an during the reign of Taizong.[4]

Alopen Comes to China

The arrival of Alopen (or Aluoben) at Chang'an in 635 is one of the few secure dates we have in Jingjiao history. This is widely used as the starting date for the history of Syriac Christianity in China, and Alopen is cited as the great missionary who traveled from Persia to first preach the gospel in the Middle Kingdom. However, a closer reading of the stele text (our only source for this information) requires us to paint a more nuanced picture of the arrival of Christianity in China.

> (At that time), the pure, bright Luminous Teaching [Jingjiao] was introduced to our Tang kingdom. Its scriptures were translated and temples built; the [spiritually] dead revived and boats gave passage [to heaven]. (Poem 27.6–27.9)

> In Da Qin there was a man of excellent virtue, his name was Alopen. He observed the heavens and carried the true scriptures here; he studied the winds and hurried past great perils. In the ninth year of the Zhenguan era [635], he arrived at Chang'an. The emperor sent his minister of state, Duke Fang Xuanling, to receive him in the western suburbs and to bring him in with a warm welcome. After his scriptures were translated in the royal library, the palace officials investigated their teaching. After thoroughly understanding it to be suitable and true, special permission was given for its propagation. (Com. 10.13–11.10)

The commentary makes it clear that Alopen and his retinue were expected when they arrived in Chang'an. An imperial delegation led by none other than Fang Xuanling (房玄齡), the emperor's top official and advisor, went out to meet and welcome the foreign arrivals. After the emperor, Fang was perhaps the most famous man in China during this period. He was part of an inner

---

4. For daily life in Tang China, see Charles Benn, *China's Golden Age: Everyday Life in the Tang Dynasty* (Oxford: Oxford University Press, 2004).

triumvirate of decision makers at the highest level of government and was also the emperor's constant companion.[5]

Religious activity, as we have seen, was closely monitored by the Tang government, just as it has been throughout China's history. With the opening up of trade with the western regions, foreigners had come to set up commercial establishments in the Tang capital. Just like local businessmen, foreigners were allowed to form merchant associations (*hang*) that were closely supervised by the government. They lived in designated sections of the city and to a certain degree were represented by their own headmen and subject to their own laws. By the time of Alopen's arrival, many Persians and Sogdians were among the foreign resident merchants and shopkeepers who lived in the Tang capital.

As we saw in chapter 1, Syriac-speaking Christians and missionaries of the Church of the East had taken the gospel into the regions east of Persia during the fifth and sixth centuries. Although it remained a minority religion, it became firmly established there, and the church had bishops and metropolitans in various cities along the Silk Road by the early seventh century. It would be only natural to expect, therefore, that some of the foreign merchants who came to live and work in Chang'an were Christian. As the community grew and became more permanent, they would have experienced the need for more organized and permanent spiritual care for themselves and their families. Ordained priests were needed to baptize their children, administer the Lord's Supper, and perform marriages and burials. And, of course, the Christians wanted to share their faith with their non-Christian neighbors, foreign-born and Chinese alike. For all of these reasons, they must have felt an increasing need to establish a more formal community of believers served by ordained and trained clergy.

We have no record of the steps involved, but at some point the Persian and Sogdian Christians in Chang'an must have sent an appeal back to Persia to the patriarch of the Church of the East: "Send priests to serve us." Even when their request was favorably received, however, much remained to be done. Communications had to be opened with the Chinese imperial court. If Christian clergy were to function inside China, official imperial approval was necessary. Since the Church of the East had official standing with the Sasanid government, the

5. On Fang Xuanling (578–648), see Howard Wechsler, "Tai-tsung (Reign 626–49) the Consolidator," in *Sui and T'ang China, 589–906, Part 1*, vol. 3 of *The Cambridge History of China*, ed. Denis Twitchett (Cambridge: Cambridge University Press, 1979), 188–241, esp. 195–96. At the time of Alopen's arrival, Fang would have been in the middle of his thirteen years of service (629–642) as vice president of the Department of State Affairs, the longest tenure of any high official in Taizong's reign.

patriarch may well have appealed to King Yazdegerd III (r. 632–651) either to assist in negotiations or even to make this request an official one from the Sasanian court. Eventually, either as a favor to the local foreign community or to further their foreign relations initiatives with the Sasanians, the Chinese court agreed to consider the request. As a matter of course, however, the teachings of this new sect would have to be examined and approved. Once that had been successfully completed, permission for priests to serve the foreign community could be granted.[6]

The result was that in 635 the Church of the East sent a delegation to China led by Alopen. The commentary's description of him as a man of "superior virtue" probably indicates that he held the office of bishop. For such an important yet delicate mission, the patriarch would have selected a priest from among the clergy whom he knew personally, or one highly recommended to him by his advisors. He may also have looked for a man with roots along the Silk Road, someone who would have understood Chinese culture better than a native Persian. The name Alopen might indicate that he was originally from Sogdia. In any case, he must have been elevated to his new position and commissioned by the patriarch himself in Seleucia-Ctesiphon before setting out on the long trip from Da Qin. The commentary goes on to describe his departure and explain that his trip was carefully planned to take advantage of optimal seasonal and travel conditions. Official communications would have preceded him, informing the Tang court officials when the formal delegation should be expected. In fact, he may well have traveled as part of a larger official embassy from the Sasanian government to the Tang court.[7] This scenario best explains the high-level reception given to Alopen by the famous courtier and imperial minister Fang Xuanling.

After the initial greeting, minister Fang escorted the retinue to lodgings near the imperial palace, and shortly afterward an official audience was conducted. Here we can add some details from another document now in the Bibliothèque Nationale. This manuscript, discovered in the early twentieth century by the French Sinologist Paul Pelliot, will be discussed at length in the next chapter. For now, we need only note that it contains two Christian writings and ends with a historical note. In that appendix, we read about

6. For the background of Alopen's mission, see Glen L. Thompson, "Was Alopen a Missionary?" in *Hidden Treasures and Intercultural Encounters*, ed. Dietmar W. Winkler and Li Tang, Orientalia-Patristica-Oecumenica 1 (Vienna: LIT Verlag, 2009) 267–78.

7. Todd Godwin has shown that there was a continuous Sasanian/Persian presence at the Tang court. See his *Persian Christians at the Chinese Court: The Xi'an Stele and the Early Medieval Church of the East* (London: I. B. Tauris, 2018).

Alopen's arrival in Chang'an and that he "humbly presented a petition in his native tongue," which was "reverentially submitted" to the emperor through Fang Xuanling and Wei Zheng, another famous court official of the period.[8] This confirms and slightly expands on what the stele text records. The delegation handed over a formal petition to preach and teach in China, and, along with it, this new sect submitted their doctrinal writings for translation and approval. Which government bureau took charge of the evaluation is not certain. The poem is using official language when it says that the emperor examined the teachings. A government bureau would have held numerous meetings at which the delegation was asked to explain some of the more intricate and sensitive points of doctrine to the appropriate official investigators. All this took time. Thus, it was almost three years later, in August/September of 638, that the new religion was approved for general dissemination. An imperial edict was issued to that effect, and Jingjing quotes a section of it in the stele text:

Autumn, the seventh month of the twelfth year of the Zhenguan reign [AD 638]; the imperial decree is as follows:

"The way has no single name;
the holy takes no single form.
When teachings vary from place to place,
they give the greatest help to the largest number of people.

Alopen is a man of great virtue from Da Qin. He has brought books and images from afar and presented them at the capital. He thoroughly explained their teachings—challenging, wonderful and serene in their operation.

When its original teaching is discerned,
it appears already mature.
Its words have no complicated meaning,
so when understood it is not forgotten.

8. Translations of the historical note in columns 19–22 of the Pelliot manuscript can be found in Matteo Nicolini-Zani, *The Luminous Way to the East: Texts and History of the First Encounter of Christianity with China* (Oxford: Oxford University Press, 2022), 231–32, and in Johan Ferreira, *Early Chinese Christianity: The Tang Christian Monument and Other Documents*, Early Christian Studies 17 (Sydney: St. Paul's Publications, 2014), 272–73.

Since it aids all creatures and profits mankind, it is proper that it be propagated everywhere. Therefore, in the Yining neighborhood of the capital, officials should immediately construct one Da Qin temple, and allow twenty-one men to serve there as monks." (Com. 11.11–13.5)

The attitude of the imperial court was simple. There is no single form of religion for all people, but each culture and land may have its own. Alopen, as representative of the delegation of the Church of the East, had properly shown their sacred texts and liturgical objects to the authorities and had explained the tenets of their faith. The results are then summarized in four couplets of poetry, each containing two four-character lines. The examiners have seen that (a) the teachers have been forthright in explaining the wondrous nature of its teachings; (b) while new to China, the faith itself has a long history; and (c) the sect does not deal in secret teachings and mysterious rites, but its tenets are simple and memorable. Finally, since their teaching can be beneficial to all, imperial permission is granted for the church to propagate its teachings everywhere in China. Therefore, the building of a monastery served by twenty-one monks is permitted in the capital itself.

The edict is a straightforward act of approval for the church. It should not be read, however, as an expression of the emperor's personal religious interest in the new teachings. The type of laudatory phrases used are similar to ones found in edicts dealing with other religions as well. Yet there are indications that the new religion was given *full* approval to the *maximum* allowable limits. Manichaeism and Zoroastrianism, two other religions from Persia, were also approved for operation in China, yet they were allowed only to function among the foreign immigrants. The edict governing the Jingjiao had no such restrictions but specifically allowed the propagation of its teachings throughout the empire. Second, Buddhism and Daoism were also regulated by the government. Their monks are mentioned in multiples of seven in other Tang-period religious texts, and twenty-one seems to indicate a large establishment or one that had received special favor. Thus the permission for twenty-one monks in the first Christian monastery in China's capital seems to be permitting the construction and operation of a major religious complex. We can be sure that the edict is unquestionably authentic and has been cited accurately in the stele since it has also been preserved in another collection of imperial decrees from the Tang dynasty, the *Tang Huiyao*.[9]

9. *Tang Huiyao* (唐會要) or *Institutional History of the Tang* was an extensive collection of one hundred books of imperial state materials edited by Wang Pu in 961. The edict about

Partnership of the Tang Dynasty and the Jingjiao

Clearly one of the objects of the stele text, written a century and a half after the arrival of Alopen, is to show that the Jingjiao church had not only been legally introduced into China but had also been a blessing to China. "One hundred blessings arose together; ten thousand regions flourished," said the text (Poem 27.10–27.11). During those years, China and its people flourished as never before, thanks to the material prosperity and peace brought about by the Tang emperors, but also, it is implied, due to the blessings of the new religion. The section on Taizong's reign ends with this thought, expressed in traditional metaphors and allusions from Chinese history. As great as the Zhou dynasty (ca. 1050–250 BC) had been, it had come to an end. And just as the great Daoist philosopher Laozi had hopped into his chariot and disappeared into the west never to return, so the Zhou was gone forever. But the Tang had now arisen and shown China the path to new heights of power, glory, and prosperity. They had been assisted in this when, from that very west where Laozi had disappeared, the Jingjiao appeared on the scene to spread the blessings of its faith across China. As the commentary put it, "The virtue of the Zhou has departed, and Laozi's chariot has disappeared into the west. But now, under the great Tang, the Way is rising, and the Luminous Teaching is blowing into the east" (Com. 13.6–13.9). Together, the Tang and the Jingjiao had brought countless blessings upon the people of China, and most especially peace, the blessing that is still treasured most in the vast country so prone to regional disharmony.

It is possible that these two four-character couplets in the commentary (13.6–13.9) are not the words of Jingjing. They may possibly have been a conclusion or addendum to the original imperial decree, meant to poetically summarize the good relationship that existed (or was expected to develop) between the Tang court and the subject religion.[10] A similar set of four-character cou-

---

the Jingjiao appears near the end (section 1011–1012) of book 49, which deals with Buddhism and other religions. For a discussion of the *Tang Huiyao* and stele versions and the minor discrepancies between them, see Forte's discussion in Paul Pelliot, *L'inscription Nestorienne de Si-Ngan-Fou*, ed. Antonino Forte (Kyoto: Scuola di studi sull'Asia orientale; Paris: Collège de France Institut des Hautes Etudes Chinoises, 1996), 349–73.

10. Because of the lack of any punctuation, the interpreter must decide where the edict quotation ends. Some (Saeki, Eccles and Lieu, Ferreira) end the edict with the announcement allowing the new teaching to be propagated everywhere (13.2). Others (Nicolini-Zani, Wilmshurst, Pelliot) extend it to include the building of the Da Qin building in Chang'an (13.5). Earlier translators (Wylie, Moule) extended it to encompass the four-line poetic com-

plets is found at the end of the section on Xuanzong's reign (18.2–18.5). On the other hand, there is no reason why Jingjing himself may not have concluded his commentary on these two emperors with a laudatory summary of the double blessing that the Tang and the Jingjiao provided for China.

The commentary on Taizong's reign concludes with additional evidence that the imperial court recognized the value of the Jingjiao. "Quickly officials were ordered to offer the imperial portrait, for copy and display upon the temple walls. The heavenly visage radiated color, it [shone] with bold brightness in the Luminous temple. The sacred image fluttered with good fortune, eternally lustrous in its rule of society" (Com. 13.10–14.2). An official copy of the emperor's portrait was given to the new Jingjiao temple for display there. This episode is given in some detail by Jingjing as an obvious mark of imperial favor. He will later mention a similar gift from Emperor Xuanzong (Poem 28.7–28.9; Com. 17.5–18.5). The writer used these incidents to further one of his goals—to remind the reader of the imperial favor that the Jingjiao enjoyed. This is especially important because Jingjing knew that not all the emperors in the past had been so favorable and that this might be the case again in the future. The documenting of past imperial edicts and benefactions might also prove instrumental in warding off attempts by the church's enemies to impose future sanctions against it.

Some Christians who have studied the early church in China have spoken harshly against the Jingjiao for their close rapport with the Tang government. They have seen this relationship as one important reason for the demise of the Jingjiao within a century of the erection of the stele. A more balanced evaluation is surely in order, however. On the one hand, the relationship was not as close as many have judged it to be. The edict, the eulogy, and the commentary, with their flowery language, must be read on the basis of the norms of Chinese governmental courtesy and the canons of public laudatory discourse. Similar positive and polite utterances are made about the other religious groups and officials as well. On the other hand, imperial portraits displayed on church walls were a definite sign not just of favor but also of governmental watchfulness over the activities of the church. (One need only think of the ubiquitous portraits of dictators found in numerous countries yet today.) Again, this was totally in line with the normal governmental oversight of all religious activity within its realms.

---

ment that ends with the Luminous Teaching blowing into the east (13.9). Since the *Tang Huiyao* (see previous note) includes the text through 13.5, ending the edict at 13.2 must certainly be wrong.

During the more than two decades of Taizong's reign, the emperor showed many favors to the Daoist elite, and he stressed his family's supposed descent from Laozi himself. He also built a Buddhist temple in Chang'an in memory of his mother and took part in its ceremonies. Yet almost simultaneously he issued several edicts that sought to control the size and importance of Buddhism and Daoism and their clergy (though not as radically as his father had). Thus, he both gave favors and exerted control on all religions. There is no evidence that his attitude toward the new Christian sect was any different, or that his favors were more than the normal piety to be shown toward all lesser religious groups. Some control must also be assumed, perhaps in the number, location, and size of churches. Jingjing simply does not mention these, as his readers would have taken them for granted—and it did not further his agenda to bring it to the notice of his readers. We must therefore be cautious in interpreting the situation and in judging it by our modern standards of separation of church and state, standards that took centuries for the post-Reformation church to develop and implement.

Yet it is also legitimate to ask whether the acceptance and display of imperial portraits on church property, perhaps even in the worship space itself, did hinder or change the church's teaching and activities in practice. Or was this merely the equivalent of having an American flag displayed in an American church? This is a subject to which we will return. Here we simply note that Jingjing takes several opportunities to stress that the Tang rulers gave their approval and support for the church and its ongoing work. This began with the arrival of Alopen in 635 and seems to have lasted throughout the reign of Taizong.

Having described to his non-Christian readers the arrival of this new religion, Jingjing takes the opportunity to enlighten them about where the church had come from. What is that Da Qin kingdom that was the original home of the Luminous Teaching? He answers this by adding a summary description of Da Qin:

According to the *Illustrated Records of the Western Regions* and to the historical records of the Han and Wei dynasties, the land of Da Qin overlooks to its south a coral sea, to its north it abuts mountains of great treasure; to its west lie the borders of the immortal realm and dense forests, to its east it meets the eternal winds and the mild waters. Its earth produces asbestos, restorative fragrances, moon pearls, and jade that glows in the dark. There is no thievery there; the people are content. No religion exists but the Luminous Teaching [Jingjiao]; no ruler is put on the throne unless he is virtuous. The land is broad and extensive, and its cultural life prosperous and enlightened. (Com. 14.3–15.6)

Jingjing states that his information about Da Qin comes from classical Chinese sources, including one entitled *Illustrated Records of the Western Regions*. Although written during the Sui dynasty (581–618), it incorporated earlier written reports from the Han (206 BC–AD 220) and Wei (AD 386–534) periods (Com. 14.3). Da Qin is pictured as a land with rare and abundant resources located far to the west, yet just east of the realms of the departed. Its people live in contentment, for their rulers are always virtuous and their society is both prosperous and enlightened. And, most importantly, everyone shares the same religion—the Jingjiao. While the last "fact" is inserted almost casually into the final section of this description, this was undoubtedly another reason for the inclusion of this fanciful description. Jingjing knew full well that there were many half-truths and imaginary elements in the Chinese accounts he had appropriated. Yet the antiquity of his sources and the respect given them within China served his purpose of elevating the Da Qin empire and its cultural heritage in the eyes of Chinese readers. Perhaps he also hoped this might spark their interest and thereby also perhaps open their ears in a positive way to consider further the Luminous Teaching that came from so far away.[11]

Continued Expansion under Gaozong (649–683)

The minister Fang Xuanling was one of the men appointed to tutor Taizong's son, Li Zhi, crown prince from 643, and to prepare him to assume imperial control. Upon Taizong's death in 649, the eighteen-year-old Li Zhi ascended the throne. We know him by his temple name Gaozong. He was to rule almost thirty-five years, at least formally. But in reality, by the mid-650s he had come under the spell of one of his father's former concubines, Wu Zetian. Wu not only became empress, but Gaozong allowed her to control imperial decisions and policies as he increasingly suffered from ill health. Intrigue within the palace and war on several boundaries of the empire made this a period of

11. Most of the book named by Jingjing has not survived. The *Book of the Later Han* (*Hou Hanshu*) has, however, and it is surely one of the Han sources used by Jingjing in his description. See the section on Da Qin in John Hill, *Through the Jade Gate—China to Rome*, vol. 1, updated and expanded edition (CreateSpace, 2015), 22–27 (text and translation), and 266–71 (notes).

political and military unrest.[12] Yet, as a whole, China continued to prosper, as Jingjing's account testifies.

> When Gaozong succeeded his father, he also erected religious buildings. Serene buildings, spacious and bright, they spread, filling the land. The true Way was proclaimed and it enlightened people; a system of clergy was established. The people were content and happy; they experienced no disasters or hardships. (Poem 27.12–28.4)

> Gaozong, the great emperor, ably and respectfully continued the policies of his predecessor, and enhanced the true traditions, Luminous temples were established in every prefecture; he honored Alopen with the title "Grand Master of Religious Teaching and Protector of the Nation." Religion spread to the ten regions, the country prospered, and its foundations flourished. Temples could be found in one hundred walled cities, and the Luminous Teaching blessed many families. (Com. 15.7–16.3)

Jingjing faced a delicate job in describing Gaozong's reign in a positive light. By the time he wrote over a century later, Wu Zetian was already viewed as the epitome of an evil ruler (as she still is portrayed today). Thus, Jingjing can say little more than that he continued the policies of his predecessors. If we did not have the commentary, we might interpret the "serene buildings" that the poem says Gaozong built as referring to the new imperial palaces built in Chang'an as well as in the increasingly important eastern capital city of Luoyang. But the commentary makes clear that Jingjing credits him with allowing the construction of new Luminous temples "in every prefecture." This may have been spurred on by the influx of Christians among the new refugees from Persia. The Muslim armies were methodically conquering the Sasanian territories during this period, and eventually their ruler, Peroz III, fled to Chang'an to plead for help; he remained an exile in China until his death.

The stele's accounts of Gaozong's actions provide us with a good example of the difficulty in interpreting the stele's text. The Eccles/Lieu translation is straightforward: "He [Gaozong] commanded Luminous temples to be built in all the prefectures." But such a literal translation conceals what really happened.

---

12. On the reigns of Gaozong and Empress Wu, see D. Twitchett and H. Wechsler, "Kao-tsung (Reign 649–83) and the Empress Wu: The Inheritor and Usurper," and R. Guisso, "The Reigns of the Empress Wu, Chung-tsung and Jui-tsung (684–712)," in Twitchett, *Sui and T'ang China, 589–906, Part 1,* 242–89 and 290–332, respectively.

During this period China was divided into 358 prefectures (州, *zhou*). The emperor neither paid for Christian churches to be built in each of these nor "commanded" that the Christians do so. Rather, the church must have appealed for official permission to build churches outside of the largest cities, and perhaps in communities with no large foreign presence. Jingjing is merely recording, in a very flowery and flattering way, to be sure, that Gaozong's government had granted that request. The result was that the Christian teaching was heard more widely in China and new churches and monasteries did appear in many parts of the land. "Filling the land," "every prefecture," and "in one hundred walled cities," however, must all be interpreted as literary hyperbole, perfectly acceptable, especially when it made the emperor look generous.

Gaozong, however, went further. Alopen by this time was a venerable figure, respected both within and outside the Chinese church. Gaozong gave him the high honorary titles of Grand Master of Religious Teaching and Protector of the Nation. (It is unclear whether these were both part of a single title.) At first reading, this seems to indicate that the Jingjiao church enjoyed a very favorable or even privileged position with Gaozong and his government. That of course is the impression Jingjing is seeking to make on his readers. But a study of Gaozong's religious policy leads us to a more measured conclusion. The emperor continued his father's attempts to achieve some nominal control over the Buddhists, but as in all else, his policies were quickly marginalized by those of his father's consort Wu. She was highly superstitious and in turn made use of shamans, Daoist sorcerers, and Buddhist holy men. She also had a new temple, the Hall of Illumination, built in honor of Shangdi, the supreme heavenly deity. Thus, there is no reason to believe that the Christians were elevated to a special place in the religious hierarchy of China or were specially favored by this emperor. The honorary titles given to Alopen were just that—honorary titles that indicated imperial favor and expectations for loyalty without actually providing any special preferment in practice. Similar titles were given by the emperors to non-Christian religious leaders as well.

Three Decades of Uncertainty (683–712)

By the time Gaozong breathed his last, Wu Zetian was in complete control of the government with the title of empress dowager. Her twenty-eight-year-old son Zhongzong (r. 684) was officially the new emperor, but when he attempted to show some independent initiative, Wu had him deposed after just six weeks of rule. She replaced him with his younger brother Ruizong (r. 684–690). The twenty-two-year-old Ruizong initially was more willing to allow his mother to exercise control on his behalf, so he lasted six years before being demoted to crown prince. It was at this point, in 690, that Wu took the bold move of declaring herself, a female, to be emperor, and declared the start of a new Zhou dynasty. This was an unprecedented step, yet she was able to hang on as sole ruler for some fifteen years until the infirmities of age allowed a palace coup to bring her son Zhongzong (r. 705–710) back to the throne and reestablish the Tang dynasty. Upon his death in 710, Zhongzong's sixteen-year-old son was made emperor briefly. But within days he was replaced by Zhongzong's brother, the former emperor, Ruizong (710–712). Ruizong only lasted two years himself before he resigned, and the young and energetic Xuanzong began his long rule (712–756). Thus ended more than a quarter century of imperial intrigue in which the only empress in Chinese history was the one consistent presence and influence.

Jingjing does not mention the empress in any way, however, nor does he even attempt to speak about the complex and sensitive political situation of this period. While the stele's poem skips this period completely, the stele's commentary artfully describes how the Jingjiao was affected by the religious turmoil of the period.

> In the Shengli period [AD 698–700], Buddhists used their influence and raised their voices in the eastern capital [Luoyang]. In the Xiantian era [AD 712–713], low-ranking scholars stirred up ridicule, spreading slander in the western capital [Chang'an]; then people arose like the head monk Luohan, and the man of great virtue Jilie; both were from a noble place and of noble heritage, otherworldly men and senior monks; together they restored the mysterious net. Together they tied up the knot that had been cut. (Com. 16.4–16.15)

Wu's religious passions, innovations, and fluctuations had become evident while Gaozong was still alive. Here is how two noted scholars of the Tang dynasty described her religious activities: "Under the influence of a succession of priests, sorcerers and wizards who became her most intimate associates, the empress became obsessed with religious ritual, symbolism and nomenclature. She ransacked tradition and created new emblems to lend supernatural authority to her position and to the dynasty which she now virtually controlled."[13]

---

13. Twitchett and Wechsler, "Kao-tsung (Reign 649–83) and the Empress Wu," 258–59.

Upon Gaozong's death, many of Wu's personal interests were reflected in government policy. She made the eastern capital of Luoyang into her permanent residence, partly because of her fear of the ghosts of high officials and royalty whose deaths she had engineered in the palace in Chang'an. She styled herself both as Heavenly Ruler and Heavenly Empress, and she sponsored and took part in a wide variety of ancient Chinese, Daoist, and Buddhist ceremonies. Starting in 685, an affair with the Buddhist monk Huaiyi resulted in Wu giving increasing favor to Buddhism, and it was elevated above Daoism in official rites from 690 on. She paid for the building of numerous Buddhist temples and appointed some senior monks to the rank of duke. In the mid-690s, the empress was even briefly entranced by several Buddhist mystics.

Jingjing's commentary focuses on two events of this period to illustrate the fluctuating fortunes of the Jingjiao under the empress and her Zhou dynasty. The first took place between 698 and 700 in Luoyang, where the empress resided during the period of her sole rule. The supporters of Buddhism caught the ear of the empress or her minions in some way that brought disrepute and imperial disfavor on the Jingjiao community. Because of the public nature of the stele, however, Jingjing gives no further details.

The second event took place a decade later. By 712, not only was Wu safely in the grave, but the brief restoration to power of both Zhongzong (705–710) and Ruizong (710–712) had come to an end. The court had moved back to Chang'an, and the much more competent Xuanzong (712–756) had taken full control of the throne and begun his lengthy reign. Already under the pro-Daoist Ruizong, laws had been passed ordering the demolition of illegally built Buddhist monasteries. Xuanzong continued the pressure by making it illegal for elite families to establish private Buddhist temples and by cracking down on illegal ordinations of monks.[14] The same Daoist leaders who encouraged these imperial decrees, "ignorant men," as Jingjing calls them, began to slander the Jingjiao to the new ruler, and this must have included attacks on church property. However, the damage was reversed sometime later thanks to two leaders of the church, the abbot Luohan and the bishop Jilie. Their pedigree, age, rank, and spiritual bearing enabled them to defend the church and ward off the slanderers.

Jingjing writes that Luohan and Jilie "restored the mysterious net" and "tied again the knot that had been cut." These expressions had been previously used in an honorific inscription describing two Buddhist sages (Asvaghosa and Nagarjuna) in their struggle against heresies. The phrases are found in

---

14. On Xuanzong, see D. Twitchett, "Hsüan-tsung (Reign 712–56)," in Twitchett, *Sui and T'ang China, 589–906, Part 1*, 333–463. On his religious policies, see especially 411–13.

the so-called Dhuta Monastery inscription, a text that was identified already by Paul Pelliot as a model that Jingjing may have imitated when composing the Chang'an stele text.[15] Jingjing used these same metaphors to describe the favorable connection between the imperial household and the Jingjiao church that had unfortunately been severed during the previous decades. When read together with Com. 17.3–17.4, they also indicate that in the absence of imperial protection, churches and monasteries had been desecrated, closed, or even seized by their religious rivals. That he quoted from an older Buddhist inscription has been seen by some scholars as an indication of Jingjing's own Buddhist tendencies. However, using an earlier approved Buddhist text at just this point may have been part of a very savvy strategy—describing the rupture between the imperial rulers and the church in as diplomatic a way as possible. It might have deflected any possible criticism of what was being said.

One of our few references to the Chinese church from Syriac historical sources deals with this same period. The fourteenth-century author 'Abdisho of Nisibis (also known as 'Abdisho bar Brikha) records that the patriarch Sliba-zkha (714–718) upgraded several bishoprics in the East and along the silk routes to the rank of metropolitan. In this regard he specifically mentions Herat, Samarkand, India, and China.[16] If the newly appointed metropolitan for China was this Jilie, he may have arrived in Chang'an about 715 (but see discussion on pp. 143–44 below). His arrival would have given the new ruler, Xuanzong, the perfect opportunity to restore the Jingjiao to favor.

Revival under Xuanzong (712–756)

The first half of Xuanzong's four-decade reign is remembered as a high-water mark of the Tang period. He ruled diligently and effectively at home, and his

---

15. On the Dhuta inscription, see Richard B. Mather, "Wang Chin's 'Dhuta Temple Stele Inscription' as an Example of Buddhist Parallel Prose," *Journal of the American Oriental Society* 83, no. 3 (August-September 1963): 338–59. For a structural comparison between it and the Chang'an Christian stele, see Glen L. Thompson, "The Structure of the Stele," in *Artifact, Text, Context*, ed. Li Tang and Dietmar W. Winkler, Orientalia-Patristica-Oecumenica 17 (Vienna: LIT, 2020), 175–80. Chen Huaiyu has identified other likely models, and there is no reason that Jingjing could not have been influenced by several other literary inscriptions. See the summary discussion of Nicolini-Zani, *The Luminous Way*, 170.

16. See the text in A. C. Moule, *Christians in China before the Year 1550* (London: SPCK, 1930), 20. See also Erica C. D. Hunter, "The Church of the East in Central Asia," *Bulletin of the John Rylands Library* 78, no. 3 (1996): 133–34.

foreign policy increased trade and commerce both along the silk routes and through maritime trade. He encouraged poetry and the other fine arts. He preferred Daoism with its emphasis on harmony over Buddhism; in an edict of 726, he decreed that every household should contain a copy of the Daoist classic, the *Dao de jing*. Jingjing also praises his rule in his stele poem: "When Xuanzong became emperor, he recovered and cultivated true rule. His imperial tablets were radiant; his celestial writings were resplendent. The imperial portraits glittered like gems; all the land was most respectful; all that was done promoted flourishing; the people relied on his benevolence" (28.5–28.12).

The commentary of Jingjing describes in some detail the rehabilitation of the Jingjiao during this period.

> Xuanzong, the emperor of perfect understanding, ordered the Prince of Ning and other princes (five in all) to personally visit the sacred building, and to restore the altar and sanctuary.[17] The sacred pillars, toppled for a time, rose straight again and to new heights; the stones, displaced for a time, were again realigned. At the start of the Tianbao era [AD 742–756], he ordered that the great general Gao Lishi be sent with five imperial portraits to be installed inside the temple. He also gave one hundred bolts of silk, for the dedication of the portraits of the emperors. Although the beard of the dragon was far away, his bow and sword could still be touched. The noble features radiated light, and the imperial face was very near to us. (Com. 17.1–18.5)

Jingjing credits the emperor with supporting the restoration of one or more Jingjiao sanctuaries. Xuanzong enjoyed a close relationship with his five brothers, including Li Xuan, the prince of Ning. They all held important (if mostly honorary) positions as governors of important prefectures. Thus, they enjoyed high ceremonial titles while having little real power at court. One of their duties was to serve as the emperor's personal assistants and representatives in various capacities.[18] According to Jingjing, Xuanzong now appointed them to oversee the restoration work of at least one Jingjiao church. Since the royal court had moved back to Chang'an, it was probably the church in the

---

17. Nicolini-Zani's translation (*The Luminous Way*, 208) says the princes visited "the places of worship" and rebuilt "the altars." That the expressions can be either singular or plural is a good example of the ambiguity of the classical Chinese that challenges translators and interpreters.

18. On the brothers, see Twitchett, "Hsüan-tsung (Reign 712–56)," 372–74.

traditional capital that received this special attention and imperial patronage. It can also be inferred from Com. 17.3–17.4 that such a restoration was needed due to the previous time of troubles and that public church activities in that building had been suspended for a time.

The second half of Xuanzong's reign was less glorious. This, of course, is not mentioned by Jingjing in his poem or commentary. The poem summarizes Xuanzong's reign by saying that everything the emperor did "promoted flourishing" and that his people enjoyed prosperity. Jingjing does, however, refer to two events in his later Tianbao period (742–756) that showed further marks of the emperor's favor. Xuanzong was a poet and artist by temperament. Early in his Tianbao period of rule, he commissioned imperial portraits of five of the Tang emperors and had them delivered by his general Gao Lishi (高力士) to the Jingjiao, probably to the cathedral church in Chang'an. Gao Lishi (690–762) was a eunuch and career court official who had risen to power under Empress Wu. Later he backed Xuanzong when he seized power and was then made head of the eunuchs who served in the palace. He remained a trusted advisor and emissary for the emperor throughout his reign. It was in the latter capacity that he carried out his visit to the Jingjiao leaders.[19] Along with the portraits, he presented the church with a hundred bales of fine silk. This kind of imperial favor was extremely beneficial to the church. The imperially given portraits that were displayed publicly in the church or monastery complex would constantly remind all who saw them that the Jingjiao had friends in high places, and that the emperor "was very near" to intervene in their behalf if called upon to do so. Note again how the poem is vague in its mention of imperial tablets, writings, and portraits while the commentary fills in the details.

Another Foreign Arrival and Imperial Gift

The second incident is precisely dated in the commentary to 744, the third year of Xuanzong's Tianbao period.

> In the third year, the priest Jihe was in the kingdom of Da Qin. Looking to heaven, he became enlightened; observing the sun, he came to pay homage at the court. The emperor commanded the priests Luohan, Pulun and others

19. On Gao Lishi, see Michael Dalby, "Court Politics in Late T'ang Times," in Twitchett, *Sui and T'ang China, 589–906, Part 1*, 561–681, esp. 571–72.

(seventeen in all), together with the man of great virtue Jihe, to perform virtuous and meritorious rites in the Xingqing palace. Then the emperor composed maxims for display in the temple, plaques carrying the royal inscriptions. These ornaments sparkled like precious jade, and glowed like the red clouds of sunset. The writings of the wise one filled the heavens, and their rays were like radiant reflections of the sun. These bountiful gifts exceeded the height of the Southern Mountains; this flood of favors was as deep as the Eastern Sea.

> There is nothing the Way cannot do,
> and what he does can be described.
> There is nothing beyond the power of the Sage,
> and what he has done can be told. (Com. 18.6–19.11)

The new delegation from Persia that arrived at the imperial court in Chang'an was led by the bishop Jihe, who was probably the newly appointed metropolitan. War had disrupted trade and communication along the Silk Road for much of the previous decade, and the arrival of Jihe and his delegation displayed the ongoing connection of the Jingjiao with the mother church. After paying his respects to the emperor, he and more than a dozen other Jingjiao clergy took part in special rites at the Xingqing palace in Chang'an.[20] This was the former family mansion that in 714 Xuanzong had expanded into an additional palace for himself. Xuanzong had also given mansions nearby to each of his brothers, and it is likely that these princes (who had earlier overseen the restoration of the Jingjiao church, Com. 17.2–17.4) were present at the special ceremonies, although the emperor was almost certainly not in attendance himself.

Following the ceremonies, the emperor presented to the church some of his own calligraphy. The presentation of several characters or a couplet or two of calligraphy from the emperor's own hand has been a mark of high imperial favor throughout Chinese history. Tourists today can still admire imperial calligraphy as it appears over the doors of many buildings in the Forbidden City and other ancient structures. This show of imperial favor caused Jingjing to effusively and hyperbolically describe the beauty of the calligraphy and the magnanimity of the gift. The section then ends with a four-line ode to "the

---

20. The Luohan mentioned here may well be the now aged head monk who had been mentioned earlier in the stele text (col. 16 as cited above), the one who had assisted Jilie in restoring the Jingjiao after the disruptions under Empress Wu.

Way" (*dao*) that seems out of place both in content and in the flow of the commentary. Could it be that these sixteen characters are not from Jingjing, but are instead the couplets composed by Xuanzong? The vague reference to the religious teaching of "the Way" and the benevolent power of "the Sage" could well be the emperor's own poetic evaluation of his support for religious institutions. Taizong had used these same two words ("way," 道, and "holy/sage," 聖) in parallel in his decree quoted earlier in the stele text (Com. 12.1–12.2).

During this later period, however, Emperor Xuanzong had become increasingly bored with his imperial duties and increasingly fell under the influence of his consort Wu Huifei. After her death, his time was spent with his beautiful concubine Yang Yuhuan (immortalized in Chinese literature as the tragic Yang Guifei). Eventually this led to major reversals. The Chinese lost the Battle of Talas (751) to the rising Islamic Abbasid Caliphate, reducing Chinese control in the northwest. And in 755 the half-Turkish, half-Sogdian frontier commander An Lushan raised a major rebellion and established the rival state of Yan in northern China. When his army marched south toward the capital, Xuanzong was forced to flee with his court retainers.[21]

Restoration under Suzong (756–762)

The author of the stele's text could not openly refer to Xuanzong's flight or to his subsequent abdication after his son was elevated by the army to become Emperor Suzong. Instead, he says in his poem, "When Suzong restored rule, the powers of heaven pulled his carriage. The wise sun unfolded its radiance; the winds of good fortune swept away the darkness. Blessings returned to the royal house; disasters vanished and permanently declined. Chaos stopped and the dust settled; our Chinese empire was reestablished" (28.13–29.6). The very brief commentary adds only a few concrete details: "Suzong, a cultivated and enlightened emperor, in Lingwu and other prefectures (five in all), rebuilt the Luminous temples. Great benefits were granted, thus the imperial fortune began; great rejoicing arrived, thus imperial rule was reestablished" (19.12–20.4).

Jingjing's mention in the poem and the commentary of the new emperor recovering and reestablishing rule only hints at the dramatic events that brought the prince to the throne in place of his father. A further intimation is given

---

21. For the An Lushan rebellion, see Dalby, "Court Politics in Late T'ang Times," 561–86. Also still useful is Edwin Pulleyblank, *The Background of the Rebellion of An Lu-Shan* (Oxford: Oxford University Press, 1955).

when it speaks of the emperor rebuilding Jingjiao temples in five commanderies (large administrative units) and specifically identifies Lingwu as one of those locations. When Xuanzong fled from the rebel army to Chengdu, Suzong (at the time still a crown prince with the name Li Heng) was left in charge at the capital. But soon the prince also fled—to Lingwu in the far northwest province of Ningxia. When in 756 the army there elevated him to the throne, his father, Xuanzong, abdicated, although retaining the title of "retired emperor." In the following year, Suzong's army recaptured the capital city Chang'an, and the rebellion slowly lost steam.

Suzong may have felt the need to solidify popular support for his rule after having been elevated under such unusual circumstances. This would have led him to seek and receive legitimation and the blessings of the local religious leaders in Lingwu, including the Jingjiao. In return, the emperor made contributions to their building projects. This incident provided the opportunity for the composer of the stele's text to imply Suzong's more general support for the Christian church. Later, in the commentary's description of Yisi, a major Christian benefactor, it gives further hints that numerous Christians fought for Suzong against the Yan rebels:

> Our great benefactor, the Great Master of the Palace with Golden Seal and Purple Ribbon, the Deputy Military Commander for the Shuofang region, the Appointed Director of the Palace Administration, the recipient of the Imperially conferred Purple Gown is the priest Yisi. . . .
>
> Later his name was inscribed at the royal tent. When Duke Guo Ziyi, Secondary Minister of State and Prince of Fanyang, first took military command in the Shuofang region, Suzong appointed him as [the duke's] attendant on his travels. (Com. 22.13–23.3; 23.11–24.3)[22]

Yisi was both a Jingjiao priest and a high-ranking military official in Suzong's army. He became a key officer under the commander of the northern army, Guo, the duke of Ziyi. Guo took command of the army in 756, and his leadership and strategy were given much credit for the defeat of the rebels and the consolidation of Suzong's power. Shuofang, with its headquarters at Lingwu, was one of the nine frontier administrative units called *commanderies* (郡, *jun*) that had been established under Xuanzong to defend the northern and western frontiers. It protected the Ordos or Guanzhong region against the Turkish tribes of the northwest and served to oversee the tribal peoples who

---

22. On Yisi's titles and honors, see p. 154 in chap. 6 below.

occupied the Ordos region. Permanent armies of Chinese and non-Chinese troops, especially cavalry, were stationed there. Yisi is the only Christian high-ranking army officer from this period whom we know by name, but others are known from later periods. This loyal service must have helped the image of the Jingjiao in the eyes of the imperial court.

Within a few years, Suzong had reestablished Tang rule firmly in Chang'an, although Yan rebels continued to control large areas in the northeast for another seven years. Although it would never regain its former power or glory, the Tang dynasty would reign for another century and a half. To Jingjing, writing a mere twenty years after the end of Suzong's reign, it might have seemed that "disasters vanished and permanently declined," that "chaos stopped and the dust settled," and that the Tang emperor had been firmly "reestablished." After all, the Jingjiao were once again able to live in peace.

The Reign of Daizong (762–779)

Suzong's eldest son, known today as Daizong, had been an instrumental leader in his father's recapture of the capitals of Chang'an and Luoyang from the Yan rebels. In 762, with his father gravely ill, he was the target of several palace plots. Upon his father's death, however, he was able to ascend the throne and bring a semblance of stability back to the palace, if not the entire empire.

> Daizong was filial and just, and his good deeds united heaven and earth. He promoted wealth, and produced peace; material wealth was beautiful and profitable. His incense was the response to merit; his kindness was the response to generosity. In the valley of dawn there was a fullness of power; in the cave of the moon darkness ceased. (Poem 29.7–29.14)

> Daizong, a cultured and warlike emperor, broadened and expanded the good fortunes of the empire, and served the principle of nonexertion. Yet every year on the morning of his birthday, he offered heavenly incense in thanksgiving for his success; he provided royal food for the illustrious Luminous congregation. Also, because of the beautiful generosity of the heavenly one, he was able to broaden life. Because he sensed the first principle, he was able to educate the people. (Com. 20.5–21.3)

Even after the ultimate defeat of the last of the Yan rebels in 763, several warlords continued to control large swathes of the countryside with impunity while palace eunuchs grew in power within the court. In addition, in 763 the kingdom of Tibet invaded China, seized the capital Chang'an and briefly put a rival emperor on the throne. Although Daizong was able to regain control of the capital, his reign continued to be plagued by external threats and internal plots. This may account for the vague nature of Jingjing's compliments in the poem and commentary.

In the mid-760s, influenced by some of his key advisors, Daizong became increasingly supportive of Buddhism. This translated into an expansion and renewed prosperity for the Buddhist communities and infrastructure in Chang'an and elsewhere. The imperial administration, however, kept up its customary respect for other religions as well. Jingjing is able to relate one example of the emperor's generosity toward the Jingjiao community. The annual celebration of the emperor's birthday included sacrifices of incense, prayers, and the distribution of food. The Jingjiao community was included in this distribution. Jingjing's point is that the comparatively small Jingjiao community continued to be recognized by the emperor and to function freely during Daizong's reign.

The Jianzhong Period (780–783) of Dezong (779–805)

As noted earlier, the temple names we use for the emperors were given them posthumously, during their funeral ceremonies. This was when their new names were inscribed on the plaques that were then officially placed into the ancestral halls of their family, where the deceased would be remembered and worshiped. We have also seen that while still reigning, emperors gave era names to the different periods of their rule, such as the Tianbao period. Thus when Jingjing writes in 781 about the reign of the still-living emperor, known today as Dezong, the poem refers only to him with the current period name Jianzhong. The eldest son of Daizong, Dezong had only ruled for a couple of years when Jingjing composed his poem.

> Rule reached its zenith in the Jianzhong period, cultivating a brilliant morality. The emperor's military action has cleared the four seas; his learning has purified ten thousand lands. His torch illuminates the secrets of men; his mirror reflects the true appearance of things. The six directions are glad and prosper; the one hundred tribes of barbarians profit from his example. (Poem 29.15–30.7)

Our Jianzhong sage is a god-like, cultured and warlike emperor; implementing the eight governmental activities, he demotes the foolish and promotes the intelligent. Following the nine categories, he restores the destiny of the Luminous ones. He learns and understands the deepest principles; he prays in his heart with a clear conscience. Then, those in high places will yet be humble; those possessing constancy will yet show mercy; broadening mercy will thus rescue many who suffer; giving good pardon will thus help many people. (Com. 21.4–22.1)

The mature Dezong, already in his upper thirties when he assumed rule, began immediately to carry out a number of domestic reforms, seeking to rein in the influence of the eunuchs and other powerful chancellors and reforming the tax laws. He also began to plan ways to deal with the major warlords that still controlled large regions of the empire. His prospects for doing so still seemed bright as Jingjing composed his text, and therefore the statements about Dezong's successes (30.2–30.3) should be interpreted more as eulogistic hopes for the future. In fact, his twenty-six-year rule did bring stability and some renewed prosperity, but he found no long-term solutions to the military and economic problems that were progressively weakening the dynasty. Jingjing also had nothing concrete to say about the emperor's attitudes toward the Jingjiao. Instead he speaks in positive but vague generalities, which is always a good policy when speaking of a living ruler.

Future Blessings from the Jingjiao

In the commentary, Jingjing concludes his parade of Chinese history with a vision of what could happen in China if the Jingjiao continued to flourish:

Thus we put into practice our great plan, implementing it gradually, step-by-step. Then wind and rain will arrive at the proper time, there will be peace in the world, people will act rationally, other creatures will be serene, the living will prosper, the dead will rest in peace, thoughts will create a warm response, emotions will be made visible and eyes become sincere; this is what our Luminous religion has the power to achieve. (Com. 22.2–22.12)

The "great plan" that God would like to implement for his church would be implemented gradually as hearts were converted. A Christian China would mean that God would have no reason to send droughts or floods or invaders.

A peaceful and harmonious society would be seen on earth, and the dead would rest peacefully. Jingjing assures his readers that a peaceful, morally pure, and prosperous China is what the Jingjiao is laboring to attain. One must not read this as an expectation or prophecy. Jingjing knew full well that, due to man's sinfulness and the pervasiveness of evil, this Christian hope could never be realized on this earth. But for the purpose of the stele, these lines are meant to reassure the unconverted reader (and the government censors) that the Jingjiao is not self-serving and has no political agenda; the church seeks only the welfare and flourishing of the country and its rulers.

The Benefactor Yisi

After his commentary on the poem concludes, the author adds a lengthy section that has no equivalent in the poem—a eulogy for the Christian military leader, benefactor, and Jingjiao clergyman Yisi, whom we introduced earlier. Though Yisi's name is not preceded by an honorary space as are the names of the emperors, he is introduced by no fewer than six epithets and titles, taking up twenty-five characters (while the emperors are normally described in three or four characters)!

> Our great benefactor, the Great Master of the Palace with Golden Seal and Purple Ribbon, the Deputy Military Commander for the Shuofang region, the Appointed Director of the Palace Administration, the recipient of the Imperially conferred Purple Gown is the priest Yisi; naturally mild and graciously disposed, he has learned the Way and followed it diligently. From the distant royal residence city he came to China; his moral principles exceed those of the Three Dynasties; his skills are perfect in every respect.
>
> At first he served loyally at the Red Court; later his name was inscribed at the royal tent. When Duke Guo Ziyi, Secondary Minister of State and Prince of Fanyang, first took military command in the Shuofang region, Suzong appointed him as [the duke's] attendant on his travels. Although trusted to serve as private chamberlain, he assumed no distinction on the march. He was the duke's claws and fangs, serving as his eyes and ears in the army.
>
> He distributes the gifts conferred on him, not accumulating family wealth. He gives away the gifts given him by imperial favor; he distributes the golden fabric given as his due. On the one hand, he repairs the old temples; on the other hand, he increases the number of religious sites. He honors and decorates the various edifices, until they resemble the plumage

of a pheasant in full flight. He further exerts himself for the Luminous community in the virtuous distribution of his wealth; every year he assembles the monks from four monasteries, for reverent service and divine worship for fifty days. The hungry come and are fed; the naked come and are clothed; the sick are attended to and healed; the dead are buried and rest in peace. Even among the pure and moral *Dasuo* [Christians] such excellence is unknown. But now among the white-robed priests of the Luminous Teaching, we see such a man. (Com. 22.13–26.5)[23]

Yisi was a native of the "royal city" of Balkh in Sogdia (today in northern Afghanistan). After coming to China, he first served in the imperial bureaucracy before transferring to the army. Jingjing credits his gracious disposition, moral principles, natural ability, hard work, and Christian morality as leading to high appointments. Eventually he became the right-hand man and intimate advisor of perhaps the greatest general of the period, Guo Ziyi (郭子儀).[24] As we have seen, Guo was the regional commander in the northwest who inflicted a serious defeat upon a Yan army in 755. When Suzong became emperor the following year, Guo was promoted to imperial commander and led the army to victory, first in the Shaanxi Province, then in retaking Chang'an from the rebels. During these campaigns the Christian commander Yisi was part of his inner circle and one of his most trusted advisors (24.3–24.7). By the time Jingjing wrote, Yisi's *curriculum vitae* listed not only his title of Deputy Military Commander for the Shuofang region, but also three other important titles granted by the emperor: Great Master of the Palace with Golden Seal and Purple Ribbon, Appointed Director of the Palace Administration, and holder of the Imperially Conferred Purple Gown. (Titles are always important indicators of status, even more so in Chinese culture than in the West.)

Yet, at the same time that Yisi was involved at the highest levels of political and military life, he was also an active member of the Jingjiao church and clergy.[25] His government position had made him wealthy, allowing him to

23. It is generally accepted that *dasuo* was a transliteration of the Middle Persian word *tarsag*, meaning God-fearer, a term used of Christians (Nicolini-Zani, *The Luminous Way*, 214n112).

24. On Guo Ziyi, see Max Deeg, "A Belligerent Priest—Yisi and His Political Context," in *From the Oxus River to the Chinese Shores*, ed. Li Tang and Dietmar W. Winkler, Orientalia-Patristica-Oecumenica 5 (Vienna: LIT Verlag, 2013), 107–21, esp. 110–12.

25. That Yisi was the benefactor for the stele and was the Yazdbozid, chorepiscopus of Luoyang, and originally from Balkh, described in the Syriac lines at the bottom of the stele, was proposed by Yoshirō Saeki (*The Nestorian Documents and Relics in China*, 2nd

become a great benefactor for the church. Jingjing mentions several specific examples. He donated the jewels and wealth he was given by the emperor to repair, refurbish, and decorate existing churches as well as to build new ones. He also provided the funds for an annual fifty-day religious retreat for the clergy from four local churches. Finally, he was known for his acts of charity to the hungry, the naked, and the sick, and for providing proper burial for the poor.

What are we to make of this long addition that doesn't seem to fit the rest of the structure of the stele? Was the benefactor Yisi the major donor for Jingjing's stele project, thus explaining this permanent tribute to him? Or was he a well-known figure even outside the Jingjiao community and so was being used as a "poster child" for the movement? The text does not provide us with an answer. Still, these lines of the commentary give us a rare glimpse into the church life of the Jingjiao.

Conclusion: One Hundred Forty-Six Years of Blessings

Jingjing's concluding lines in both the poem and the commentary end on a high note.

> The Way is spread widely, and with great effect;
> there is no better name or description [of it] than the Three-One.
> The Lord is able to act, his servants but record;
> we erect this great stele in praise of his fundamental goodness.
> (Poem 30.8–30.11)

The true Way of the Three-One God has been faithfully preached by the white-robed clergy of the Jingjiao and has successfully spread in China. The great stele looming in front of the reader honored that God, the men who proclaimed his message, and the emperors who approved of its proclamation. The facts given in detail on the stele speak for themselves, and God's humble

---

ed. [Tokyo: Toho Bunkwa Gakuin/Academy of Oriental Culture, Tokyo Institute, 1951], 37), and he has been followed by all modern interpreters. See Max Deeg's article, "A Belligerent Priest," 108. In his article (109), Deeg also equates Yisi's son Adam (S14–15) with the stele's author, Adam/Jingjing, a suggestion that has not, to my knowledge, found acceptance elsewhere.

servants can only stand in awe with their thanks and praise. As the poem and commentary say in their final lines:

> The Lord is able to act, his servants but record;
> we erect this great stele in praise of his fundamental goodness.
> (Poem 30.10–30.11)

> We desire to engrave this magnificent stele to eulogize such great deeds. (Com. 26.6–26.7)

The second year of Dezong's Jianzhong period was the year of the chicken, according to Chinese reckoning; we call it AD 781. On Sunday, February 4 of that year, the newly erected stele was unveiled, probably with a dedicatory service. The church dignitaries in attendance probably included many of the officials named on the bottom of the stele and some of the priests whose names are inscribed on the sides of the stone. Local government officials would also have been invited to attend. Perhaps Lu Xiuyan was also there to receive compliments on his beautiful calligraphy. Jingjing's poem and commentary might have been read aloud just as it would be read by passersby in the following decades. Some sixty-five years later, however, the Jingjiao would be suppressed. Thinking that this persecution might also soon pass, the stone was carefully buried for the moment. Those who did so could never have imagined that the stone would wait eight hundred years before being rediscovered.

The stele's text remains our most valuable single source of information about the earliest Christian church in China. Significant additional writings of the Jingjiao would not be discovered until the twentieth century. While those new documents do not enlighten us much about the history of the Jingjiao, they are invaluable in what they tell us about the church's message. As a result, we will now turn to a description of those documents. After doing so, we will endeavor to combine what they teach with the theological section of the stele in order to elucidate the teachings and church life of the Jingjiao.

Chapter 4

NEW EVIDENCE EMERGES

For several centuries after the discovery of the Chang'an stele, the story of the Jingjiao and its place as an imperially sanctioned religion during the Tang dynasty seemed incredible to many European scholars. By the early nineteenth century, the text had been translated into several European languages, and yet many still questioned its authenticity. In China, it was republished in 1805 by Wang Chang in his vast collection of ancient Chinese inscriptions. His concluding comment was simply, "Such was the introduction of Christianity in China which, since the Tang until this day, has spread in all the empire."[1] Yet all further evidence of the Tang-era Christian church seemed to have been lost. Thomas Yeates, for example, in his 1818 book entitled *Indian Church History*, repeated the claims that the Syriac church had brought the gospel to China yet remained doubtful "whether any . . . remains or vestiges of Christianity are discoverable in China."[2] His view seemed to be justified throughout the nineteenth century when Great Britain forced itself into China to expand its trade and brought with it major advances in the West's knowledge of the Chinese language and history. During the same period, the Protestant mission movement had also made China a focus, increasing interest in its religious history. It was not until the early twentieth century, however, that new evidence was uncovered to significantly add to our knowledge of the Jingjiao and its teaching.

1. Cited in Henri Havret, *La Stèle Chrétienne de Si-Ngan-Fou*, vol. 2, Variétés Sinologique 12 (Chang-hai: Impr. de la Mission catholique, 1897), 318.
2. Thomas Yeates, *Indian Church History . . . with an Accurate Relation of the First Christian Missions in China* (London: A. Maxwell, 1818), 76.

Explorers and Linguists

A steady if small stream of books, pamphlets, and notices on the stele and the "Nestorian" church in China was published during the nineteenth century. Protestant missionaries working with the Chinese gave some attention to the stele. The American Asahel Grant, for example, concluded that it described a church whose worship and teachings were "more simple and scriptural than the Papal and the other Oriental churches." William Milne of the London Missionary Society, however, was skeptical about the stele since it had first been mentioned by "some Romish Missionaries" and in the following centuries there had not been any further "monuments, inscriptions, remains of old churches, &c. . . . noticed by any Chinese writer." He concludes: "It is a singular circumstance that, if they really were there for so great a length of time, Chinese History never mentions them." The British orientalist Alexander Wylie, on the other hand, investigated the Chinese historical sources thoroughly and found no fewer than seventeen references to the stele; he wrote that not a single one of them showed "the slightest hint of a suspicion as to its genuineness or authenticity."[3]

During the eighteenth and nineteenth centuries, a few crosses and Christian tombstones had come to light in northwestern China and the surrounding areas. Yet, by the end of the century, when the Jesuit Henri Havret published his three-volume study of the stele, *La Stèle Chrétienne de Si-Ngan-Fou*, he could only list again Wylie's collection of Chinese references to support the stele's testimony that a church had existed in China under the Tang.[4] Thus the Chang'an inscription remained the single greatest proof and the only substantial testimony to the early Syriac church in China. The inscription's importance, and the enthusiasm it evoked, is well illustrated by the story of the Danish aristocrat and adventurer Fritz Holm, which we summarized above in chapter 2.

While Holm was in China trying to "rescue" the stele for posterity, China's last dynasty, the Qin, was imploding. Russia, Japan, and the European powers were all competing for increased influence in the Middle East and Central Asia. To make that influence a reality, however, they needed better knowledge

---

3. Asahel Grant, *The Nestorians; or, The Lost Tribes: Containing Evidence of Their Identity* (London: John Murray, 1841), 6; William Milne, *A Retrospect of the First Ten Years of the Protestant Mission to China* (Malacca, Malaysia: Anglo-Chinese Press, 1820), 7–9; Alexander Wylie, "On the Nestorian Tablet of Se-Gan Foo," *Journal of the American Oriental Society* 5 (1855–1856): 335.

4. Havret, *La Stèle Chrétienne de Si-Ngan-Fou*, 2:253–61.

of the peoples, geography, and resources of this vast area; the blank spots needed to be filled in on the map of Asia. This led to a succession of exploratory expeditions in the last half of the nineteenth century and first decades of the twentieth century. Although most of the explorers were primarily motivated by their own ambitions for geographical discovery and the lure of finding ancient manuscripts and artistic treasures, many were also patriotic nationalists and players in what came to be known as "the Great Game." Exploring and mapping that region became important to all sides. Two of the most illustrious explorers of the period, Aurel Stein and Paul Pelliot, were destined also to play important roles in uncovering the history of the early Chinese Christian church.[5]

Originally from Budapest, Stein (1862–1943) pursued the study of oriental languages at the universities of Vienna, Leipzig, and Tübingen, earning a doctorate when he was just twenty-one years old. After several years of postdoctoral work in England, he left for India, where the precocious young scholar held posts at Oriental College and Punjab University in Lahore. He became a British citizen and spent most of his adult life in Kashmir (northern India), endearing himself to the local people by his insatiable interest in their language and cultural heritage. Between 1900 and 1930 he made a series of important expeditions farther afield into Central Asia. He mapped new areas; discovered oases, cities, and languages; and conducted primitive archaeological digs.[6]

He left India in 1906 on his most ambitious trip—a ten-thousand-mile, thirty-one-month exploration that began in Pakistan and traversed the remote Swat Valley (the stronghold of the modern-day Taliban). Arriving in Kashgar (today just inside the western border of China), he hired a Chinese assistant; after they had crossed the Taklamakan Desert, he paused to excavate the ruins of the Chinese military outpost of Loulan, founded before the time of Christ and abandoned in the fourth century AD. Next he discovered important Buddhist frescoes in the ruins of the oasis town of Miran, then mapped several hundred miles of ancient Chinese border fortifications stretching toward Dunhuang, the western end of the famous Great Wall. When Stein finally arrived at the oasis town of Dunhuang in March of 1907, he could hardly imagine that still greater discoveries awaited him.

5. On the Great Game, see Peter Hopkirk, *Foreign Devils on the Silk Road: The Search for the Lost Cities and Treasures of Chinese Central Asia* (Oxford: Oxford University Press, 1984). For Stein, see 68–110 and 145–76, and for Pelliot, 177–89.

6. See the complete biography of Jeannette Mirsky, *Sir Aurel Stein: Archaeological Explorer* (Chicago: University of Chicago Press, 1977). On the expedition of 1906–1907, see 225–330.

Dunhuang, now in Gansu Province in western China, had been a major stop along the Silk Road since its earliest development. Here, the road to the west split, with one branch going northward and the other southward along the edge of the Taklamakan Desert before reuniting on its western end. By the fourth century, this thriving commercial emporium had also become a center of Buddhism, providing a rest stop for pilgrims traveling between India and China. The early pilgrims took shelter in the caves that dotted the surrounding mountains, and it became customary for travelers, in order to ensure divine protection on their perilous journey across the desert to the west, to pay for the production of Buddhist paintings and statuary before they left. Over the centuries, hundreds of caves were hollowed out and their walls covered with thousands of religious sculptures and frescoes. Today they are known as the Mogao Caves and have been designated as a World Heritage Site.

Stein had heard a description of the caves from a previous Hungarian expedition, but what had especially piqued his interest were rumors about a secret cache of ancient manuscripts recently discovered in one of the grottoes—manuscripts that were in numerous languages and scripts. As the explorer began touring the most spectacular caves, his attention was soon drawn to the one called the Cave of the Thousand Buddhas. A local Daoist monk named Wang Yuanlu had made it his life's work to restore and preserve the cave, using the money he collected from pilgrims. It was Wang who had discovered inside the larger cave a small side room full of ancient manuscripts. Apparently, the scrolls had been hidden for protection during a foreign attack or were discarded with the advent of printed Buddhist texts. In either case, the chamber, now known as Cave 17, or the Library Cave, had been filled floor-to-ceiling with manuscripts before it was sealed shortly after AD 1000. It was not opened again until Wang discovered it nine hundred years later.[7]

It did not take Stein long to confirm the existence of this hoard. Wang, however, was rightly suspicious of the foreigner's intentions. Yet he was no match for the inventive and passionate scholar. Stein found out that Wang revered the seventh-century monk Xuanzang, who, thirteen centuries earlier, had traveled through Dunhuang on his way to India, returning decades later laden with precious Buddhist manuscripts. Stein convinced the modern monk that it was by divine providence that he himself had arrived and that he would assist Wang by taking those same manuscripts back to the devout in India while at the same

---

7. On the discovery of the cave, see Hopkirk, *Foreign Devils*, 156–76, and lecture 3 of Rong Xinjiang, *Eighteen Lectures on Dunhuang*, trans. Imre Galambos (Leiden: Brill, 2013), 79–108, esp. 79–85 and 100–108.

time contributing money to help Wang restore the caves. Soon Stein and his Chinese assistant were not only examining large numbers of the documents but receiving permission to carry many away. Passing through the area again four months later, the monk agreed to Stein's request for still more bundles. When the explorer finally headed home, he had with him twenty-four large crates of the precious documents as well as five bundles of paintings, most of which ended up in the British Museum. Stein's plan was marred only by the fact that he and his Chinese companion lacked the expertise to choose the most important of the manuscripts. As a result, their treasure trove included hundreds of duplicate copies of the most common Buddhist writings.

This was not a mistake that his French rival would make. Unlike Stein, Paul Pelliot (1878–1945) had specialized in Chinese studies from the beginning of his career. After studies in Paris, he served at the French School of the Far East in Hanoi and happened to be in Beijing in 1900 at the outbreak of the Boxer Rebellion. His selfless actions during the siege of the city led to decorations for bravery. By his mid-twenties he had been appointed a professor of Sinology (the study of China and its languages) in Paris. In 1906, he mounted a large expedition to explore the western regions of China. Arriving in early 1908 at Dunhuang, just months after Stein's departure, he too won the confidence of caretaker Wang. But unlike Stein, he was able to evaluate more thoroughly the Chinese manuscripts that remained. After several weeks of examination, he purchased about three thousand of the most interesting documents. These were safely brought back to Paris by Pelliot, where today they are housed partly in the Bibliothèque Nationale (the French national library) and partly in the Guimet Museum of eastern art.

At first Pelliot was accused in the press of having wasted public funds on his expedition and of returning with forged manuscripts (since, it was claimed, Stein had carted off the genuine ones). Eventually Pelliot was not only cleared of those charges but it became evident that he had obtained items of significantly more interest than many of Stein's. Meanwhile, additional manuscripts from Dunhuang were taken by Japanese and Russian explorers, and others ended up in the hands of private collectors. Finally, in 1910, Chinese government officials took the remainder to Beijing for safekeeping. Altogether, some forty thousand manuscripts and paintings emerged from Cave 17, and many thousands more came from the surrounding area, well preserved in the dry desert conditions.[8]

8. Scholars from many countries and virtually all the institutions that hold texts found at Dunhuang are now cooperating on their study, preservation, and publication via the International Dunhuang Project (http://idp.bl.uk/).

Collectors and Forgers

In the years following, as the Dunhuang treasures were studied in Europe, word began to surface that there were Christian texts among them. According to a story in the *New York Times*, Pelliot triumphantly arrived back in Paris in 1909 with thirty thousand volumes! It quoted the adventurer as already claiming that his discoveries would show "that Buddhism and Christianity must have existed . . . side by side" in ancient China.[9] A tenth-century scroll in Chinese (now labeled *Pelliot chinois 3847* in the French national library) contained two Christian texts in Chinese—a hymn to the Trinity and a liturgical list of Christian leaders to be remembered in the prayers of the church, and a list of Christian books and scriptures. Another set of documents, seemingly from the same cave, ended up in the collection of Li Shengduo of Tianjin and was soon sold to a Japanese collector named Tomioka. Yet another manuscript was purchased in 1922 by another Japanese man named Dr. Takakusu. These documents were Christian theological treatises that by all appearances were composed in China in the seventh and eighth centuries by leaders of the Jingjiao. In addition, three hundred miles to the northwest, German scholars uncovered Christian texts in several Central Asian languages in the vicinity of the Turfan Oasis. Over the years, additional Christian texts and inscriptions have also been found in several places in the steppes of northwestern China.

In the years after Pelliot's announcement of his discoveries, texts and translations of these newly discovered documents slowly began to appear. In 1930, A. C. Moule, a career missionary and Sinologist, gave the first extensive account of them in his *Christians in China before the Year 1550*.[10] Four of the Christian documents from Dunhuang were published the next year by the Japanese Kyoto Institute of the Oriental Culture Academy. The Japanese Christian and scholar P. Saeki then published English translations of most of the documents in a groundbreaking book published in 1937.[11] While the documents have remained controversial in many ways, and some of these Christian manuscripts have been suspected of being forgeries, the genuine texts clearly support the story told in the stone monument from Chang'an.

---

9. The article from the November 28 paper is available online at https://timesmachine.nytimes.com/timesmachine/1909/11/28/106723777.pdf.

10. A. C. Moule, *Christians in China before the Year 1550* (London: SPCK, 1930).

11. An updated version appeared as Yoshirō Saeki, *The Nestorian Documents and Relics in China*, 2nd ed. (Tokyo: Toho Bunkwa Gakuin/Academy of Oriental Culture, Tokyo Institute, 1951).

A Christian *Dharani* Pillar

Almost a century passed before another important witness to the Jingjiao was discovered. This one came from near a set of caves in Henan Province. The Longmen Grottoes, carved into the cliffs along the Yi River, are eight miles south of Luoyang, which served as the eastern capital city during much of the Tang period. The Longmen Grottoes were declared a World Heritage Site in 2000 because "the high cultural level and sophisticated society of Tang Dynasty China is encapsulated in the exceptional stone carvings" found there.[12] They contain some 1,300 caves and recesses that contain over 100,000 stone figures and 2,800 inscriptions.

In May of 2006, Zhang Naizhu, a staff member of the Longmen Grottoes Institute, found what appeared to be a Christian artifact while perusing the wares of an antique seller in Luoyang. Ancient inscriptions are valued not just for their historical content but also for their beautiful calligraphy, and this has given rise to the industry of stone rubbings. In this process a stone containing an inscription is covered with wet rice paper. A fine brush is then used to beat the paper into the engraved characters. Ink is then tapped over the still exposed surface of the paper, with only the indented characters remaining white, providing a near perfect representation of the ancient writing. (See the rubbing of the Chang'an stele in figures 2–4.) This process has remained virtually unchanged since used by Zhang Gengyu to make the first copy of the Chang'an stele in 1623, nearly four hundred years earlier. Now Zhang Naizhu saw a rubbing of an octagonal pillar not quite one meter in height and a bit more than a meter in circumference. It had originally stood upright but had been broken off at some time so that the bottom was damaged and a portion of its text was missing.

From its shape and size, Zhang immediately recognized it as a *dharani* pillar, a memorial stone that became popular among Chinese Buddhists in the Tang period. Normally such a pillar would be engraved with Buddhist imagery and religious texts (*sutras*)—magic spells and other short devotional texts. However, on this rubbing, Zhang found a cross rising out of a lotus blossom, with two winged figures facing it. Zhang purchased the rubbings and alerted the office of national relics, giving them his description and pictures. Later it was found out that the pillar had originally been uncovered by grave robbers.

---

12. "Longmen Grottoes," UNESCO, accessed April 4, 2023, https://whc.unesco.org/en/list/1003/.

Fortunately, Chinese officials succeeded in tracing the pillar to Shanghai before it disappeared on the black market. The pillar is now back in Luoyang, where it is displayed in the archaeological museum (see figure 5).

The pillar text describes its original dedication in AD 814 in memory of a Christian matron and her uncle. The inscription contains a section describing how the family of a deceased Christian lady had erected the pillar in her honor. Most of the surface, however, was covered with the text of a Christian tract that had been discovered earlier among the Dunhuang documents. This writing was one entitled *On Book of the Luminous Teaching of Da Qin on Revealing the Origin and Reaching the Foundation.* Not only does the text add to our knowledge of the Jingjiao, but the pillar's discovery provides important new information about the Christian presence in Tang China.[13] The pillar confirms several facts about the Jingjiao community: it was not limited to Chang'an; the communities exchanged written texts; and adherents were still to be found in the early ninth century. Later we will discuss the light it sheds on the church's ethnicity and social standing.

The Christian Documents from Dunhuang

Preliminary texts and translations of most of these new Jingjiao documents had been made available already in the 1930s in the books of Moule and Saeki. However, the Japanese invasion of China and the world war that followed on its heels were just two factors among many that interfered with a full study of these precious "relics" (as Saeki termed them) in the decades since. Except for the Pelliot manuscript, the others all quickly disappeared into the hands of private collectors, mostly in Japan. By the end of the Second World War, they could no longer be located. At the same time, a profitable black-market trade in Dunhuang manuscripts led to a flourishing forgery industry, and some scholars increasingly labeled these Christian texts inauthentic. Since even good

13. On the discovery of the pillar, see the English translation of Zhang Naizhu's account, "Note on a Nestorian Stone Inscription from the Tang Dynasty Unearthed in Luoyang," in *Precious Nestorian Relic: Studies on the Nestorian Stone Pillar of the Tang Dynasty Recently Discovered in Luoyang,* ed. Ge Chengyong (Beijing: Wenwu chubanshe, 2009), 17–33. On the text itself, see Li Tang, "A Preliminary Study on the *Jingjiao* Inscription of Luoyang: Text Analysis, Commentary and English Translation," in *Hidden Treasures and Intercultural Encounters,* ed. Dietmar W. Winkler and Li Tang, Orientalia-Patristica-Oecumenica 1 (Vienna: LIT Verlag, 2009), 109–32.

photographs of the manuscripts were unavailable, frustrated scholars were forced to continue their analysis of the texts and their authenticity without the necessary tools.

Fortunately, this situation changed almost overnight when, in 2010, most of the missing manuscripts reappeared in a Japanese exhibition of manuscripts. It turned out that the "lost" material was part of a "Dunhuang Secret Collection" of manuscripts owned by a Japanese foundation. In cooperation with Kyoto University, the Takeda Science Foundation mounted an exhibition of some of its manuscripts and published a multivolume catalogue of their entire collection, including high-quality photographs. Among them were nearly all the lost Christian texts. Now scholars are finally in a position to reevaluate the documents and expand our knowledge of the Jingjiao as never before. Although it has not yet been ascertained whether all the new material (except the Luoyang pillar) did in fact come from the Dunhuang cave, for convenience we will still refer to the whole group as the Dunhuang Jingjiao documents.[14]

Table 3. The Dunhuang Christian Documents

TITLE	PREVIOUS OWNER/ LOCATION
*Book of the **Lord Messiah***	Takakusu Junjirō [1923] Kyoto Dunhuang Secret Collection no. 459
Discourse on the One God [name given to the following three works as a whole]	Tomioka Kenzō [1917] Kyoto Dunhuang Secret Collection no. 460
*On the **One Godhead**, Number 1*	
Metaphorical Teaching, Number 2	
*Discourse of the Honored One of the Universe on **Almsgiving**, Number 3*	

14. On the rediscovery, see Matteo Nicolini-Zani, "The Dunhuang Jingjiao Documents in Japan: A Report on Their Reappearance," in *Winds of Jingjiao*, ed. Li Tang and Dietmar W. Winkler, Orientalia-Patristica-Oecumenica 9 (Vienna: LIT Verlag, 2016), 15–26.

TITLE	PREVIOUS OWNER/ LOCATION
Hymn in Praise of the Salvation Achieved through the Three Majesties of the Luminous Teaching Book of the **Honored**	Paris, Bibl. nationale *Pelliot chinois 3847*
Book on Profound and **Mysterious Blessedness**	Li Shengduo Kyoto Dunhuang Secret Collection no. 13
*Book of the Luminous Teaching of Da Qin on Revealing the **Origin** and Reaching the Foundation* **Pillar** historical notice	Li Shengduo Kyoto Dunhuang Secret Collection no. 431; and Luoyang *dharani* pillar

Kojima documents [still considered forgeries]

Hymn of Praise to the Most Holy One of the Luminous Teaching of Da Qin through which One Penetrates the Truth and Turns to the Doctrine	Kojima A [dated AD 720, at Shazhou]
Book of the Luminous Teaching of Da Qin on Revealing the Origin and Reaching the Foundation	Kojima B [dated AD 717]

While most of the writings have Chinese titles provided in the manuscripts, the variety of ways these have been translated into English has led to some confusion when discussing them. In addition, even if they were all to be judged authentic, a lack of unanimity about their dates of composition remains. Table 3 lists the Christian works from Dunhuang in the order in which we will discuss them. The titles given match those found in the recent translation and study of Nicolini-Zani.[15] The original owner (where appropriate) and

---

15. See Part II: The Texts in Translation, Texts B–F, 222–303, in Matteo Nicolini-Zani, *The Luminous Way to the East: Texts and History of the First Encounter of Christianity with*

the current location are also listed. Because of the lengthy titles and to avoid confusion, I will reference these works by the key words in their titles, which are in boldface in the chart, followed by the column number(s) to indicate where the citation is found within the extant manuscript. As just mentioned, the supposed dates of composition are still a subject of debate. This overview, however, should provide context for when they are quoted and discussed in coming chapters. Readers are urged to consult all these documents in the new translation of Matteo Nicolini-Zani in his recent work *The Luminous Way to the East*.[16] Note that the short historical notice at the end of the Luoyang Pillar text will be referred to as "Pillar."[17]

Book of the Lord Messiah (序聽迷詩所經一卷)

This document has been preserved on a nine-foot-long scroll, first published by the Japanese Sinologist Prof. Haneda Tōru in the *Bulletin of the Metropolitan Library* (of Peking) in 1928.[18] Moule, Saeki, and others had considered it the oldest of our extant documents and thought that it may have come from the hand of Alopen himself. Moule stated: "The extraordinary style, which in very many places quite baffles the translator, and the large number of wrongly written words justify Professor Haneda in guessing that it is the work of a foreigner

---

China (Oxford: Oxford University Press, 2022). The author worked closely with Nicolini-Zani to agree on the best English translation for each document so as not to confuse future readers. We hope in the near future to make available on a website all the Jingjiao documents together with translations in several languages.

16. Nicolini-Zani, *The Luminous Way*, 222–303. Since Nicolini-Zani also includes the column numbers, one can both observe the differences in translational possibilities and examine my citations within their larger context.

17. For the only English translation of the historical section of the Luoyang Pillar, see Tang, "A Preliminary Study," 119–25.

18. Excellent photographs of the manuscript are now available in Kyōu shooku, ed., *Tonkō hikyū: Eihen satsu* [Dunhuang secret collection: Photographic volumes] (Osaka: Takeda kagaku shinkō zaidan, 2009–2013), 6:83–87. Moule provided a partial translation under the title *Book of the Jesus Messiah* (*Christians in China*, 59–64). Saeki translated the title as *Jesus-Messiah Sutra* and published the first complete English translation (*The Nestorian Documents*, 125–46). *Book of Jesus the Messiah* was the title in the more recent translation of Li Tang, *A Study of the History of Nestorian Christianity in China and Its Literature in Chinese: Together with a New English Translation of the Dunhuang Nestorian Documents*, 2nd rev. ed. (Frankfurt am Main: Lang, 2004), 145–56.

who had not progressed very far in the study of the Chinese language and that no educated Chinese helper can have been available to write it out."[19]

Saeki argued that it was written even "prior to the proclamation of the imperial Rescript on the Nestorian Teaching" cited in the stele (i.e., AD 638). In fact, Saeki concludes that its contents were designed "to give the Emperor the outline or general sketch of the whole Christian Teaching" and that therefore this was the first Jingjiao document ever written in China.[20] It would seem, however, that the wrongly written characters might just as well reflect the abilities of the copyist rather than those of the author, and that this question should be addressed in any discussion about its "extraordinary style." Recent analyses have confirmed that the extant manuscript was once part of the same scroll as the three tracts making up the *Discourse on the One God*. However, estimates of the date of the manuscript and the date of the original composition of *Lord Messiah* are now quite varied, and the link to Alopen has been strongly challenged.[21] While some uncertainty remains as to whether the manuscripts all emanated from the single cave at Dunhuang, no one has put forward a credible alternative location. And although some of the textual problems would logically be the result of later copyists, the amount of time and expertise required of a forger make it unlikely that the texts are anything but the descendants of Jingjiao authors (see figure 6).[22]

Dating aside, *Lord Messiah* indeed does have peculiarities. It is the only surviving Christian document that at times uses the Chinese character for "Buddha" (佛, *fo*) to refer to the Christian God—a linguistic choice that was abandoned in future compositions. Scholars have also taken note of the way biblical names are found in this text. It has been a common practice in the Chinese language to render foreign proper names using phonetic transliterations. Thus "Messiah," *Mšyḥ'* in Syriac pronunciation, is rendered with the Chinese sounds *Mi-shi-he*. The Chinese language, however, is full of homophones, words that have different meanings but sound exactly the same—like English "to," "too,"

19. Moule, *Christians in China*, 58.

20. Saeki, *The Nestorian Documents*, 116.

21. See the summary of research by Rong Xinjiang, Lin Wushu, Tōno Haruyuki, Chen Huaiyu, and Sun Jianqiang, in Nicolini-Zani, *The Luminous Way*, 152–69. Nicolini-Zani's own conclusions are not clearly spelled out.

22. Most recently the entire corpus has been given much later dates by Sun Jianqiang, "Redating the Seven Early Chinese Christian Manuscripts: Christians in Dunhuang before 1100" (PhD diss., Leiden University, 2018).

and "two." And as written English distinguishes homophones by different spellings, written Chinese uses different characters for each. In Chinese, however, the number of homophones is immense, and so the number of characters that an author has to choose from when transliterating names is also considerable. The writer thus usually seeks to choose characters appropriate to the name.

The two characters chosen in *Lord Messiah* for "Jesus" (*Yšwʿ* in Syriac) were 移鼠 (*yi shu*), a fairly good correspondence of sound but with the literal meaning "remove rat." In subsequent documents, more pleasant characters were selected with the more neutral meaning of "feather-screen" and "number." The three characters chosen more than twenty times in *Lord Messiah* to represent *Mi-shi-he* are 彌師訶. Saeki translated these as "full," "teacher," and "upbraid," respectively. But he notes that in two other places the document uses 迷 (*mi*) for the first character, which he translates as "confused." These and similar literary choices further convince Saeki that this document is in fact a first attempt to clothe the Christian message in the Chinese language and that this was done by newcomers who at the time had only begun to master the language and had not yet standardized a Christian vocabulary in Chinese.[23]

The problem is highlighted already in the document title: 序聽迷詩所經, *xu ting mi shi suo jing*. Prof. Haneda thought the first two characters were improperly written and should read *Yi-shu*, "Jesus." He further regarded the fifth character, *suo*, as faulty, substituting *he* to form *Mi-shi-he*, as in the rest of the document. Thus he rendered the full title as *Book on Jesus the Messiah*. His interpretation was accepted by Moule, Saeki, Li Tang, and others. By suggesting different emendations, Max Deeg came up with *Book of the One Preaching the Regulation of Errors*. Matteo Nicolini-Zani originally read *Book on Listening to the Messiah* but more recently has interpreted the first two characters as a phonetic rendering of a Sogdian term for "Lord." We have followed him in translating *Book of the Lord Messiah*.[24]

Turning to the text's content, Moule already notes that the opening is modeled on that of a Buddhist sutra—"at that time the Messiah spoke the law of the Lord . . . saying. . . ."[25] While admitting that the language of the text seems very difficult to attribute to a Christian author, Moule decides that the writing emanates from a "Persian missionary with little knowledge of Chinese language and

---

23. Saeki, *The Nestorian Documents*, 118–21.

24. Nicolini-Zani, *The Luminous Way*, 265n1. Max Deeg recounts the history of the title's interpretation and offers his own tentative reconstruction. See "Messiah Rediscovered: Some Philological Notes on the So-called 'Jesus the Messiah Sutra,'" in *The Church of the East in Central Asia and China*, ed. Samuel N. C. Lieu and Glen L. Thompson, China and the Mediterranean World 1 (Turnhout: Brepols, 2022), 111–20, and especially 112–14.

25. Moule, *Christians in China*, 59.

thought" who "struggles to make a Chinese friend of very humble scholastic gifts" acquainted with the Christian message. He concludes that "more strange results . . . have, I think, been produced by modern translators, both missionary and secular whose orthodoxy has been above suspicion."[26] Although many passages still puzzle interpreters, and contemporary scholars are not in agreement about the precise occasion of its composition, there is little question that this is indeed a Christian text and that it certainly appears to be an early attempt to communicate the Christian message in the Chinese language. It may indeed still be the earliest text that we have for the Church of the East mission.

The one manuscript we have of this text is 2.75 meters long and 26 centimeters high; unfortunately, it is incomplete, breaking off midsentence in column 170. After the opening line cited above, the first section (cols. 3–35) describes the attributes of the Lord of Heaven—invisible, all-powerful, the one who gives life to humans. After sin entered the world and corrupted them, God still provided a path (道, *dao*, the character used for the Daoist religion) for humankind to reach heaven (36–39).

Then follows a section that gives a Chinese paraphrase of the Ten Commandments, with commentary (77–92).[27] The second "obligation" and the fourth through the tenth are all specifically mentioned. However, the correspondence is not exact, with the third commandment entirely omitted. This section is followed by a discussion (reminiscent of sections of the Sermon on the Mount) on how to use one's money properly in helping the weak, the poor, laborers, and the sick (92–107), followed by other admonitions to proper Christian living (107–113).

Another major section describes the life and work of the Messiah (115–149). This begins with a detailed description of the incarnation and birth of Jesus through Mary and the Holy Spirit (115–127). Jesus's baptism by John is also described in considerable detail (129–136), followed by a summary of Jesus's teaching and healing ministry (136–145). Finally, the rejection of Jesus by evil men, his arrest, his trial before Pilate, and his execution are narrated in considerable detail (145–169). The text then breaks off in midsentence, calling its readers to trust in this Messiah (169–170).

While Lin Wushu has joined others in pointing out the text's scribal mistakes and lacunae, his conclusion that this results in a text that is "counterfeit"

---

26. Moule, *Christians in China*, 60n70.

27. Since the first commandment/obligation is not specifically mentioned, it is unclear where in the text the discussion begins. Nicolini-Zani has the first "vow" starting in column 77 and the tenth ending in 92 (*The Luminous Way*, 272–74).

and has "almost meaningless content" is unwarranted.[28] As we shall see in the other Dunhuang documents such as *Discourse on the One God*, the early missionaries clearly struggled with the complex problem of using classical Chinese literary forms to accurately express Christian teaching in a culturally appropriate way. The *Lord Messiah* text clearly reflects those same issues, and it would be incredible to think that even the most educated and skilled of forgers could imitate this. Thus, we are forced to conclude that although Lin may be correct and the manuscript is a later copy, it reproduces much of an earlier genuine text and, therefore, can and should be used to shed light on the Jingjiao and its teaching.

Discourse on the One God (一神論)

This name is given to the writings contained in a 6.4-meter-long, 25-centimeter-high scroll, originally even longer, as it originally included our extant text of *Lord Messiah*, as noted earlier. The title *Discourse on the One God (yi shen lun)* appears at the end of the scroll.[29] The first tract to appear has the title *Metaphorical Teaching* followed by the notation "number two," then follows *One Godhead* with the additional characters "number one," and finally *Almsgiving*, followed by "number three." The logical conclusion is that these numerical designations indicate the order in which the writings originally appeared, but that the first two were accidentally reversed at some point in transmission, and the notations were added to point this out. We have followed Nicolini-Zani in discussing them in what appears to be the original order.[30]

Prof. Haneda first published the text in 1918, dating it to 642. Lin Wushu has argued that the manuscript itself is a twentieth-century copy. The three tracts within the manuscript do not appear to form a harmonious whole; however, all three normally refer to the Christian deity as "one God" (一神, *yi shen*, seventy-eight times) rather than as "Lord of Heaven" (天尊, *tian zun*), as *Lord*

---

28. His conclusions are given in English translation by Nicolini-Zani, *The Luminous Way*, 157.

29. For photographs of the manuscript, see Kyōu shooku, *Tonkō hikyū*, 6:88–96. The first English translation was that of Saeki, who translated the manuscript title as "A Discourse on Monotheism" (*The Nestorian Documents*, 161). Li Tang entitles the entire manuscript "On the One God" (*Study of the History of Nestorian Christianity*, 157).

30. Li Tang keeps the tracts in the order in which they are found in the manuscript, including putting the title at the end of each. "On the One Heaven, Part 1" is found in her *Study of the History of Nestorian Christianity*, 160–70.

Messiah does some sixty times. This justifies the title at its end and may explain why the three works were at some point grouped together.

On the One Godhead, Number 1 (一天論,第一)

The five characters in the title of this tract of 146 columns are literally translated as *Discourse on the One Heaven, Number 1.*[31] However, the expression "one heaven" never appears in the tract itself or anywhere else in the corpus of Jingjiao texts. Yet the character "heaven" does appear some sixty times in this tract; in forty-six of those, it is part of the expression "under heaven" (天下, *tian xia*), a common Chinese phrase indicating all of China, or the inhabited world. It also appears seven times in the tract in the phrase "Lord of Heaven" (天尊, *tian zun*). For example, in column 139 we read, "Worship the Lord of Heaven with an honest heart." Thus, it is possible that the character 尊, "Lord," was somehow omitted from the title during transmission or was merely assumed, and that the title should be understood as *On the One Lord of Heaven.* Nicolini-Zani, however, sees 天 (Heaven) as being synonymous with 神 (*shen*), and so translates "Godhead."[32]

The treatise begins in the form of a catechism, providing rhetorical questions followed by their answers. What are humans made of? Of invisible things and of the four visible elements (61–63). What was made from the four elements? Everything in the universe through the power of God (63–70). Are there created things that he did not make? No, the single true God made everything, despite the extreme diversity of creatures—including two kinds of people (70–77). Are there then two Gods? No, the God of heaven, not a god of this world, made man and joined man's spirit to his body (78–81). The spirit is given by God to animate man and his five senses, and together they function as a unity (81–90). This is followed by an excursus on the five senses or components (蔭, *yin*) related to the soul and body (91–99).

The text then turns to a further discussion of death, resurrection, and eternal life (99–115). Can humans know about the next world (115)? Yes, and even though they cannot see it now, they should know it is coming (115–130), and they should prepare for it by doing good in this world (130–139). Worshiping the

31. The text occupies columns 61–206 in the extant manuscript, and we will cite it using those column numbers. Saeki provides the title "Discourse on the Oneness of the Ruler of the Universe" (*The Nestorian Documents*, 174, with translation and notes, 174–205). Li Tang provides the title "On the One God" for the entire manuscript, but gives no additional title for the tract (*Study of the History of Nestorian Christianity*, 157).

32. Nicolini-Zani, *The Luminous Way*, 245n69.

true God will bring forgiveness and peace (139–145). Who can know if they will be forgiven? Just trust and serve the one God and do good, and you will have a solid foundation, for he knows all and he is just (145–165). Humans were created good but became as irrational as four-footed beasts, confused by Satan and the other evil demons who fell into sin and who still lead them astray (166–199). There is still evil everywhere in this world, but the one God wants all people to be holy (200–205). Thus, the author seeks to describe God's power and control of the world in relation to the questions of the origin and composition of the world and of human beings, and to explain the ubiquitous presence of evil.

Metaphorical Teaching, Number 2 (喻,第二)

The first section of *Metaphorical Teaching* (*Parable* and *Analogy* are possible alternate translations) is the shortest of the three tracts in the manuscript, running some sixty columns.[33] As its title suggests, it uses comparisons or analogies to explain Christian teaching about the true God. God created all things, visible and invisible, and their continued existence and the function of the heavens testify to this (cols. 1–5). God's power is seen in how the sky continues to stand without supporting beams (5–12). As an arrow falling from the sky proves the existence of an unseen archer, so creation gives proof of an unseen creator (16–22). As a house can have but one master, so there can be but one God in the world (29–33). Although invisible, God exists, just as the soul in a human being is invisible (33–36). God is omnipresent, unchanging, and eternal (37–49). As a single tree may have two branches, human beings have a twofold nature, body and soul (51–56). The tract ends with an enigmatic reference to the world consisting of four elements (a phrase that appears early in columns 2–3 of the following tract).

In the manuscript, the text of *Metaphorical Teaching* ends a quarter of the way down column 60, and the title appears a few spaces below. The next document begins at the top of the next column. Yet, although it does not appear that the end of *Metaphorical Teaching* was lost, the final line leaves the reader hanging, indicating that this was not the original ending. The title, which appears only at the end of the text, is followed by "number 2" or "second part" (第二), as mentioned above, clearly delineating it from the third tract that follows.

33. As noted earlier, this text appears first in the extant manuscript, occupying columns 1–60. Saeki translates the title as "The Parable" (*The Nestorian Documents*, translation on 161–68 and notes on 169–73); Li Tang gives it as "Parable" (*Study of the History of Nestorian Christianity*, 157–60).

Discourse of the Honored One of the Universe on Almsgiving, Number 3 (世尊佈施論,第三)

The final tract in the manuscript, the longest of the three, spans 199 columns.[34] From early on, it has most often been referred to simply as *Almsgiving* because of its opening admonition to charity.[35] In fact, the entire first forty-two columns of the treatise (208–249) appear to be an enculturated paraphrase of sections of the Sermon on the Mount as recorded in Matthew 6:1–30 and 7:1–14.

This is followed by the statement "This is how the Messiah acted" and the calculation that his work took place over a three-and-a-half-year period (250). Attention is then turned to the unbelieving Jews, and an extended account is given of their plots and eventual success in having Jesus arrested, brought before Pilate, and executed (251–286). Embedded in this long narrative is a recounting of the fall into sin and the need for a Messiah to come and die (263–278). The burial and resurrection of the Messiah, his appearances to the disciples, the Great Commission to evangelize the whole world, and the promise of Pentecost follow (286–313). The author then returns to the Messiah's story, elucidating the theological necessity of his suffering and death (313–317) and calling on his hearers to believe this message (317–319). He emphasizes that both those believers living and those who had already died will be resurrected (319–322).

The ascension and fulfillment of the Pentecost promise (322–327) are then recounted, including what might be a summary of Peter's Pentecost sermon (327–332). The tract continues with the prophecy of eventual judgment as proclaimed by the Messiah (332–339), the rejection by the Jews and the destruction of Jerusalem as a punishment (339–347), and the trials and martyrdom that face some believers (347–353). The work of the Messiah, however, will survive and spread on earth as a witness to the truth (353–369). Then, after repeating the Great Commission (370), the tract concludes with a plea for faithfulness to the Messiah's teaching and for avoidance of false gods until the end of time (370–404).

In many ways this tract is the one that resonates most easily with Western Christian readers today and shows that its author was well versed in tradi-

34. Columns 207–405 in the extant manuscript.
35. Saeki, the first translator, translates the title as "The Lord of the Universe's Discourse on Almsgiving" (*The Nestorian Documents*, 206–30, notes on 231–47). Li Tang translates "Sermon of the Lord of the Universe" (*Study of the History of Nestorian Christianity*, 170–81).

tional Bible history and teaching. At one point the author says that "641 years have not yet passed" since the Messiah's birth, and yet his message has spread everywhere (366–367). This statement led scholars to date this writing, along with the other two tracts in the same scroll, to the period shortly after Alopen's arrival in China, thus forming an "Alopen corpus" of four tracts (*Lord Messiah* and the three tracts in *Discourse on the One God*). As we have seen, other factors have more recently caused Nicolini-Zani and others to question or reject such an early dating of these works.

Hymn in Praise of the Salvation Achieved through the Three Majesties of the Luminous Teaching (景教三威蒙度讚)

This hymn of praise (*zan*), together with the other Jingjiao texts that follow it, was in a scroll retrieved by Paul Pelliot in three pieces from Dunhuang. Therefore they are the only Christian texts that can be directly confirmed as coming from the so-called Library Cave. Today the scroll resides in France's Bibliothèque Nationale in Paris under the designation of *Pelliot Chinois 3847*.[36] The scroll is just over 1 meter long and 26 centimeters high, and it has forty-six columns. Its contents are as follows: (1) an initial hymn, (2) a list of revered holy men and religious writings, and (3) a final historical note. The paper sheet on which the initial hymn was written was later joined to several subsequent sheets that contained the list of men and writings and the concluding note, which indicates that thirty of the books in the preceding list had been translated at the time of the Jingjiao leader Jingjing.[37] Since the stele text composed by Jingjing dates to 781, the second and third texts in the Pelliot scroll cannot date much earlier than that period. But the first text, the *Hymn*, may be still earlier. (See figure 7.)

The first item in the scroll, occupying columns 1–24, has the title *Praise-hymn for the Salvation Obtained by the Trinity of the Luminous Teaching*.[38] It

36. A photograph of the manuscript can be viewed at https://gallica.bnf.fr/ark:/12148/btv1b8303183c.

37. See Nicolini-Zani's summary of the research of Lin Wushu in *The Luminous Way*, 159–61.

38. The first English translation was that of A. C. Moule, who called it the "Tun-huang *Gloria in excelsis Deo*" (*Christians in China*, 52–54). In Saeki's translation it was entitled "A Nestorian Motwa Hymn in Adoration of the Holy Trinity" (*The Nestorian Documents*, 266–72). Li Tang renders it as "The Mighty of Three Receiving Great Praises" (*Study of the History of Nestorian Christianity*, 182–84), and Johan Ferreira simply as "Hymn to the Trinity" (*Early Chinese Christianity: The Tang Christian Monument and Other Documents*, Early Christian Studies 17 [Sydney: St. Paul's Publications, 2014], 377–79).

has forty-four poetic lines, all but one consisting of seven characters, and most of these divided into two smaller clauses of four characters followed by three.[39] The careful construction is illustrated by the fact that the one exception to this pattern, line 23, is at the very center of the *Hymn* (12), which has eight characters and reads "O Messiah, most holy Son, Honored One of the Universe." Already in the early twentieth century, the *Hymn* had caught the attention of Alphonse Mingana, a Syriac Christian scholar who from 1915 to 1932 worked for the John Rylands Library in Manchester, England. Mingana identified the text as a Chinese version of the Syriac *Gloria in Excelsis*, a hymn regularly sung as part of the liturgy on Sundays and feast days, similar in form and function to the Latin *Te Deum Laudamus*. Recent studies have concluded that the Chinese text is a translation of the Sogdian version, which in turn was based on the Syriac text. The Chinese version, however, also was made to conform to Chinese poetic meters that caused it to be very different from a rote translation. The existence of this liturgical text is also evidence that at least in certain places and on some occasions, Jingjiao worship took place in Chinese.[40]

Book of the Honored (尊經)

After column 24 of the Pelliot manuscript, there is a space of about four columns in width before a new work begins. The two characters of its title, 尊經 (*zun jing*), could be translated as "honored persons" and "classic writings," respectively (1).[41] Moule thus originally translated the title as *Honored Persons and Sacred Books*, and more recently, Ferreira opted for *Saints and Scriptures* to reflect the two subsections of the writing.[42] But since the

39. The forty-four lines are divided by Nicolini-Zani into eleven four-line verses. In the analysis here, I refer to line numbers in the poetry, while the position within the manuscript is still signaled by the column numbers given in parentheses.

40. On recent research, see Nicolini-Zani, *The Luminous Way*, 171–73.

41. Rather than counting columns from the beginning of the manuscript, as he did in the previously discussed *Discourse on the One God*, Nicolini-Zani, in his translation of the *Book of the Honored* and the note that follows it, opted to use numbers 1–22 to refer to their contents even though they occupy columns 25–47 of the manuscript (*The Luminous Way*, 226–32). For ease of comparison, I will follow Nicolini-Zani.

42. Moule, *Christians in China*, 55–57; Ferreira, *Early Chinese Christianity*, 47, 267–73, and 381–83. Saeki's rendition was *The Book of Praise Dedicated to the Living and the Dead*, since "to be honoured or to be honourable is nothing but to have given high respect or to be glorified by others" (*The Nestorian Documents*, 277). Li Tang opted to translate as "Honored Persons and Sacred Books" (*Study of the History of Nestorian Christianity*, 184–88).

character *jing* is used in several other titles among the Jingjiao writings as a descriptor for the kind of writing designated (i.e., used in Chinese as a descriptor of classic texts and compilations), it is probably used in that way in this title as well. That leaves the one character *zun*, "holy" or "honored." Since both persons and books that the church honored are listed here, the title *Book of the Honored (Ones)*, that is, people and books, would seem appropriate.

After an opening four-clause invocation of the Trinity (2–3), twenty-two names of revered Christian leaders are given (4–9). This appears to be an official list of the men who were to be included in the liturgical prayers of the church. The list includes biblical figures from the Old and New Testaments as well as later martyrs and church leaders. This is followed in columns 10–18 by a list of thirty-five sacred and theological writings. This catalogue includes books of the Bible as well as noncanonical writings.

Finally, the manuscript concludes with a four-column historical notice indicating that the Jingjiao had a total of 530 sacred books in a foreign language,[43] that Alopen came to China and humbly submitted a petition to allow the Jingjiao entry, and that afterward Jingjing (the author of the Chang'an stele text) had received an imperial order to translate thirty of the books from the list in columns 10–18 (18–22).[44]

Book on Profound and Mysterious Blessedness (志玄安樂經)

This scroll, about 2.8 meters long and 26 centimeters high, was purchased in 1916 in Suzhou by the Chinese collector Li Shengduo.[45] It was first published by Prof. Haneda in 1929. The tract is written in 160 columns, but the first 10 columns were already damaged, and so the text of the lower two-thirds of those columns is missing. The title is found at both the beginning and end of the manuscript, and the first translation, that of Saeki, rendered it as *Sutra on Mysterious Peace and Joy*.[46] Besides their use in the titles, the characters

---

43. The Chinese text quite clearly shows 500 and 30 (五百卅), the number that Moule (*Christians in China*, 57), Saeki (*The Nestorian Documents*, 276), and Ferreira (*Early Chinese Christianity*, 272, 383) all give. The "130" given twice in Nicolini-Zani's translation (*The Luminous Way*, 148, 231) is clearly a misprint.

44. Nicolini-Zani's translation makes it sound as if Alopen and Jingjing were near contemporaries. Ferreira's rendering, "Afterwards, by the imperial orders, Priest Jingjing, bishop of this religion, was summoned," is a better alternative translation.

45. Photographs are found in Kyōu shooku, *Tonkō hikyū*, 1:128–33.

46. Saeki, *The Nestorian Documents*, trans. 281–302, notes 303–11. Li Tang likewise gave

"peace," 安, and "joy/blessedness," 樂, are used as a combined phrase nineteen more times in the text, and often appear to be the goal awaiting followers of the Jingjiao. The Church of the East (like the Greek and Latin churches) refers to its sacraments and some other teachings as "mysteries" (i.e., truths that can only come to humankind through God's revelation). Thus the character 玄 might be understood by Christian readers in this sense, rather than simply as indicating something that is secretive or enigmatic. "Blessedness" also better captures the Christian connotation of 樂, a state of spiritual contentedness even when hurdles are encountered in daily life. Therefore, the title might be paraphrased as *On the Peace and Blessedness Which Come Mysteriously* (i.e., only by revelation). The rendering given above is that of Nicolini-Zani.

This writing, however, lives up to its title in another sense as well—its contents are the most "mysterious" of all our texts. Many lines are difficult to decipher in terms of the Chinese grammar and the word choice, not to mention from the standpoint of Christian teaching. Saeki notes the strong Daoist flavor of the work, and it may well be that the author wrote for Daoist readers or that a Daoist was involved in the translation. This same title is also found near the beginning (col. 10) of the list of honored religious books in the Pelliot manuscript. This would seem to indicate that, despite some of its contents being difficult to square with traditional Christian theology, it was officially numbered among the sacred texts of the Jingjiao. This makes it even more unfortunate that the damage to the manuscript makes the opening ten columns virtually unintelligible.

The *Mysterious Blessedness* text is constructed in the form of a dialogue between a certain Monk Cenwen (岑穩) and the Messiah. Scholars have not come up with a satisfactory explanation of who this Cenwen might be, although Nicolini-Zani in his new translation has adopted the suggestion that Cenwen is a transliteration of the Sogdian name for Simon Peter. As with the work's title, this name also appears separately in the *Book of the Honored* section of the Pelliot manuscript, this time as the fifteenth of the "saints" to be included in the liturgical prayer list. There the name appears in the middle of a list of patriarchs of the Syriac church (col. 7). Yet in the text Cenwen appears to speak directly with the Messiah, so some conclude that he must be one of the twelve apostles, such as Peter. In the text Cenwen is not just referred to with the term 僧, *seng*, as all other Christian monks in the stele and Dunhuang texts are, but instead he is always referred to with the more specific 僧伽, *seng*

---

the title as "Book on Mysterious Peace and Joy" (*Study of the History of Nestorian Christianity*, trans. 188–99).

qie (a Chinese equivalent of the Sanskrit *sangha* or *samgha*, a term specifically used for the order of celibate Buddhist clergy/monks). This would support the conclusion that this work was designed as an apologetic tool for Jingjiao outreach to Chinese Buddhists (and perhaps Daoists).

One often-overlooked characteristic that is useful for interpreters of this "mysterious" text is that it is the most carefully constructed of all the Dunhuang Christian texts. The macrostructure consists of Cenwen asking four questions and the Messiah responding with answers of various lengths. We have just enough text preserved in the opening ten damaged columns to conclude that Cenwen's first question, about the path to salvation, begins in column 4, and the Messiah's answer begins in columns 7–8. That answer continues all the way to column 47. Then, in his second question, Cenwen asks for clarification about what it means that people have "nothing" to bring to God (47–51), and the Messiah gives a second, rather lengthy answer in columns 52–72. The third question is about how one is to cultivate a spiritual life (72–77), and it results in the longest of all the answers (cols. 78–154). Cenwen's final request, for further teaching (154), is followed by a brief denial of his request (155–157). The narrator then provides a curt ending: "They [Cenwen and his companions] were overjoyed, saluted him [the Messiah] respectfully, and withdrew to carry out his commands."

The text's microstructure displays even more meticulous design. The answer to the first question is made up of four shorter responses. Each starts with a four-character address to Cenwen, followed by an opening statement of teaching in six to twelve units of four characters each. Then comes the three-character rhetorical question "Why is this so?" (何以故), followed by sixteen to thirty-two units of additional explanation, the majority of which consist in four-character lines. The second question of Cenwen is also followed by four shorter responses. The first of these follows the same pattern of opening teaching, rhetorical question, and final teaching. The other three skip straight to the final teaching, following a pattern in each of those similar to what was found in units 16–47.

The final of these four subanswers, however, flows seamlessly into a much longer response. After addressing Cenwen by name again (col. 83) and giving a brief admonition about the confusion found among people (83–86), the Messiah says that humans need to practice "ten types of reflection" (十種觀法) to remove such confusion. This is followed by a discussion of these ten types (cols. 87–113). Each is listed in order, beginning with a six-character line, and then is described in nine lines of four characters each.

In the short conclusion to the "ten reflections," the Messiah says that learning these ten reflections allows a person to progress further, to the "four kinds of teachings" (113–114). He then launches into a description of these in columns 115–135. Again, each of these four sections is carefully constructed with seven four-character lines of introduction followed by the three-character rhetorical question "Why is this so?" and then fourteen or fifteen mostly four-character lines in the final answer.

The "four kinds of teachings" section is followed by the narrator's comment that "the Messiah spoke again" (136), introducing a final section of the Messiah's teaching (136–154). After an opening statement (136–137), there follow three monologues, each introduced by the two four-character couplets: "Only this Jingjiao is the most superior teaching. . . ." The first two of these statements is followed by twelve four-character lines explaining how the Jingjiao is superior, the final one by six such lines. Then comes a long conclusion of four-character lines. After the short final request and denial for teaching (154–155), the narrator provides the concise closure for the work. In sum, the tract is carefully crafted and balanced, a fact that should not be neglected when its origin and transmission are being studied.

The intricate design of the tract would indicate that our manuscript has quite faithfully preserved the original text. The main questions posed in this work might well be ones that a Daoist would ask about the path to peace and blessedness—how it could be achieved by emptying oneself of desires, actions, merits, and demonstrations (50), and whether the sinful chaos of the world will not prevent one from reaching the goal (76–77). The answers are not at all what we would expect from a Christian teacher. The "ten reflections" and the "four types of teachings" do not seem to be very different from Daoist and Buddhist teachings. Yet the narrator/Messiah concludes that "only Jingjiao teaching" can help someone achieve true peace and blessedness, and only this teaching can provide true light and brighten one's journey through life and even into foreign lands (148–149).

Book of the Luminous Teaching of Da Qin on Revealing the Origin and Reaching the Foundation (大秦景教宣元至本經)

The final Christian Dunhuang scroll in the Kyoto Secret Collection contains only twenty-six columns over a length of just under a half meter and is just over twenty-five centimeters in height. It was once a longer scroll, however, and would have contained perhaps another dozen columns to complete this tract. Until recently, only the first ten columns had been published by Haneda and Saeki. The latter gave it the title "Ta-Ch'in [Da Qin] Luminous Religion Sutra on the Origin of Origins."[47] In 1995 Lin Wushu presented the first complete transcription of all twenty-six columns, based on a photograph of Prof. Haneda's that was only published in 1958 after his death.

In 2009, a second copy of the same text was published. It was engraved on the memorial *dharani* pillar from Luoyang described earlier in this chapter. The octagonal pillar had been broken, and some of the text on several of its faces near the base was lost. Fortunately, by using both incomplete copies, nearly the entire text can be reconstructed, with only the last few characters missing. The discovery of the pillar, erected in AD 814/815, has also made it clear that the text was composed no later than the early ninth century. Note that we will normally cite *Origin* by giving the column number from the more complete Luoyang pillar text rather than the more fragmentary Dunhuang manuscript.[48]

Nicolini-Zani translates the title of the tract as *Book of the Luminous Teaching of Da Qin on Revealing the Origin and Reaching the Foundation*. The manuscript gives the title with a space between two sets of four characters. The pillar has all eight characters together and adds one additional character (至, *zhi*) before the final two characters, but this has little effect on the meaning. These final five characters (with the 至, *zhi*) are also given as a title in the list of religious books found in Pelliot's manuscript *Book of the Honored*. Having two copies preserved in two totally different settings, and the title surviving in a list of Christian texts, also confirms that this text was both known and had some official status within the Chinese Christian community.

The tract portrays a great teacher from Nazareth called Jingtong (4– 5) who has gathered humanity to teach them about the true origin of all things. He says that Aluohe (a transliteration of the Syriac version of the

47. For photographs of the manuscript, see Kyōu shooku, *Tonkō hikyū*, 5:396-97. For Saeki's translation, see *The Nestorian Documents*, 312–13. Li Tang, referring to it as Fragment I-A, provides a translation of the same part of the original manuscript as "Book on declaring the origin of the Jing religion of Da Qin" (*Study of the History of Nestorian Christianity*, trans. 200–201; discussion on 118–23). She also translates what she calls Fragment I-B, the Kojima document B, as "Book on declaring the origin to the origin of the Jing religion of Da Qin" (201–2). On the latter, see below.

48. The pillar text was published in Zhang Naizhu, *Precious Nestorian Relic*, 19–20. For the text of the entire tract, combining the Luoyang stele text with the Dunhuang manuscript, see Matteo Nicolini-Zani, "The Tang Christian Pillar from Luoyang and Its Jingjiao Inscription, a Preliminary Study," *Monumenta Serica* 57 (2009): 129–30, and his updated translation (*The Luminous Way*, 298–303).

Hebrew word *Elohim* used in the Old Testament for the God of Israel) existed before there was anything else (7), and that he then brought all things into existence (8). Although evil arose, through Aluohe humans can be restored (12). All this is revealed through his spirit (15). Listeners were enlightened by the true wisdom that Jingtong imparted to them through his teaching (19). The shortness of this text leaves one wondering about its purpose and use. Once again we find a text imbued with Chinese imagery, and perhaps it was designed to be used with new contacts who were inquiring about the Christian faith, to open a conversation rather than provide all the answers.

The Kojima Documents

Two additional documents were included among the Christian Jingjiao documents in the 1951 second edition of Saeki's book. Not wishing to change the pagination from the 1938 first edition, he inserted new "*Origin*" material on pages numbered 313A–D, after the ten lines of the Dunhuang *Origin of Origins* text that he had included in his first edition. Then he added a new *Transfiguration Hymn* on pages 314A–C. He told the readers that in late 1943 he had received photos of these two manuscripts from his Japanese friend Kojima Yasushi who was then in China. Saeki gave the title of the first as being identical with that of the Dunhuang *Origin* text, yet with the missing *zhi* character that would appear in the still-undiscovered Luoyang pillar. He entitled the second text *The Nestorian Hymn in Adoration of the Transfiguration of Our Lord*; it had a postscript with a date of AD 720. The new "*Origin*" text was dated in a colophon to AD 717. Lin Wushu, Rong Xinjiang, and others have argued convincingly that both these documents are forgeries. Like the other Dunhuang manuscripts discussed earlier, these disappeared shortly after their existence was first noted. In this case, however, the originals have never resurfaced. In addition, we have no complete photographs of them. In his 1951 edition, Saeki provided only his own translations. Because of these doubts and our inability to study the manuscripts further, we will not include the content of these two works in the rest of our study.[49]

49. For a translation of Kojima A and B, see Saeki, *The Nestorian Documents*, 313A–D and 314A–C, respectively, and Li Tang, *Study of the History of Nestorian Christianity*, 203–4 and 201–2, respectively.

Questions of Authenticity

As mentioned earlier, ever since the Dunhuang Christian documents came to the notice of scholars, some have questioned their authenticity. This was partially because they could not be consulted. It was also due to the reality of a lively black-market business in forged manuscripts claiming to come from Dunhuang. Finally, the fact that Japanese collectors possessed most of these manuscripts made some Chinese scholars especially suspicious, partly because of ongoing hostility toward Japan for their still-unacknowledged wartime atrocities in China. These factors combined to create a situation in which, until very recently, the authenticity of many of the documents could not be confirmed. While the Pelliot manuscript could be carefully studied and authenticated and was thus spared this fate, most of the other writings were considered suspect at best.

In the past decade, however, after most of the manuscripts resurfaced in Japan, their authenticity has received a new and fairer scrutiny. The Dunhuang scholar Rong Xinjiang has led the way in this and has shown the complexity of the issues involved. For example, it was well established that the same ownership seals of the twentieth-century collector Li Shengduo as were found on the *Mysterious Blessedness* and *Origin* documents were also present on numerous forged documents. However, Rong found that many of these seals were added after Li's death. He demonstrated that Li Shengduo himself was not responsible for any forgeries, and that the mere presence of his seals on a manuscript could not be used as conclusive evidence of forgery either. Many genuine Dunhuang documents had been carefully purchased, collected, and catalogued by Li during his lifetime, including the two Christian ones just mentioned. Thus, there is no reason to doubt their authenticity. Commenting on the *Lord Messiah* text and the three tracts that make up *Discourse on the One God*, Hidemi Takahashi dismisses any thought that the texts are forgeries and finds much to support their dating to the time of Alopen.[50]

When Rong turned his attention to the Kojima forgeries, however, he came to the opposite conclusion. Working together with Prof. Lin Wushu, Rong concluded that these documents, which were said to have come from Li's collection but were first seen by Saeki and others after Li's death, were in fact forgeries, probably composed for the market that arose when Li's famous collection began to be sold.

---

50. Hidemi Takahashi, "Representation of the Syriac Language in Jingjiao and Yelikewen Documents," in Lieu and Thompson, *The Church of the East in Central Asia and China*, 24–25n6.

Despite the ongoing questions, we have reason today to consider the majority of the surviving documents genuine. As a result, we can use them to provide a more complete and more reliable picture of the Jingjiao than ever before. They can aid us in learning more about the Christian teaching that was proclaimed in ancient China and how its leaders tried to express the Christian message in a way that was meaningful within the Chinese culture. This understanding of the target audience is also welcome when compared with our other major source, the Chang'an stele, which presents its own problems in interpretation because of its dual audience (see chapter 2 above). These new documents have also removed any lingering doubts some may have had that for several hundred years a form of Syriac Christianity really did have a presence in Tang-dynasty China. In the next chapter, we will use some of these additional Christian documents to examine the spiritual teachings that they and the Chang'an stele present, and so shed more light on the character of the Jingjiao during the Tang period.

Chapter 5

THE TEACHINGS OF THE JINGJIAO

Now that we have surveyed the surviving source material from the Jingjiao, let us turn to the Christian teaching found in those documents. To properly situate their teachings, we will review the main religious options in China during the Tang period. Then we will trace the elements of Christian theology and biblical history found in the extant Christian documents by excerpting them and organizing them thematically to illustrate which traditional Christian teachings are in fact found in the documents. Although this method is not ideal, it must serve as a temporary expedient until we have a complete theological study available to us. By providing many direct citations, I hope the reader will get a sense of the Chinese character of the texts. I have mostly incorporated my own translations, attempting to keep some sense of the typical classical Chinese forms and style. For the most part, they are written in short rhythmical lines that are quite poetical and often more ambiguous than we are used to in Western theological discourse. Wherever possible, I have attempted to preserve that form in the excerpts we cite. At the same time, I have made some allusions more concrete for the Western reader.[1]

Worldview Options in Tang China

China is often admired for the stability, unity, and millennia-long continuity of its traditional culture. While there is much truth in this, conformity could

1. For complete translations with notes, see part 2 of Matteo Nicolini-Zani, *The Luminous Way to the East: Texts and History of the First Encounter of Christianity with China* (Oxford: Oxford University Press, 2022), 193–303. I speak of "my own translation," but in reality it is my rendering after consulting the translations of Saeki, Tang Li, and others, and following long discussions with scholars much more proficient than myself (see the acknowledgments on pp. ix–x above).

still never be complete in any area so vast. Its religious situation is a case in point. While "traditional Chinese religion" is a meaningful category, that term also hides a multiplicity of differences and peculiarities across both time and space. And while the Middle Kingdom was quite successful in keeping out foreign cultural influences for much of its history, it was eventually infiltrated by Buddhism, with lasting effects. So, when the Syriac Christian mission arrived in Chang'an, it would have merely added yet another religious worldview to the ones already competing for the hearts, minds, and adherence of the Chinese people.

In the second millennium BC, during the so-called Shang-dynasty period, the Chinese were venerating nature deities, seeking communication with a spirit world of angry ancestral ghosts, and utilizing shamanistic intercessors to bridge the gap between the living and the dead. The legendary founding ruler(s) of the dynasty had already become deified under the name *Shangdi* (上帝), meaning "supreme deity." The concept of Shangdi gradually morphed into the idea of a cosmic creator and preeminent emperor, and became more personal in the first millennium BC in the form of "heaven" (天, *tian*). The human emperor became the "Son of Heaven." The divine was seen as entering this world through a host of nature deities (sun, moon, wind, etc.) and other semidivine royal ancestor-heroes, all of which needed to be placated through periodic sacrifices by religious specialists whose knowledge was gradually enshrined in sacred written texts. A concept of human immortality also developed. It taught that the human soul survived death—its spirit soul (魂, *hun*) rose to heaven while its physical soul (魄, *po*) descended with the body to the underworld. This is the background for the immense importance in Chinese culture of remembering and showing respect to one's dead ancestors, and this in turn brought about the development of ancestor tablets and shrines and a strong emphasis on all aspects of filial piety. However, because this underlying cultural worldview was somewhat malleable and nebulous and in places even contradictory, numerous other important Chinese philosophical and religious movements that developed in the following centuries could be grafted onto it.

One of the most important of these, dating to the fifth century BC, was Confucianism. Confucius's overt goal was to produce a method of living one's earthly life that would create an atmosphere of social and political harmony. Yet it did have its religious aspects, and, while its adherents were of many stripes, mainstream Confucianists were normally theists. The master's teaching stressed harmony within the "five relationships" (ruler-ruled, father-son, husband-wife, elder brother–younger brother, friend-friend), the virtues of human kindness (仁, *ren*), and proper observance of ritual conduct (禮, *li*). Practicing such virtues would produce a morally superior person (君子, *junzi*). One can see how these emphases could easily push traditional religious beliefs to emphasize even further outward compliance with rituals and respectful relationships at the expense of inner change. And China's strong family/clan societal structure meant that one's success in exhibiting such virtues would bring either honor or shame upon a person and his family. By the Tang period, upper-class Chinese men were receiving training in the Confucian writings in order to become gentlemen officials or scholars who were then entrusted with the imperial bureaucracy (these later became known to Westerners as *mandarins*). The imperial examination system that tested and ranked new applicants centered on a mastery of Confucian thinking.[2]

A contrast to Confucianism was the developing movement of Daoism (or Taoism). The Chinese word *dao*, 道, means road, path, or way, and it is used in many contexts in daily life, as well as in most Chinese philosophies and religions. Laozi (ca. 500 BC) is usually credited as the first major figure in the development of this multifaceted movement. Unlike Confucianism's stress on social harmony in the present life, the Daoists sought an inner harmony both under present circumstances and for eternity. The Way/Dao was seen as the eternal first principle of the universe with which each person must reestablish his or her own harmony. Through teaching, meditation, and proper breathing and other exercises, the three life principles in each person—one's breath/energy (气, *qi*), vital essence (精, *jing*), and spirit (神, *shen*)—could be brought into harmony with the cosmic Dao and become pure potentiality, like "uncut wood." At the same time, this is achieved in a more mystical way through nonaction (*wuwei*). One's inherent character (德, *de*) is cultivated in this way. These philosophical concepts were wedded to other traditional Chinese ideas, like the twin but antithetical forces called *yin* and *yang* as well as honoring other traditional gods and rites, and so produced a variety of sects, each with its own pantheistic amalgam. Daoism had received official backing and encouragement under the short-lived Sui dynasty, and the Tang ruling family that followed it claimed to have Laozi as an ancestor. As a result, Daoism gained a more official status during the Tang period.[3]

2. For a fascinating introduction to the major Chinese philosophical and religious traditions, see A. C. Graham, *Disputers of the Tao: Philosophical Argument in Ancient China* (La Salle, IL: Open Court, 1989).

3. In addition to Graham, Isabelle Robinet ably describes the development of Daoism in *Taoism: Growth of a Religion*, trans. Phyllis Brooks (Stanford, CA: Stanford University Press, 1997), esp. 184–211 on the Tang period.

The final main strand of Chinese religious identity came from outside China in the form of Buddhism. There were many reasons to think it would not gain traction in China. Its vegetarianism was quite countercultural to traditional Chinese eating habits; its monasticism was viewed as contrary to filial piety; and its doctrine of reincarnation and transmigration of souls seemed to fly in the face of ancestor worship. Yet, Buddhist monks began spreading its teachings in China already in the first century, and by the Tang period it was becoming truly Sinicized and began to grow rapidly. Two newly developed varieties would especially take hold in China—the Zen (*Chan*) and the Pure Land (*Jingtu*) sects. Monks translated classic texts from their Indian originals into Chinese and composed new texts as well. Soon after Buddhism entered China, Chinese Buddhists began to borrow freely from Daoist ideas and traditional Chinese religious and cultural concepts, incorporating them freely into their own religious systems. By the Tang period there were so many Buddhist monks and nuns, and so many sites designated as temples and shrines (all outside the taxation system), that the emperors periodically placed limitations upon the Buddhists and several times tried to suppress Buddhism more completely, all to no avail. Buddhist monks served as medical doctors, chanted magic spells, said prayers for the dead, and served as guardians for temples and family shrines.[4]

Thus, by the time of Alopen's arrival, the religious life of China was vibrant and varied. Confucian, Daoist, and Buddhist written texts were all referred to as *jing*, 經, variously translated as "books," "classics," or "sutras." Confucian teaching had long been enlisted in the education of government officials, and their priests received front-row seats at public ceremonies. Daoist teaching produced hermits, priests, and practitioners who sought harmony with nature away from society and politics, yet their prayers, spells, and potions were valued by many Tang rulers. Because the Tang claimed a clan relationship with Laozi, the Daoist leaders stood close to the emperor (but behind the Confucian priests) at public ceremonies. Buddhist monks usually had to stand in the rear (behind the Daoist priests) on public occasions, yet their increasingly large public following and the support of some emperors allowed them to play an ever greater role in the religious life of China, as well as to be periodically influential in political affairs.

4. See Stanley Weinstein, *Buddhism under the T'ang* (Cambridge: Cambridge University Press, 1987), and the classic of Erich Zürcher, *The Buddhist Conquest of China: The Spread and Adaptation of Buddhism in Early Medieval China*, 2 vols., reprint with additions and corrections, Sinica Leidensia 11 (Leiden: Brill, 1972).

Enter the Luminous Teaching

It was into this complicated amalgam of worldviews that Alopen came with his new "Luminous Teaching." When he arrived, he was carrying with him books of sacred teaching written in Syriac. He himself was probably not fluent in the Chinese language, although members of his party may have been. As the stele text tells us, the Tang officials had to translate these books and understand them before the Jingjiao teachings could be given a stamp of approval and their priests permission to begin teaching. Yet Alopen and his colleagues would have had the same struggle to translate their teaching into Chinese. Christianity is unique among the major world religions in requiring potential converts to undergo a significant amount of teaching before they are initiated into the faith. Nor were the existing Chinese religions monotheistic or as exclusive in their conception of what was pure religion. The Jingjiao team had much to learn to do their job properly.

Throughout the history of Christianity in China, missionaries have struggled with putting the Semitic and Greek terms and the concepts of Holy Scripture into the Chinese language. In the seventeenth century, the Jesuits argued among themselves and with the other Roman Catholic mission orders on many such points. In the following centuries, intense controversy erupted about which Chinese words should be used to refer to the Christian God. The results caused divisions between the Roman Catholics and Protestants and further dissension between Protestants, often within the same denomination. When a "union" Bible translation was completed by a diverse group of Protestants in 1919, it still required two different editions for just that reason! Thus, we should not be surprised that Alopen and the Jingjiao leaders who followed him struggled with these issues. Communicating the Christian gospel accurately required clothing its concepts in a language and culture whose categories were quite different from those of the Middle East and Europe. Since our surviving documents probably date from different periods within the two centuries of Jingjiao presence in China, we should not expect to find a unity of terminology or approach within them. At the same time, we should expect to find the main teachings of Christianity as given in the much more copious writings from the heartland of the Syriac church.

The One God and His Attributes

Our texts make it clear that the Jingjiao religion was monotheistic. The documents suspected of being the earliest use the expression "one God" (一神, *Yi shen*) as another name for the "Lord of Heaven" (天尊, *Tianzun*), or simply "Lord" (尊, *Zun*). In the *Hymn*, the Jingjiao deity is referred to by numerous names and epithets: six times as the "Great Master" (大師, *Dashi*, 31, 33–37), four times as "Merciful Father" (慈父, *Ci fu*, 4, 10, 33, 42), twice as "Most Holy Universal Lord" (大聖普尊, *Dasheng pu zun*, 23, 41), and once as "Master God" (師帝, *Shi di*, 11). *Mysterious Blessedness* uses both the more generic "God" (神, *Shen*, 25, 32) and "One Lord" (一尊, *Yizun*, 48, 51, 73, 78). By the late eighth century, the stele calls him "True Lord" (真主, *Zhenzhu*, 3.9, 26.9), or simply "Lord" (主, *Zhu*, 30.10). And in the early ninth-century historical text inscribed on the Luoyang pillar, we find another reference to the "True Lord" (真主, *Zhenzhu*, 23). Thus *Lord Messiah*'s initial experimental use of the Chinese word *Fu*, 佛 (78), the common way to refer to the Buddha in Chinese, must have created enough confusion to be rejected as a term for the Christian God. Instead, the Jingjiao God was increasingly designated by the terms mentioned above, or by transliterations. *A-luo-he* (阿羅訶), a transliteration of the Semitic Old Testament plural word for God (Hebrew *Elohim*; Syriac *'lh'*), is found in five different documents of the period—*Hymn, Honored, Origin*, the historical note at the end of the Luoyang pillar text, and on the Chang'an stele. In the same way, *Mi-shi-he* (i.e., *Messiah*) is used over seventy times in the Jingjiao documents as the most common way of referring to Jesus Christ.

Yet, just as one would expect, our texts also associate the all-powerful monotheistic God with a triple personality. He is called in the title of the *Hymn* the "Three Powered" (1), and the *Hymn* itself praises the "Three alone, merciful Father, Aluohe" (3). Later, and even more clearly, the *Hymn* addresses the "merciful Father, illustrious Son, pure Spirit—the Supreme One" (6) and "Most holy and honored Messiah, . . . merciful Father, and . . . most holy and meek Pure Spirit" (21–22). *Honored* begins also with an invocation of "Father Aluohe, . . . Son Messiah, and . . . Spirit," concluding that "these three persons are united in one being" (2–3). *Almsgiving* speaks of coming to the water of baptism in the name of "the Father, the Son and the Pure Spirit" (308). In the stele text, the Jingjiao God is referred to four times simply as the "Three-One" (三一, *Sanyi*). Interestingly, the first occurrence is in connection with Aluohe (3.8), the second with the Messiah (6.4), and the third with the Pure Wind (7.2). The final reference comes in the conclusion to the poem itself: "There is no better name or description [for the Jingjiao God] than the Three-One" (30.9). There is no mistaking that the Christian God is the one being referred to.

The three persons of the Trinity are mentioned by a variety of names. Curiously, except for four references to the "merciful Father" in the *Hymn*, the first person of the Trinity is only referred to as "Father" in one other Trinitarian reference (*Almsgiving* 308), and three other references in *Almsgiving* (326, 334, 336). More commonly, he is referred to as the Creator (see the next section). The Son is most often referred to as Messiah, with only the *Metaphorical Teaching* and *One Godhead* texts not using this name. *Honored* refers to the Messiah with the additional epithets of "royal Son" and the "Promised One" (2). "Yishu," the transliteration of the Syriac personal name for "Jesus," appears twice in *Lord Messiah* with the characters 移鼠 ("remove rat," 121, 124), and then twice in *Almsgiving* with the less offensive characters "feather-screen number" (翳數, 214, 363). The Holy Spirit is referred to five times in *Lord Messiah* as "Cool Wind"—four times in connection with the Messiah's birth, and once in the retelling of Jesus's baptism. This was modified slightly in *Almsgiving* to "Pure Wind," where it is used once in a Trinitarian formula (308) and four times in the story of Pentecost. The same expression is used twice in the *Hymn* text. The "wind/spirit" character (風) was also used by itself in the Chang'an text in a reference to baptism as a washing "with water and spirit" (8.6). *Lu-he* (盧訶), a transliteration of the Syriac *rwḥ'* (Hebrew *Ruach*), meaning "Spirit," is also used once in *Origin* (15).

Other attributes of God are brought out in the texts—both those familiar to our traditional theological language and some new ones. The poem of the stele begins with God's eternal nature: "The True Lord is without beginning" (26.9), and the commentary explains he is "first of the first . . . last of the last . . . without beginning" (3.3; 3.5; 3.9). He is invisible to man (*Lord Messiah* 6), has unlimited divine power (*Lord Messiah* 15, 17), has unfathomable and all-knowing wisdom (*Metaphorical Teaching* 35–36; *Stele* 3.4), is omnipresent (*Metaphorical Teaching* 36) and all-compassionate (*One Godhead* 67), the Creator of all things, and the great preserver of what he has created (*Metaphorical Teaching* 18; *Hymn* 19–20; *Origin* 11). He dwells in a place of tranquillity and happiness (*Lord Messiah* 11). More unusual are the thoughts that in heaven "there is no life or death, no encounters with the beautiful" (*Lord Messiah* 16), perhaps meaning that the eternal realm is beyond such things that pertain only to the created world. *Metaphorical Teaching* also says that because of the One God "there is neither border nor the beginning of action" (42–43). This may be an attempt at describing God's eternity in a way that would communicate with people imbued with Daoist and Buddhist ideas. The same might be said about the stele text's comments that God possesses a profound tranquillity and stillness (3.2; 26.10), perhaps seeking to relate the immutability and impassibility of God taught in the West with Daoist ideas. Clearly, however, there is not simply a recasting of Semitic or Hellenistic categories of thought, but an attempt to express God's attributes in language that encompasses Chinese religious and philosophical discourse.

The Jingjiao documents have numerous references to the Christian God as the creator of all things. After beginning his stele poem with God's eternity and constancy, Jingjing continues: "Like a craftsman, he began to create, bringing forth the earth and setting the sky in place" (26.11–26.12). To this the commentary adds that "the dark and void were changed, and heaven and earth came into being; sun and moon began to move and day and night commenced. Working skillfully, he created 10,000 creatures, and then he created the first man" (4.1–4.4). Additional details are added by the Dunhuang documents: he was the creator of both the visible and invisible parts of creation (*Metaphorical Teaching* 3–4), and nothing exists in heaven and earth that was not created by him (*One Godhead* 64). Other details preserved from the Genesis account include the original garden with its fruit and animals (*Lord Messiah* 41), and that the first man, Adam (阿談, *a tan*), disobeyed and ate from the tree and was punished for wanting to be like God (*Almsgiving* 265–267). Again, however, we find a Chinese slant. In *Origin*, a proclamation is read about the mysterious creation and the Creator: "There was no beginning, no words, no way [道, *dao*], no original cause; only the mysterious existence that was non-existent" (7). Here Buddhist and Daoist phraseology is used to convey the *ex nihilo* aspect of creation, the totally uncaused existence of God, a creation that was solely his idea.

Humankind and Their Attributes

When it comes to human beings, "all that a person has—body, life, organs and spirit—come from the Lord of Heaven" (*Lord Messiah* 23). Humans were made up of elements, soul and spirit (*Metaphorical Teaching* 52–54), or with a visible part and an invisible part (*One Godhead* 61–63). The first person was created with a knowledge of God (*Lord Messiah* 42), and his original nature was good with "an absence of [evil] desires" (*Stele* 4.10). In *Almsgiving*, there is a description of the man's fall into sin: he wavered in his heart and wanted to be like God, so he ate from the tree; this ended his fellowship with God, resulted in Adam's lie and a punishment of death (265–268). Since then, "all beings live in sin" and "dare not approach the Lord of Heaven" any longer (*Lord Messiah* 30–32). Jingjing attributes the delusions of sin directly to the work of "Satan," who "planted the idea of equal greatness inside the one man" (*Stele* 4.11–4.13); originally a celestial angel, the devil fell and turned to a life of evil (*One Godhead* 181–182), leading lost people ever further into evil (*One Godhead* 188–190). The sinful state of humans, in turn, led them to trust in prayer and sacrifices, to ascetic practices, or to a pretense of goodness (*Stele* 5.6–5.8); others cast horoscopes, or worshiped fire or devils (*Almsgiving* 382–384). In this new, confused state, corrupted humans began worshiping images of gold, silver, bronze, clay, and wood, or of animals and humans (*Lord Messiah* 48–52; *Stele* 5.5).

In his earthly life, man was intended to do good and "sow" good deeds that could be "rewarded or judged" in the next world (*One Godhead* 119–120); and "an evil heart, evil thoughts, evil repayment along with jealousy—all should be eliminated while still in this world" (*One Godhead* 136–137). Those who do not do so "will live forever in hell under fire" (*Almsgiving* 178). When humans recognize their sin, God's power can raise them up again (*Lord Messiah* 21–22). For there is another world when "the soul returns to the body . . . needing no food or clothing, happily existing" (*One Godhead* 100–101). While many texts speak of doing good and avoiding evil as the path or way to heaven (*Lord Messiah* 34–35), it is also clear that salvation is intimately connected with the Messiah (*Lord Messiah* 137). He is still portrayed as the pivotal figure in salvation history. Thus, these texts are more similar to the New Testament's Letter of James in giving space to the fruit of faith than to the apostle Paul's emphasis on God's grace given as a free gift. Yet the Jingjiao texts still presuppose the substitutionary work of Christ, which is given to the Christian by faith. To make this more readily apparent, we will give more extended citations in the sections that follow.

The Messiah and His Work

The incarnation, God becoming man in the person of Jesus, is one of the most central mysteries of Christian revelation. It was a counterintuitive event that had no more parallel in Chinese religion or mythology than in Western spirituality. It can also be seen as the opposite of Buddhism, which concentrates attention on how a person can become a godlike Buddha. Therefore, it is not surprising that this teaching is mentioned in several of the surviving documents—most completely in the Chang'an stele, in *Lord Messiah*, and in *Almsgiving*. There is no doubt that when the texts speak of the Messiah, they are referring to the Jesus of Christendom as his name is also given in transliteration (*Lord Messiah* 121, 124; *Almsgiving* 363).

While just one four-character line in the stele poem refers to the incarnation, still it says much: "Dividing his being he came to earth" (26.13). This translation can be justified in light of the way the commentary has expanded on it in the following four lines:

> Therefore, our Three-One divided being,
> the luminous and honorable Messiah,
> concealing his true majesty,
> appeared as a human being. (6.4–6.7)[5]

Almsgiving provides a further description of the incarnation:

> Therefore, the Messiah did not remain with God,
> but he made himself become a man;
> the Lord himself made him man;
> because the power of the Lord is unbounded;
> it is not like what humans can make,
> the Lord has a body subject to passions
> which he shares with Adam. (268–271)

The familiar details of his conception and birth are provided in *Lord Messiah*:

> The Lord of Heaven sent the Cool Wind [Holy Spirit]
> to a virgin called Mary.
> Then the Cool Wind entered into the womb of Mary,
> just as the Lord of Heaven had instructed,
> and Mary became pregnant immediately.
> Therefore, the Lord of Heaven sent the Cool Wind
> to wait upon this virgin,
> and she got pregnant without a man.
> Let everyone know
> that this conception came about without a man. (115–118)
>
> Mary later gave birth to a baby boy
> whose name was Yishu [Jesus].
> His father was the Cool Wind. (120–121)

The stele commentary further makes mention of the star that announced Christ's birth. This story was of particular importance in the Church of the

---

5. The Eccles-Lieu translation renders the expression in col. 26 as "A part of his divided-self entered the world to bring salvation to all without limit." And in line 6, "Thus, one of the three the radiant Míshīhē, concealing his true majesty, appeared as a man." See http://www.unionacademique.org/content/files/10362790247079243.pdf.

East, as they believed the magi (Matt. 2:1–12) had come from Persia and were therefore their own spiritual ancestors.

> God in heaven proclaimed a celebration;
> a virgin gave birth to a sage in Da Qin.
> A luminous star announced the good news;
> in Persia they saw it shining and came with tribute.
> Thus, he fulfilled the ancient words told by the 24 sages,
> regulating both family and nation through his great plan. (6.8–7.1)

That star is further described in *Lord Messiah*:

> At the time the Messiah was born,
> the surrounding world
> all saw a bright star in the sky above the earth.
> A new bright star was known to be in the sky.
> The star was as big as a wagon wheel,
> in the bright and clean place
> where the Lord of Heaven dwells. (124–126)

The Messiah's Ministry

Although the Messiah's teaching is discussed in many of the documents, the actual events of his ministry are given much less attention. The stele says nothing of them. *Almsgiving* gives only the briefest of summaries:

> The Messiah did these deeds
> imparting his teaching everywhere;
> for three years and six months
> he did his work just like a disciple,
> and died among his own people,
> and was hanged up high. (250–251)

Lord Messiah is the only source to give a few more details about the Messiah's life and ministry. It begins by mentioning Jesus's visit to the temple at age twelve (Luke 2:41–52): "When he was twelve years old, he explained the law to the people so that they would do good" (128).

The text then goes into substantial detail in describing John the Baptist and his baptism of the Messiah.

> He immediately came to Ruohun [John] and entered the water in
>   the valley.
> John was at the beginning a younger brother of the Messiah and
>   submitted to the Holy One.
> He lived in the valley.
> Since his birth,
> he had never taken wine nor meat,
> but ate only raw vegetables and honey,
> honey from the earth.
> At that time, there were many people
> who came to John and were baptized
> and received the teaching again.
> At that time John
> sent for the Messiah
> and baptized him in the Jordan.
> As the Messiah went into the water and then came out,
> the Holy Spirit immediately appeared
> coming from heaven,
> in appearance like a dove
> which sat on the Messiah.
> From the emptiness a voice said:
> "The Messiah is my son.
> All beings in the world
> should follow the Messiah's teaching." (129–136)

John's lifestyle, the descending dove, and the voice praising the Messiah as "my son"—all clearly reflect the accounts found in the canonical Gospels. If the last two lines, however, are part of the quotation, rather than the Christian author's admonition, the reference seems to reflect Matthew's version of the similar words spoken at Jesus's transfiguration. Only there does the voice conclude with the command, "Listen to him!" (Matt. 17:5). There may have been good reason for *Lord Messiah* to include these closing words and to provide such detail for this one story. Baptism was a new and strange custom in China. The missionary author may have felt that the example of the Messiah and the command from his Father to follow this teaching would bear fruit in convincing local believers to receive baptism themselves. One might add that

Matthew was the gospel that was used most often in the Syriac church's Sunday Gospel readings in the liturgy.

A few lines later, *Lord Messiah* again mentions the Savior's age:

> The Messiah, at age twelve
> and again when he passed age thirty-two,
> sought to ask everyone who had done evil,
> to turn back and do good. (139–141)

The miracles and signs performed by the Messiah are then briefly summarized:

> The dead were made alive;
> the blind had their vision restored;
> those with diseased skin were gradually cured;
> the sick were healed;
> those afflicted by demons had them cast out;
> the crippled received special healing.
> All who were sick
> came to appeal to the Messiah.
> They touched his clothes
> and were always healed. (142–145)

This brief summary stresses Christ's healing ministry and omits mention of his stilling of the storm, multiplication of the loaves, and other nonhealing miracles. Healing, however, was central to the Messiah's ministry, and thus we should probably not read too much into what is not mentioned. Almost in passing, *Lord Messiah* refers to the twelve apostles (141). The stele, meanwhile, gives only the vaguest descriptions of the Messiah's earthly ministry:

> Thus, he fulfilled the ancient word told by the 24 sages,
> regulating both family and nation through his great plan.
> Thus, he established the new teaching unspoken by the Three-One
>   Pure Spirit,
> modeling good practice through proper belief. (6.12–7.3)

Arrest, Crucifixion, and Burial

The stele gives only a one-line explanation of the denouement of the Messiah's work on earth: "He saved and expiated without limit" (26.14). In describing the earthly life of Jesus, both *Lord Messiah* and *Almsgiving*, on the other hand, devote extensive sections to Jesus's arrest and execution—columns 145–170 and 251–292, respectively, or about 15 percent and 20 percent of their total texts. This parallels the emphasis of the four canonical Gospels, which all devote from one-fourth to one-third of their length to the final week of Jesus's life. If there is an unusual emphasis in the Chinese texts, it is the space devoted to the plotting of the unbelieving Jews. The reason for this lies in the catechetical purpose of the writings rather than in some supposed anti-Semitic attitude of their authors. One of the many "stumbling blocks" for the Chinese to believe that this Christian Messiah was a worthy figure of worship was his condemnation and death as a criminal. Thus, a detailed account had to be provided to show that his death was not due to any crimes of his own but was rather a miscarriage of justice that was still part of God's plan of salvation.

In *Almsgiving* this lengthy section follows directly on the author's summary of Jesus's Sermon on the Mount. He speaks of both the plot of the unbelieving Jews and Jesus's own prediction that what would happen to him was in response to prophecy. Nicolini-Zani's translation shows the clear references perfectly.[6]

> Three days before his death,
> he had already predicted his imminent end,
> so that all people would later rise from the dead
> and ascend to heaven.
> And this is precisely what his sanctifying action
> brought about in this world. (252–253)
>
> He set a time of three years and six months
> for a proclamation of these things under heaven.
> Now it is up to you to judge what happened. (254–255)
>
> The Jews captured him
> and discussed the fact that he had said
> he was the Son of the Honored One:
> "[He says] 'I am the Messiah,'
> [but] who can say such a thing?

6. See columns 252–263 in Nicolini-Zani, *The Luminous Way*, 254–55. While I reproduce his translation, I have printed the text to show the poetic line structure, whereas Nicolini-Zani does not.

He is not at all the Messiah.
He lies, and we want him to be arrested.
It is up to you to do the right thing." (255–258)

This last section appears to reflect the trial of Jesus at the house of the Jewish high priest. The author continues by explaining how he was brought before a Roman court. Pontius Pilate is referred to as Caesar and king since, as the imperial official in charge locally, he spoke and acted for the emperor.

> . . . even if the Caesar had not consented to his arrest,
> [the Messiah] could not have escaped death.
> In fact, he was captured and arrested
> in accordance with [the judgment of] the doctors of the law,
> was meticulously interrogated by them,
> and [as expected] from the beginning
> [condemned to be] hung up high.
> . . . .
> [The Caesar had said], "You say
> That among you there is a law,
> according to which he must die
> because of what he said about himself,
> [because] who can say,
> 'I am the Honored One of the Universe'?
> Let us therefore cease to argue." (258–263)

Lord Messiah further describes how the unbelievers and evildoers rejected the Lord of Heaven's teaching and in their jealousy plotted against the Messiah (145–149). Although their plots at first failed (150–151), they did not give up:

> They then spoke evil [against him] before the great king.
> The evildoers calmly do their evil.
> Messiah does good;
> he goes even further
> and teaches all beings.
> When Messiah was only thirty-two years old,
> those evildoers
> then came and spoke to the great king Pilate.
> Coming before Pilate they said:

"The Messiah deserves to die."
The great king then made inquiries
about the evil reason for testifying against Messiah,
and they came before the great king Pilate
to persuade him that the Messiah should receive the death penalty.
(151–156)

The text continues with Pilate's examination of Christ:

Then the great king was about to make his judgment:
"Should this person be put to death?
I have really not seen nor heard anything!
This person does not deserve death."
It was decided by the evildoers themselves.
The great king said,
"I cannot execute this person!"
The evildoers then said:
"If this person does not die,
then our men and women [should die]."
The great king Pilate
asked for water and washed his hands
and then went to the evildoers saying,
"I really cannot kill this person."
Those evildoers
increased their appeal,
"It is impossible not to kill him." (156–161)

After recounting so many details from the Gospels, as well as references to Old Testament prophecy, *Lord Messiah* describes unambiguously both the actual crucifixion and death of the Messiah and its soteriological meaning:

The Messiah offered his body up to this evil,
for the sake of all beings;
he was sent into this world
knowing that all people had lives as short as candles.
He preached to the people in this world
and died in their place.
The Messiah gave his own body

and received death willingly.
The evildoers then took the Messiah to another place.
To a place of execution
called Qiju [Golgotha].
Then they tied him to a tree
together with two criminals
on his left and right sides.
On the same day,
they bound Messiah for five hours;
on the sixth day of fasting,
he was bound at dawn.
Until sunset,
it was then dark all over.
The earth quaked; mountains collapsed.
All the tombs were opened,
and all the dead rose to life.
When people see these things,
should they not believe these teachings?
Death and life are in the hands of the Messiah. (161–170)

Almsgiving not only states that the Messiah was executed but explains the reason for it by using very biblical imagery:

He died among his own people,
and was hanged up high. (251–252)

But the lamb was taken to the slaughterhouse
without making any sounds,
without any shouting,
he remained silent;
but when his body was hung according to the sentence,
he gave you the love which he himself received [from God].
And the sinfulness of Adam and his offspring was passed to him.
   (272–274)

The Messiah carried the suffering.
It is not that he has no strength to bear,
or no strength to do anything,
but he obeyed the law and was hanged [crucified]. (277–278)

Almsgiving then continues by describing the signs and wonders that took place at the time of the Messiah's death:

> At that time,
> as a result of giving his life,
> the earth and mountains were shaken.
> The rocks were split and the curtain that hung
> at that place, the holy temple,
> was torn in two pieces.
> At that place tombs also opened themselves,
> and it was heard that those who had died in a blessed state
> rose from death to life,
> and approached many people. (279–282)

The text continues by describing the burial of Christ and the guard placed at his tomb:

> Thus, the Messiah was hanged,
> in order to demonstrate the truth of the Lord of the universe,
> just as it was foretold.
> When it was dark,
> the Messiah's human body
> was granted to the Lord of the universe.
> Therefore, a man named Joseph,
> a councilor, took his body home,
> using a clean shroud to wrap it.
> He had a new tomb in a field,
> newly cut from the side of a hill,
> and a large stone cover was placed there,
> and a seal was put on the stone.
> The Jews asked that men be placed as watchmen,
> for the Messiah had said
> that he would rise from the dead in three days.
> "So do not be fooled;
> his disciples will come
> and the coffin will be stolen
> and they will say
> that he has risen from the dead." (284–291)

Resurrection and Ascension

In the only surviving manuscript of *Lord Messiah*, the text breaks off in mid-sentence after the account of the signs accompanying Jesus's death. As a result, *Almsgiving* is our only surviving source to inform us how the resurrection was taught among the followers of the Jingjiao. Again, the many parallels to the gospel accounts come through clearly in Nicolini-Zani's translation:

> And so it was:
> the Jews had the tomb guarded for three days,
> watching over the seal from outside.
> The women who had followed [the Messiah]
> even after hands had been raised [against him]
> testified to what they had seen.
> Then also some other followers [did the same].
> A flying immortal clad in garments as white as snow,
> was sent by the Honored One of the Universe.
> He appeared from the heavens, approached the guards,
> went to the great stone,
> rolled away the rock that had been placed on the door,
> and sat on it.
> The guards, recognizing [that figure] as a flying immortal,
> entered the tomb and searched for the body,
> but did not find it.
> They discussed [the matter] among themselves
> and then abandoned the tomb,
> going to report to the Jews everything they had seen.
> From the Jews [the guards] received great wealth,
> so that they would not respond to questions
> and would not say what they had seen.
> But the guards said, "Everything was as it had been proclaimed:
> The Messiah rose from the dead as he had said."
> Then the women went there according to the law,
> and some Jews also went to the tomb on the third day
> to make sure [of the end of the Messiah].
> There, [the women] clearly saw that the Messiah had departed,
> and together they went to inform the disciples. (291–302)[7]

7. Nicolini-Zani, *The Luminous Way*, 257–58.

The Chang'an stele also mentions the results of Christ's death and resurrection in enculturated, soteriological terms, ending with what appears to be a reference to Christ's ascension.

> He opened the door of the three constants,
> initiating life and extinguishing death.
> The Luminous Sun was hung up to dispel the darkness,
> and so the devil and the arrogant were totally destroyed.
> He rowed a voyage of mercy so they could enter the bright palace,
> and thus the people could finish crossing.
> When he had finished his work,
> at midday he rose into the air. (7.6–8.3)

Of special note is the clear reference to the substitutionary nature of the Messiah's death and its atonement for sin that is found in *Almsgiving*, ideas totally foreign to Chinese religion:

> So, Adam and his offspring can avoid [eternal] death.
> They die, and do so justly,
> but rather with the help of a holy act
> through the Messiah, they can avoid death.
> It is appropriate to receive [forgiveness/life],
> for Messiah carried the suffering. (276–278)[8]

Thus, even with our limited number of surviving documents, and although they come from a variety of genres, we can verify that the Jingjiao expounded the traditional picture of the Messiah's life and work in some detail, as well as its theological meaning. Indeed, the use of the term "Messiah" itself some seventy times in the texts attests to their Christocentric nature.

The Way to Heaven

How do the texts convey the Messiah's work to humankind? The Jingjiao texts do not seem to have found a good Chinese equivalent to the biblical concepts of *sin* or of *grace*. At the same time, numerous texts make it clear that freedom

---

8. The last several lines are translated as follows by Nicolini-Zani: ". . . that the Messiah should suffer, and that he should act in weakness so that others would [no longer] be subject to weakness" (*The Luminous Way*, 256).

from death and evil comes through God's work and not humankind's. In *Lord Messiah* we read:

> Clearly knowing evil, man can no longer communicate with heaven,
> but God's power can still raise up a human being. (21–22)

And in *Almsgiving*:

> Through the Messiah they [humankind] can avoid death.
> It is appropriate to receive [forgiveness/life],
> for Messiah carried the suffering. (278)

And again:

> Therefore, he suffered greatly,
> afraid that people might be alienated from the Lord of the
>   universe.
> Get ready and turn toward Messiah.
> All who have faith
> should come to the Lord of the Universe. (316–318)

And in the liturgical *Hymn*:

> You give yourself up for the sins of all people. . . .
> Send down a raft so we avoid sinking in the river of fire. (14, 16)

While a good life is constantly encouraged and seen as an outcome of following the path of Jingjiao, enlightenment through its teachings must first come from God. As it says in *Lord Messiah*:

> All humans are by themselves unable to see the Lord of Heaven,
> but if they themselves do good,
> and do not follow the evil way to hell,
> then they can obtain the heavenly way (*dao*). (34–35)

> The Lord of Heaven has power!
> And he will send to many
> a pure faith
> and they will return to the good. (119–120)

Almsgiving links that faith with the good works that flow from it:

> Therefore, you have faith,
> and you have done good works.
> Has anyone followed this way with all his heart?
> Then he will go to heaven. (396–397)

The word "faith" (信, *xin*) appears eight times in *Lord Messiah* and nine times in *Almsgiving* in the context of Christian faith, and once each in *Mysterious Blessedness* and *Origin*.

The Role of the Church

The character 寺, *si*, used in Chinese of traditional Chinese temples as well as Buddhist and Daoist shrines and monasteries, is used eleven times in the Chang'an stele to denote the buildings of the Jingjiao. In some places it seems to refer to church buildings, in others to monasteries (temples and monasteries are often not distinguished in Buddhist terminology). In the Chang'an stele inscription, the stele's erection is dated to the time when Ningshu was patriarch of the "Luminous people" (景眾, 31.2). The word in the other texts that comes closest to the abstract concept of the "church" as the community of believers, or the corpus of teaching, is 教, *jiao*, religion or teaching, the second character in Jingjiao. For instance, we read in *Almsgiving* that "The *teaching* (教, *jiao*) of the Lord was proclaimed" (339) to the people. There is no hope for "those who do not believe the *teaching* (*jiao*) of the Lord of Heaven" (*Lord Messiah* 146; also 59, 170). If one follows the Jing teaching, one will help oneself and "help save all creatures" (*Mysterious Blessedness* 129).

Here and elsewhere the words used to describe the Luminous Teaching (經, *jing*, and some equivalent characters) are at times almost interchangeable in meaning with "faith" (信心, *xinxin*; *Almsgiving* 170), similar to how the Greek word *pistis* has the dual meaning of "believing/trusting" and the body of teaching, that is, the Christian *faith*. Thus, *Mysterious Blessedness* says that when people hear this "teaching" (經文, *jing wen*) being preached, it will bring them joy, nourishment, and support (66). This is crucial because "only the supreme transcendent doctrine of this Luminous Teaching" (as the Messiah repeats three times to his audience in the *Mysterious Blessedness* text) can "protect living beings from the enemy [forces] that afflict [*sic*] them" (137–138), can "lead living beings across the ocean of mortality to the other shore, the place of blessedness" (140), and can "ensure that living beings return to life . . . in the knowledge of truth" (144–145).[9] Therefore, the Messiah urges:

> You disciples
> and all other listeners,
> spread throughout the world
> and practice my teachings (經, *jing*).[10] (150–151)

Faith and Practice

This brief overview must suffice to indicate some of the many parallels of the Jingjiao texts with Christian doctrine. But other essentials are also contained in the documents. The lengthy account of the "Ten Obligations" (願者) in *Lord Messiah* is a Chinese paraphrase of the Ten Commandments (ca. 60–92). *Almsgiving* opens with an extensive adaptation of many important sections of Jesus's Sermon on the Mount (1–43). Further on in that text we have a creed-like summary:

> That he who was with your Father came down from heaven
> and did his sanctifying work;
> that in order to assume in his divine nature our condition of sin
> he suffered death;
> that on the third day . . . [he] rose from death,
> thanks to the energies of the Honored One of Heaven,
> and he ascended into heaven.[11] (326–329)

All of this teaching is clothed in Chinese terminology, pictures, and phraseology. Favorite Chinese themes are stressed. In the section of *Lord Messiah* that recounts the Ten Commandments, the commandments on loving God and honoring parents are greatly expanded in comparison with the others. The readers are told repeatedly that one cannot love and honor God without also a consistent commitment to filial piety and obedience to the emperor (62–77 and 81–85). Not only *Metaphorical Teaching* but many of

---

9. Translation of Nicolini-Zani, *The Luminous Way*, 295.

10. Note the character 經, *jing*, is also used to denote a book, as in the titles of *Lord Messiah, Honored, Mysterious Blessedness, Origin*.

11. Adapted from the translation of Nicolini-Zani, *The Luminous Way*, 259–60.

the other texts use metaphorical language as a matter of course, a common feature of classical Chinese moral texts. Comparisons from nature and daily life are used to illustrate abstract and concrete truths: man's confused spiritual vision is like a moon reflected in dirty water (*Mysterious Blessedness* 10–11); God's presence and man's life force are both invisible like the wind (*Lord Messiah* 6–7, 26–28; *One Godhead* 68); the creation proves the existence of a Creator in the same way that a falling arrow is certain evidence of an unseen archer (*Metaphorical Teaching* 16–21); a single man has a soul and spirit in the same way a single tree can have two branches (*Metaphorical Teaching* 53–54); all created things are as insignificant as grains of sand (*Origin* 10). Complex distinctions are made in typical Chinese style when discussing growth in Christian knowledge and sanctification. They are like "ten types of reflection" (*Mysterious Blessedness* 87), "four kinds of superior teaching" (114), or "four ways of understanding" (171).

In these texts, foreigners attempted to present the Christian message in a culturally meaningful way for their Chinese hearers. To accomplish this in written form, they needed to use the highly ambiguous forms of classical literary Chinese. As a result, they have left modern readers with many difficult passages to decipher. It is not surprising that this has led scholars to interpret such passages according to their own theories about the Jingjiao. Some see the Syriac monks as being similar to the Buddhist missionaries who took their religion in bold new directions as they enculturated it within Chinese traditional religions. Others see Alopen and his successors through the lens of modern entrepreneurial Protestant missionaries and look to evaluate them on the simplicity of their message and their success in planting a new church in China. With the reemergence of the Dunhuang manuscripts, we can hope that scholars will soon produce both translations and more objective arguments for their competing interpretations. Until then, we must withhold ultimate judgment about many passages in the documents, and therefore we must also be cautious about making final conclusions about the charges of syncretism often leveled against the documents and their authors. Some additional light, however, can be thrown on the Jingjiao by looking at its further life and history under the Tang and in still later periods.

Chapter 6

THE JINGJIAO UNDER THE TANG

Judging by the notices in the Chang'an stele, a reader might infer that the Jingjiao was quite successful in spreading its teaching across China. Taizong's edict of 638 certainly allowed it to do that, saying that, since their teaching "profits mankind . . . it is proper that it be propagated everywhere" (13.1–13.2). But this lofty pronouncement initially mentioned only the establishment of a single church and monastery in Chang'an itself (13.3–13.5).

The stele commentary, however, claims that under the next emperor, Gaozong (649–683), Jingjiao churches "were established in every *prefecture*" (州, *zhou*, 15.10). It is doubtful, however, that the church spread so rapidly as to be represented in all 360 prefectures that made up the Tang realm at this period. A few lines later, we read that the Jingjiao "spread to the ten regions" and its "temples could be found in one hundred walled cities" (15.12; 16.2). All these statements reflect typical hyperbole common in classical Chinese texts, yet Jingjing would not have been allowed to use such expansive language in a public document of this kind if there had not been at least a moderate spread of the faith. Such an expansion would have required a similar increase in the number of clergy within the church, and this might be what the stele poem is telling us when it says that "a system of clergy was established" during Gaozong's reign (28.2).[1]

---

1. The phrase again is difficult to understand with certainty. Samuel N. C. Lieu and Lance Eccles, http://www.unionacademique.org/content/files/10362790247079243.pdf, translate "leaders of religion were duly appointed" (8); Matteo Nicolini-Zani translates "a Lord of the Doctrine was appointed": *The Luminous Way to the East: Texts and History of the First Encounter of Christianity with China* (Oxford: Oxford University Press, 2022), 215. On China's administrative structure during this period, see Mark Edward Lewis, *China's Cosmopolitan Empire: The Tang Dynasty*, History of Imperial China 3 (Cambridge, MA: Belknap Press of Harvard University Press, 2009), 72–77, who states that the average *zhou*, 州, contained about 25,000 households (72).

By the latter half of Gaozong's reign, however, the Jingjiao experienced a major setback, as Wu Zetian increasingly controlled state affairs. The instability deepened after Gaozong was debilitated by a stroke in 660, and it was further augmented after his death in 683. After serving as regent for the two brief reigns that followed, she declared herself empress of a new Zhou, 周, dynasty in 690. When she died fifteen years later, the Tang dynasty was revived, but court intrigues continued to bring instability until Xuanzong took the throne in 712. It was during this tumultuous period at the end of the seventh century and in the early eighth century that rival religious leaders, as we have seen, "raised their voices" against the Jingjiao (16.4–16.9). It was only after Xuanzong had consolidated his power in 713 that the Christians could again worship freely. The commentary's reference to the sacred pillars and stones being "toppled" and "displaced" during the previous period (17.3–17.4) indicates that some churches had been vandalized or even closed. But under Xuanzong, and with the arrival of bishop Jihe from the mother church in Da Qin, a spirit of optimism again filled the church (19.8–19.11).

But Xuanzong's long reign also went downhill in later years, leading up to the revolt of An Lushan in 755, the emperor's flight, and his abdication the following year. His son and successor, Suzong (756–762), however, is credited by the stele text with building or rebuilding Jingjiao churches in northwest China (20.1–20.2); it was there that he consolidated his power and began his march back to reclaim the capital of Chang'an from the rebels. The stele also gives praise to his two successors—first Daizong (762–779) and then Dezong (779–805), the ruler when the inscription was composed and erected. The church's powerful member and benefactor, Yisi, apparently served under all three of these emperors, providing further indication that the church and its adherents were not being shunned in society, at least at the imperial level.[2] Yisi is also praised for repairing old churches and building new ones, further evidence of the church's prosperity and expansion (25.1–25.2).

---

2. Todd Godwin's arguments are unconvincing in trying to show that the Church of the East played a major role in the Sasanian/Persian presence at the Tang court. See his *Persian Christians at the Chinese Court: The Xi'an Stele and the Early Medieval Church of the East* (London: I. B. Tauris, 2018).

The Organization of the Jingjiao

As mentioned earlier, a large number of clergy and church leaders are listed in the stele text. The Chinese and Syriac text on the bottom and sides of the stone mentions more than fifty monks and members of the clergy. Most are simply identified in the Chinese text as *seng*, 僧, the term used for Buddhist monks and priests, and in the Syriac as priests (*qšyš'*). However, the additional titles contained both in the stele text and in the lists that surround it provide vital information about the organization and makeup of the Jingjiao church, even if they leave us with numerous unsolved questions.

By the seventh century, the Church of the East had a well-defined hierarchy of officials and clergy.[3] As with the Greek and Latin churches, the Syriac church had begun with three basic offices: deacon, priest, and bishop. Gradually the Church of the East subdivided each of these into three ranks, making a total of nine. The diaconate was subdivided into reader, subdeacon, and deacon. The office of presbyter or priest was divided into priest, chorepiscopus, and archdeacon. The office of bishop was expanded with the addition of two higher ranks: a number of regional metropolitans and a single patriarch or catholicos. The catholicos, who resided in Seleucia on the Tigris River in central Iraq, served as both the chief administrator and the chief spiritual officer for the entire Church of the East. Beneath him were metropolitan bishops, who oversaw geographical regions of the church, with multiple bishops under them. Ordinary bishops had charge of the churches in a city or region.

The archdeacon was an executive assistant to a bishop, and he would also assist the bishop in conducting worship services. Each chorepiscopus also served under a local bishop. While originally the main function of the chorepiscopus was overseeing the Christians and churches in the surrounding rural areas, soon he was assisting the bishop in a variety of other functions. The council of 410 decided that each bishop should have one chorepiscopus assigned to him. Within each bishop's geographical area or diocese, numerous priests did the ordinary pastoral work of attending to the daily and weekly worship services and the other needs of the local Christian community.

The priests were in turn assisted by deacons. Originally charged with over-

---

3. On the offices of the Church of the East, see Bishop Mar Awa Royel, *Mysteries of the Kingdom: The Sacraments of the Assyrian Church of the East* (Modesto, CA: Edessa Publications, 2011), 86–122.

sight of the charitable work of the church, the deacons distributed alms to the poor and needy. Soon, however, they also began assisting in the church's spiritual work, visiting the sick and assisting in the worship services. Deacons-in-training were called subdeacons. Before that office was attained, one started by being a reader. This first step into the clergy involved, among other basic duties, gaining enough literacy and familiarity with Scripture to confidently and fluently read the Scriptures aloud in the church service.

It appears that this hierarchical stratification was in place in the Church of the East by the seventh and eighth centuries, although we are less sure about the ministerial functions that accompanied each rank at that time.[4] The ongoing contact between the Jingjiao and its mother church would have ensured that a very similar system of ranks and functions grew up within China. Barring good reasons to make official exceptions, the patriarch in Seleucia would have expected uniformity. In fact, we have evidence for just such a system in the stele and our other Jingjiao documents. Table 4 lists the various ranks and other clergy identifiers mentioned on the stele both in Chinese and Syriac (remember the column numbers preceded by S refer to the Syriac text).[5]

The Syriac terminology indicates that the Jingjiao's structure reflected quite closely that of the Church of the East elsewhere. Of the nine clerical ranks mentioned above, only the metropolitan and subdeacon are not specifically mentioned.[6] On the other hand, the chart shows that the Chinese texts on the stele provide scant illumination about how those positions and offices were described in Chinese. The Dunhuang and Luoyang texts add little additional information, for they too are rather sparse in their references to church offices. The historical note appended to the *Origin* text on the Luoyang pillar is somewhat more helpful. The references from these other Jingjiao texts are tabulated in table 5.

---

4. For a more complete discussion of the evidence for offices in the Jingjiao, see Nicolini-Zani, *The Luminous Way*, 85–97.

5. Nicolini-Zani (*The Luminous Way*, 207n75) has suggested that the stele's description of Luohan as "head of the priests" (僧首, *seng shou*) may be the Chinese term for archdeacon. On the possibility that the description of Jingjing as "*p'pšy* of China" may also indicate a bishop or metropolitan, see p. 44 above.

6. Nicolini-Zani postulates that because Bishop Johanan heads the list of clergy on the sides of the stele, he may have been the metropolitan in 781 (*The Luminous Way*, 87), but the text gives no specific designation to show that. I also follow Nicolini-Zani (218–19) and David Wilmshurst in translating *mšmšn'* as "deacon." See pp. 72 and 74 in the latter's paraphrase of the stele text, "A Monument to the Spread of the Syrian Brilliant Teaching in China," in Eccles-Lieu, "Stele on the Diffusion of Christianity," 63–78.

Table 4. Offices in the Church of the East mentioned on the Chang'an stele

	HIGHER CLERGY	
patriarch/catholicos	ܩܬܘܠܝܩܐ ܦܛܪܝܪܟܝܣ	S2
	法主僧	31.2
metropolitan	ܦܐܦܫ	S1
bishop	ܐܦܝܣܩܘܦܐ	S22
	大德	12.5, 16.11, 18.10
	PRIESTHOOD	
archdeacon	ܐܪܟܕܝܩܘܢ	S19, S65
chorepiscopus	ܟܘܪܐܦܝܣܩܘܦܐ	S1, S5, S15, S17, S64
priest	ܩܫܝܫܐ	S1 [+ 30x]
	僧	2.1 [+73x]
	LOWER CLERGY	
deacon	ܡܫܡܫܢܐ	S14, S38
subdeacon		
reader	ܡܩܪܝܢܐ	S65
	OTHER	
priest of the tomb	ܩܫܝܫܐ ܕܩܒܪܐ	S37
solitary/hermit	ܝܚܝܕܝܐ	S33-S36, S38
priest monk	ܩܫܝܫܐ ܝܚܝܕܝܐ	S33-34
head of the church	ܪܫ ܥܕܬܐ	S20
sacristan	ܩܢܟܝܐ	S74
elder	ܣܒܐ	S73
monk	僧	(see above)
head monk/priest	僧首	16.10
chief monk/priest	主僧	38
senior monks/priests	高僧	16.13
venerable one	老宿	75

Table 5. Clergy titles and offices found in the Dunhuang and Luoyang texts

bishop	大德	*Honored* 20, 21
		Pillar 41 (2x)
monk/priest	僧	*Honored* 7, 20, 21
		Pillar 39
monk	僧伽	*Mysterious Blessedness* (14x of Cenwen)
saint	法王	used 24x of biblical authors, patriarchs,
		etc. in *Honored* (4-9; 14; 16-17)
mar (title of respect)	摩	*Honored* 6; 7; 18
	ܡ	*Stele* S2; S16; S55; S58; S64; S80
monastery head	寺主	*Pillar* 41

Here, however, we encounter some interpretational problems. It has been generally accepted that the term 大德, *da de*, denotes a bishop. So when we find those terms in the note at the end of the Pelliot manuscript used to describe Alopen and Jingjing, it is what we might expect (*Honored* 20–21). However, the same term is used in the historical section of the Luoyang pillar of a man named Xuanqing and another named Zhitong (Pillar 41.5). Xuanqing is described as "dignified *da de*" and Zhitong as *da de* "of the ninth rank." This has led some to interpret these as Buddhist monastic titles taken over into Jingjiao usage.[7]

Titles play an extremely important role within traditional Chinese culture. The many titles of the Christian benefactor Yisi mentioned on the stele (22.13–23.3) are a good example of that. It is thus not surprising that titles for clergy or monks in our Jingjiao texts seem to go beyond those used in the Church of the East in other regions. And if the Christian community did indeed feel the need to create them, they would have naturally modeled them on already existing equivalents within other Chinese religious communities. So until we have further evidence, it is best merely to say that the general structure of the Church of the East was preserved in the Jingjiao, but that it probably was

---

7. Nicolini-Zani also argues that *da de* ("[man of] great virtue") may have been used by the Chinese as "an honorific title, something like 'monsignor' or 'Excellency'" (*The Luminous Way*, 94). However, it is also our only candidate for a Chinese word equaling "bishop." I will interpret it as indicating the latter, believing that it may have served both functions.

augmented and adjusted with titles and functions that had more "Chinese characteristics."[8]

The Names on the Stele

Besides the indications of offices and titles, we can glean other useful information from the names of Christians on the stele. On the bottom of the stele is a notice about Yazdbozid and his family (S3–15); Yazdbozid's Chinese name is Yisi, the great benefactor described on the stele.[9] He is part of a multigenerational family of Christian clergy. His father, Milis, was a Christian priest in Balkh, an important city on the southern branch of the Silk Road (four thousand kilometers west of Chang'an in north-central Afghanistan). Syriac Christians had long resided in Balkh, which had its own bishop in the Church of the East for several centuries. The Christian community had been disrupted (at least temporarily) when the Arabs conquered the city in 715. The move of Yazdbozid's family eastward into China may have been caused by those political factors, or perhaps Milis was sent eastward to take a position in the expanding Jingjiao community in China. Yazdbozid's main career was as a soldier, as the stele's extensive description depicts. Perhaps it was later in his life when he began serving also as a Jingjiao priest and eventually as chorepiscopus of Chang'an. Whether he actually functioned in the latter position or was given the title as an honor cannot be determined. By 781 when the stele was erected, Yazdbozid had a son, Adam, who was already serving as a deacon in the church.[10] This reminds us that celibacy was not required

8. Note also in the bottom portion of table 4 the variety of terminology (or ranks?) used to describe monks in the stele lists of names.

9. On Yisi, see Max Deeg, "A Belligerent Priest—Yisi and His Political Context," in *From the Oxus River to the Chinese Shores*, ed. Li Tang and Dietmar W. Winkler, Orientalia-Patristica-Oecumenica 5 (Vienna: LIT Verlag, 2013), 107–21.

10. Erica Hunter notes the progression of names over the three generations from Syriac (Milis), to Iranian (Yazdbozid), to Hebrew (Adam), which "may reflect the trajectory of the family's dislocation from Persia to Central Asia and thence to China." See "The Persian Contribution to Christianity in China: Reflections in the Xi'an Fu Syriac Inscriptions," in *Hidden Treasures and Intercultural Encounters*, ed. Dietmar W. Winkler and Li Tang, Orientalia-Patristica-Oecumenica 1 (Vienna: LIT Verlag, 2009), 77. In the Syriac text at the bottom of the stele, between the acknowledgment of Yazdbozid's role with the stele and the mention of Adam as deacon and son of Yazdbozid, there are the three Chinese characters 僧靈寶 (monk Lingbao). Although this may have been a separate person, it could also be the

of priests in the Church of the East, except for the rank of bishop and above. Although we do not have specific geographical backgrounds on most of the other clergy mentioned in our texts, it is likely that a significant number, like this family, had ethnic roots farther west along the Silk Road and were not native Han Chinese.

What can we learn from the list of names on the two sides of the stele? The left side contains 41 names—11, 6, 13, and 11 in its four rows. In the first row a bishop is named followed by 10 priests; the second row has 4 priest-monks, a priest of the tomb, and a deacon-monk; persons in the third and fourth rows have only their names given in Syriac, followed by the character 僧 ("monk") and their Chinese names. Thus, the names on the left side provide 1 bishop, 10 priests, 4 priest-monks, 1 priest of the tomb, 1 deacon, and 24 monks. Might it be that these men make up the diocese where the stele was erected, with a local bishop, 11 secular (married) priests and 4 monastic priests, 1 deacon, and 24 regular (unordained) monks living within the diocesan complex?

The right side of the stele has 29 names divided into three rows of 11, 13, and 5. In the first row (S63–73) every name is described in Syriac as a priest, and all but the first and last as 僧, "monk," in Chinese. The first is described in Chinese as 老宿, "venerable," the second is described in Syriac as "priest and chorepiscopus *šy'ngtsw'*" (either a title or place), the third as a "priest and archdeacon of Kumdan (Chang'an) and reader," and the final name has no Chinese description or name, only a name and "priest and elder" in Syriac. The second row begins with a Syriac name of a "sacristan," who is further described with a Chinese name preceded by "monk," 僧(S74, 85), and then 12 more Syriac names (S75–86), each followed by the Chinese designation for monk, 僧, together with his Chinese name (85–97). The last line lists 5 names without further description in Syriac (S87–91), with only the first, third, and fifth given the title monk, 僧, and a Chinese name (98–100). Thus, on the right side we have a total of 11 priests (with several holding other offices as well), 16 monks, and 2 men who have no description besides a Syriac name. Were these men part of one or more dioceses separate from those on the right side, or perhaps serving in a different geographical part of the city or diocese? If the two sides list men from the same diocese, it would have had a total of 22 secular priests, 4 monastic priests, and some 40 monks. It is also possible, of course, that the

---

Chinese name for deacon Adam. Its link with and position before the Hebrew "Christian" name would be further evidence of the family inculturation indicated by Hunter.

names constitute the current clergy roster of a larger area of the Jingjiao. In any case, since the inscriptions on the sides appear to be contemporaneous with the main text of the stele, this would provide evidence of a small but flourishing community in the late eighth century. Besides the mention of Chang'an (*Kumdan* in Syriac, S3–4, S20), the inscription also mentions a Gabriel who served as an archdeacon and "head of the church" in both Chang'an and Luoyang (*Sarag* in Syriac, S19–21); Gigoy, a "priest and archdeacon" in Chang'an who was also a "reader" (or "teacher of reading"?) (S65); and the priest Mar Sargis, who was also a chorepiscopus possibly in a place called "*Shangtsua*," perhaps Shazhou (沙州), the Chinese name for Dunhuang during the Tang period (S64).

Several scholars have analyzed the names given in Syriac on the stele to determine the ethnicity of the Jingjiao clergy. Erica Hunter concludes that many of the names of the clerics and monks were Syriac or Middle Persian, thus indicating that they had come from the Middle East or at least had roots there.[11] Hidemi Takahashi notes that eight of the names are at least partly of Persian origin, and many of the rest were biblical names common among East Syrians, as one would expect among monks and clergy.[12] Matteo Nicolini-Zani notes that the names of the known bishops and archdeacons make it clear that they "were chosen from among the non-indigenous missionary clergy who came from Persia and Central Asia."[13] A generation later, the names of Christians in Luoyang mentioned on the pillar are Sogdian in origin.[14] It is difficult to know whether the names on the stele and pillar merely reflect the immigrant communities where the two monuments were erected or the makeup of the Jingjiao in general. However, the data does indicate an ongoing connection with the mother church and its Silk Road communities.

---

11. Hunter, "The Persian Contribution," 80, 83.

12. Hidemi Takahashi, "Representation of the Syriac Language in Jingjiao and Yelikewen Documents," in *The Church of the East in Central Asia and China*, ed. Samuel N. C. Lieu and Glen L. Thompson, China and the Mediterranean World 1 (Turnhout: Brepols, 2020), 28. While it has normally been assumed that the stele list shows mostly Syriac monks, many of whom then took Chinese names, it is also possible that the reverse happened. Converts to Christianity in many cultures take Christian names at the time of their baptism.

13. Nicolini-Zani, *The Luminous Way*, 88.

14. Li Tang, "A Preliminary Study on the *Jingjiao* Inscription of Luoyang: Text Analysis, Commentary and English Translation," in Winkler and Tang, *Hidden Treasures and Intercultural Encounters*, 130.

Bishops and Metropolitans

The stele says that Alopen was a man of "excellent virtue" (*shang de*) in 634 or early 635 when he left for China (10.13–11.1). He would have been elevated to the rank of bishop (*da de*) for this new assignment, and the historical note at the end of the Pelliot manuscript confirms that he was *da de* at that time (*Honored* 20). He was still active in ministry during the reign of Gaozong (650–683), when the court awarded him the honorary title of "Grand Master of Religious Teaching and Protector of the Nation" (*Stele* 15.11). We do not have the name of Alopen's successor, and the bishopric may have been vacant for some years during the troubled times under Empress Wu when the church was persecuted in both capitals, Luoyang and Chang'an (*Stele* 16.4–16.9).

The expansion within China of the Luminous Teaching is confirmed by a Syriac historical work that records that the Church of the East patriarch Sliba-zkha, catholicos from 714 to 728, appointed the first metropolitan for China. Metropolitans in the Church of the East were seldom selected from the local clergy. Almost invariably they came from the Syriac heartland (modern Iraq) and often from the monastery at Beth 'Abe.[15] So, when the stele highlights the arrival in China of new leaders, it is reasonable to suppose that they included a new metropolitan. After the situation surrounding the demise of Empress Wu had quieted down, the stele specifically mentions the arrival sometime after 712 of new leaders, the head monk (or archdeacon) Luohan and the bishop Jilie (16.10–16.15). If Sliba-zkha sent out a metropolitan soon after his elevation to catholicos, this may well have been the unnamed monk who arrived at the Tang court in 719 as part of a Persian delegation.[16] The Chang'an stele also mentions the arrival of *da de* Jilie, seemingly early in Xuanzong's reign, so perhaps he was the newly appointed metropolitan. Two Chinese sources mention a bishop Jilie who accompanied a Persian royal envoy to the capital in late 732. The emperor granted the royal envoy an honorary title, while he gave the monk "a purple robe and 50 pieces of silk and sent them home."[17] Was this the same Jilie? If so, he might have been appointed at the end of Sliba-zkha's reign (728), which would mean it took him a number of

---

15. David Wilmshurst, *The Martyred Church: A History of the Church of the East* (London: East & West Publishing, 2011), 82.

16. The incident is recorded in the *Old Book of Tang* (舊唐書). See Nicolini-Zani, *The Luminous Way*, 76.

17. It is difficult to tell whether the emperor gifted this Jilie with a magnificent robe, or whether he honored him with the same "Imperially conferred Purple Robe" that the stele says was received by Yisi (23.3) and the chief monk Yeli (37).

years to arrive in China. The reference to the emperor sending "them" home would also then have to refer to the delegation as a whole and exclude Jilie. Such scenarios are highly speculative, and it is just as likely that the Chinese sources are speaking of a different Jilie.

The stele commentary mentions a third bishop, Jihe, 佶和, who came in 744 from Da Qin to serve in China (18.6–18.11). He may also have been a new metropolitan, perhaps the direct successor of Jilie. The main stele text records no other 大德, but, as mentioned earlier, the names on the left side of the stele begin with "Mar Johanan, bishop" (in Syriac), followed in Chinese by 大德, Yaolun, also possibly a metropolitan according to Nicolini-Zani.[18]

Table 6. Jingjiao bishops and metropolitans

DATE	BISHOP(S)	METROPOLITAN
635–?	Alopen	
715/728?–744?	Jilie	Jilie?
745–?	Jihe	Jihe?
781	Jingjing Yaolun/Johanan	Jingjing?
ca. 820s–830s	Xuanqing? Zhitong?	David

Column 2 of the stele text gives the name of the author in Chinese as "the monk Jingjing," and in Syriac as "Adam, priest and chorepiscopus and *p'pšy* of China." In the historical note at the end of the Pelliot scroll, unfortunately undated, Jingjing is spoken of as if he were still living. There he is referred to as a bishop (大德, *da de*) and credited with translating thirty of the Christian books listed in the manuscript (*Honored* 21). About fifteen years later, a Buddhist text says Jingjing took part in another translation effort, this time translating a Buddhist scripture with a famous Buddhist monk. It is not easy to sort out the evidence for his career. But one would surmise that he was a priest who became a chorepiscopus, and later bishop, and possibly even metropolitan—although his scholarly and literary pursuits might better fit

18. Nicolini-Zani, *The Luminous Way*, 87.

someone who did not have the duties of a metropolitan to deal with. What is clear is that he was a famous Jingjiao leader in the last two decades of the eighth century and clearly the literary expert tasked with composing the stele text.

Two men are described in the historical note at the end of the Luoyang pillar (early ninth century) as *da de*—"disciplinarian of *da de* Xuanqing, of the Mi clan," and "ninth rank *da de* Zhitong, of the Kang clan." Li Tang and Matteo Nicolini-Zani have translated these lines as if *da de* does not indicate a bishop but rather some other monastic title influenced by Buddhism. This is because the context seems to imply that they are both monks living in the Da Qin monastery in Luoyang. However, while it is difficult to square the additional description with the office of bishop, nothing precludes there being two contemporaneous bishops in China by that period. Nothing in the context makes it clear that these men were both serving the church in Luoyang except their presence at the funerary activities. The importance of the deceased, family connections, and several other reasons could be deduced for their presence. Thus, we must leave the question open at this time.[19]

Table 6 summarizes what we can glean and shows that we actually know a fair amount about the highest officials in the Jingjiao during its first century and a half. Even if we cannot be certain about dates, there is evidence for the appointment of a metropolitan within a century of Alopen's arrival, and therefore we would expect several contemporaneous Jingjiao bishops to be serving in various parts of China by its second century of existence. Since the stele indicates that *da de* Jihe arrived from Da Qin about 745 (18.10), it is plausible that he too came as a newly appointed metropolitan, perhaps after the death of Jilie. A Syriac writer in Persia, Thomas of Marga, noted that a Persian monk named David was sent to China as metropolitan in the early ninth century. When we combine all these bits of information, we can see the development we would expect in a growing church. The initial team sent from Da Qin included one bishop, but during the following century, as the church grew, multiple bishops were needed and, by the eighth century, also a metropolitan to oversee them.

According to Syriac sources, a metropolitan was still in China at the end of the eighth century. In conjunction with a synod in 790, Patriarch Timothy I reorganized the metropolitans of the Church of the East into two categories: those in the heartland or "interior provinces" and those in the far-off

19. On the Luoyang pillar titles, see the discussions of Tang, "A Preliminary Study," 124, and Nicolini-Zani, *The Luminous Way*, 95–97.

regions now termed "exterior provinces." Because of the distances involved, the latter were not expected to travel to Persia for patriarchal elections and synods. Instead, they were told to submit a written report at least every six years. Those ten provinces were then listed—Fars, Merv, Herat, Rai, Armenia, Barda'a (in modern Azerbaijan), Samarkand, India, China, and Damascus. This policy was probably not new but rather a formal recognition of the realities that had been experienced since the office of metropolitan had been established in these far-flung locations. By 893, when the metropolitan of Damascus, Eliya ibn 'Ubaid, made a list of exterior provinces, China was no longer included.[20]

Bosi—Da Qin—Jingjiao

We can piece together a bit of additional evidence on the spread of the Jingjiao from references in Chinese sources. In all the surviving documents we have studied, the Christians of the Church of the East in China refer to themselves and their teaching as the Jingjiao, the Luminous Teaching. However, this was not how the Chinese authorities referred to them. From early on they were referred to as the 波斯教, *Bosi-jiao*, a transliteration of *Persian*. This is how we find Alopen described in the *Tang huiyao*'s reproduction of the 638 edict of Taizong permitting the Christians to establish themselves in China. The same *Bosi* is found in several other Chinese documents of the early eighth century, such as the notices about the Persian embassies that arrived in 742, as mentioned earlier. In October of 745, however, an edict of Emperor Xuanzong mandated an official name change for the Jingjiao.

> The texts and teaching of Bo-si [Persia]
> originated in Da Qin.
> They were transmitted from outside,
> but now have long circulated in China;
> when their monasteries first were established [in China],
> they were named accordingly [i.e., Bosi].
> Wishing to show men that they should demonstrate their origin,
> let the monasteries of Bo-si in the two capitals

20. On the administrative structure of the metropolitans, see David Wilmshurst, *The Martyred Church: A History of the Church of the East* (London: East & West Publishing, 2011), 158–67.

properly change their name to Da Qin.
In every prefecture and commandery of the Empire
it is suitable for them to do likewise. (*Tang huiyao* 49.28)

Why the name change? And who instigated it? If done at the request of the Jingjiao authorities, it may have been because the Persian Empire was now long gone, swallowed up by the expanding Islamic caliphate. Or perhaps it was to more clearly distinguish the Christians from the two other religions that had originated in Persia—the Manichaean and Zoroastrian sects. Both of these had also been granted permission to operate within China, although they were only to serve their own adherents who had immigrated into China. It may also not be insignificant that Islamic forces were still massed on the western border at this time. China had managed to defeat them in two early encounters in 715 and 717, but tensions were ongoing. The Jingjiao may not have wanted to be associated with these new masters of Persia. T. H. Barrett, on the other hand, has suggested that it may have been a ploy of the anti-Buddhist government faction that was then in power. A legend circulating at the time held that the dynasty's supposed ancestor Laozi had profited from a visit to Da Qin after leaving for the West. Thus, the Jingjiao might have benefited from this Daoist connection.[21]

There may have been other reasons that caused the government itself to initiate the change. In any case, the name change was made, and so Chinese sources and some Jingjiao sources (such as the stele) use the new name from this point forward, often in conjunction with its own preferred name, Jingjiao. Thus, when several decades later the stele was erected, it proudly proclaimed in the large characters that graced the top of the stone "Stele about the Spread of the Da Qin Jingjiao in China."

The Extent of the Jingjiao Presence

The heading of the stele claims its text documents the spread of the faith within China—that is, the Middle Kingdom, as the stele heading proclaims, or Chinastan (*dzynst'n*), as the first Syriac line on the stele expresses it. Exactly how much did it spread? As mentioned earlier, the stele's claims that a generation

---

21. T. H. Barrett, "Buddhism, Daoism and the Eighth-Century Chinese Term for Christianity," in *Jingjiao: The Church of the East in China and Central Asia*, ed. Roman Malek, Collectanea Serica (Sankt Augustin, Germany: Institut Monumenta Serica, 2006), 48–49.

after Alopen's arrival there were already churches in every prefecture (15.10) and in "one hundred walled cities" (16.2) must surely be hyperbolic. But the bits of information we have do indicate that a gradual spread did occur.

The edict of 638 approved the building of a church or monastery in the capital city of Chang'an (*Stele* 16.9). More precisely, the first church was to be built in Chang'an's Yining district or ward (13.3) on the western side of the city. It was still in existence a century later, being mentioned in a gazetteer of the capital produced in 740.[22] Another gazetteer mentions that a Bosi monastery had been approved in 677 for construction in the city's Liquan ward and that it was later moved to the Buzheng ward about 710.[23] So it seems there were at least two monasteries and congregations in the capital by the early eighth century.

The stele also mentions a Christian group in Luoyang (Syriac *srg*, *Stele* S21), the eastern capital for Tang emperors, and especially favored by Empress Wu. The stele's reference to voices being raised there against the Jingjiao during Wu's reign also confirms the existence of a church there (16.5–16.6). The earliest definitive mention of a Luoyang monastery or congregation comes in the edict of 745, which changed the name from Bosi to Da Qin; it specifically mentions monasteries in the two capitals, Chang'an and Luoyang.[24] Christians still resided in the Luoyang area in the early ninth century when the Luoyang *dharani* pillar was erected, and it links the Christian presence there with the Sogdian immigrant community in the area known as Gande township.[25]

A few other specific locations of Jingjiao churches can be added. A complaint of 714 about a Persian monk named Jilie (not to be confused with the previously mentioned bishop of that name) indicates that by the early eighth century there were Christians far to the south in the Lingnan region near modern Guangzhou.[26] Moule further cites a Chinese work composed about 1050 that mentions a "very old Da Qin monastery" standing near the

---

22. A. C. Moule, *Christians in China before 1500* (London: SPCK, 1920), no. 5, p. 66.

23. Moule, *Christians in China*, no. 10, p. 71.

24. Moule, *Christians in China*, no. 6, p. 67.

25. See Matteo Nicolini-Zani, "Luminous Ministers of the Da Qin Monastery: A Study of the Christian Clergy Mentioned in the Jingjiao Pillar from Luoyang," in Tang and Winkler, *From the Oxus River to the Chinese Shores*, 50–53.

26. Moule, *Christian in China*, no. 4, pp. 65–66; more recently translated and discussed by Godwin, *Persian Christians*, 85–88. This may well be a different Jilie from the one mentioned in the stele, especially if it is a transliteration from Syriac of the commonly used biblical name Gabriel.

Pearl Tower in Chengdu in southwestern China.[27] In the main Chang'an stele text, we also hear about Jingjiao churches in the northwest, at "Lingwu and other prefectures" (20.1). We also have physical evidence surviving from a Christian monastery at Turfan on China's northwest border. The many fragmentary texts recovered from that site make it clear that it was active during the later Tang period. Martin Palmer has more recently claimed that the so-called Da Qin Pagoda at Louguantai, about sixty kilometers southwest of Chang'an, was an eighth-century Jingjiao building. His claims, however, have yet to be verified.[28]

Beyond this, our evidence is limited. The edict of 745 does say that the name change should not be limited to the capital cities but should also take place in "every prefecture and commandery of the Empire," thus indicating a network of Jingjiao congregations. Thirty-six years later, Jingjing states in the stele text that the great general Yisi, who also served as a Jingjiao priest, both repaired old temples and increased their number (25.1–25.2) and that he sponsored an annual worship festival that gathered the monks and clergy from four temples or monasteries (25.7–25.8). Since Yisi/Yazdbozid was chorepiscopus of Chang'an, it would be logical to assume that the four monasteries that took part in this annual festival were in the greater Chang'an area.

Two last pieces of evidence come from outside the Jingjiao itself. In a monastery inscription dated to 824, a Buddhist named Shu Yuanyu claimed that the Da Qin, Zoroastrian, and Manichaean monasteries were very few in number compared with those of the Buddhists.[29] Yet the number was relatively small only in comparison to the immense number of Buddhist monks. When a few years later those "three foreign religions" were banned in China, a historical chronicle asserted that the closing of the Zoroastrian and Da Qin monasteries led to some two thousand to three thousand monks returning to lay status.[30] Thus, while the Jingjiao never became a serious rival in size to the Buddhists, evidence indicates a small but somewhat widespread Christian presence in China by the mid-ninth century.

---

27. Moule, *Christians in China*, no. 11, pp. 71–72.

28. Martin Palmer, *The Jesus Sutras: Rediscovering the Lost Scrolls of Taoist Christianity* (New York: Ballantine Books, 2001), 11–38. A facsimile of the Xi'an stele was erected at the site, together with signage for tourists. However, Chinese archaeological investigators have published no confirmation of Palmer's claims of the presence of a Syriac graffito and Christian statuary.

29. See the English translation in Moule, *Christians in China*, no. 8, pp. 69–70.

30. Moule, *Christians in China*, no. 9, p. 70. The two related accounts differ in putting the number at two thousand or three thousand.

How Foreign Did the Jingjiao Remain?

Officially, the Tang came to group the Jingjiao as one of three "foreign" or "barbarian" religions (三夷教, *san yi jiao*), along with Manichaeism and Zoroastrianism. All three had been introduced from Persia, and none of them was ever totally indigenized into Chinese society. This was unlike Buddhism, which, precisely during the Sui and Tang periods, was developing new forms that deeply integrated into itself aspects of both the Confucian and Daoist worldviews. Chinese Buddhism became a reality that has lasted down to the present day. Zoroastrianism, the ancient Persian worship of the god Ahura Mazda, was officially allowed into China in 621, fourteen years before the arrival of Alopen, when the government permitted a temple to be built in the Chonghua district of Chang'an. However, unlike the approval for Christianity, permission was only granted for Persians, not native Chinese, to worship at the Zoroastrian fire temples. Enough Persians were present in the capital that eventually as many as six Zoroastrian temples were located there. Yet the few references to them in Chinese sources would indicate that they were tolerated only for the sake of the foreigners living in the country.[31]

The earliest Chinese mention of a Manichaean missionary comes from the second half of the seventh century during the reign of Gaozong. Somewhat later, a Persian priest brought a Manichaean scripture to his royal audience with Wu Zetian. She was so pleased that she allowed him to remain at court giving lessons, much to the displeasure of the Buddhist clergy. The teachings of Mani were quite malleable and able to be adapted to local cultures. Its scriptures were translated into Chinese, and a few of those survived, to be discovered in the Dunhuang caves. This resulted in a small following among locals as well as Persian immigrants. Its success caused a reaction among Buddhist leaders, for Chinese sources record that in 732 Emperor Xuanzong issued an edict prohibiting Han Chinese from practicing the religion: it was "an evil doctrine and it falsely declares itself to be Buddhism" and so "bewilders and cheats the public and shall be banned totally." The edict continued, "among the Western barbarians, however, those who practice this sect shall not be punished, since it is indigenous to them."[32] The military support given the Tang rulers by the Uyghurs led to the first imperial decree (of 768) permitting the

31. On Zoroastrianism in Tang China, see Donald D. Leslie, "Persian Temples in T'ang China," *Monumenta Serica* 35 (1981): 275–303, esp. 280–82.

32. Lin Wushu, "A Study of Equivalent Names of Manichaeism in Chinese," in *Popular Religion and Shamanism*, ed. Ma Xisha and Meng Huiying (Leiden: Brill, 2011), 62.

building of a Mani temple. Several more followed.[33] We do not know to what extent the new law was enforced. One Manichaean temple on Huabiao Hill in Cao'an, between Quanzhou and Xiamen in Fujian Province, has survived as a local religious center right up to the present day. The local Chinese who worshiped there, however, did not realize they were offering incense to the Persian prophet Mani until scholars made that identification and it was subsequently registered as such on China's list of protected historical sites. The confusion was already evident in the sixteenth century when a Chinese gazetteer referred to it as a temple of "the Buddha Mani"![34]

So, we must ask, was the history and success of the Jingjiao, the third "foreign" religion, parallel to or different from the other two? One significant difference between the Jingjiao and the other two "Persian" religions was that the Jingjiao was part of a much more tightly structured organization. Unlike the others, it always remained an arm or subsidiary of a larger organization, its mother church. Properly ordained clergy who formally administered sacramental rites were central to its spiritual mission and to its ability to connect its members with the grace and forgiveness of the eternal God. While it had some freedom in how its teachings were expressed to the local population, it would have always felt bound by the traditional interpretation of scriptural truths and by its own creedal statements. The stele text ends with a colophon in which it dates itself in both Chinese and Syriac by providing the name of the church's leader back in Persia—"the Father of Fathers, Mar Hananisho, Catholicos-Patriarch" (31.2 and S2). The Syriac at the bottom of the stele also clearly gives an imprimatur to what was written on the stele text: it was "the teaching of our Savior and the preaching of our fathers to the emperors of China" (S11–13). This close connection can further be seen in the fact that the top leadership of the Jingjiao was consistently appointed by and probably brought in from the Church of the East headquarters in Persia, as the stele's comments about Jihe indicate (18.6–18.11). Erica Hunter notes that "the distinctly 'Persian' components of several of the Syriac names listed on the stele intimate that some of the men had indeed traveled along the silk route from the Mesopotamian 'homeland' to China."[35]

Yet, while this would have been the norm for the metropolitans, most other foreign clergy came from much closer regions. A study of the names

33. Leslie, "Persian Temples in T'ang China," 62. On Manichaeism in Tang China more generally, see Samuel N. C. Lieu, *Manichaeism in the Later Roman Empire and Medieval China: A Historical Survey*, 2nd ed., Wissenschaftliche Untersuchungen zum Neuen Testament 63 (Tübingen: Mohr Siebeck, 1992), 231–39.

34. Lin, "A Study of Equivalent Names," 57–60.

35. Hunter, "The Persian Contribution," 83.

of the clergy on the stele and elsewhere, and studies of the vocabulary and loanwords used in the Christian texts that survive, have led scholars to believe that the Sogdian connection was substantial. Hidemi Takahashi's recent exhaustive study of the Syriac language in the Jingjiao material led him to conclude that, during the Tang period, the Jingjiao literati probably started with materials "in Iranian languages (presumably mainly Sogdian) to compose the extant Chinese Jingjiao texts."[36] From secular Chinese historical sources we can determine that the four clergymen mentioned at the end of the Luoyang pillar inscription were all from among the nine Sogdian clans known to be immigrants to China.[37] Hunter has also found Sogdian and other related languages in the names of the Jingjiao clergy. The same church leaders and saints listed in the *Honored* of the Pelliot manuscript would have been included in the liturgical prayers in any Church of the East congregation. Thus, long after the first mission team had arrived with Alopen, the connection with the mother church and other Silk Road Christian communities, the active participation of non-Chinese clergy, and the use of the traditional liturgical rites would have helped prevent the Jingjiao from veering away from the Church of the East's teachings and practice. *Da Qin Jingjiao* was more than a term to Jingjing and his colleagues; it reflected the reality that their church was part of a larger entity.

This may then be a second factor to help explain why the Jingjiao remained a "foreign" barbarian religion. Our texts certainly show serious attempts to enculturate the language of Christianity into Chinese thought patterns, vocabulary, and worldview. Yet we are unsure whether Syriac continued to be the dominant liturgical language of the church, as might have been expected, at least initially. Takahashi found little evidence of even that.[38] The *Hymn* and *Honored*, on the other hand, seem to have been produced as Chinese translations of liturgical texts. Were they then used in a Chinese liturgy or just as aids to help Chinese worshipers understand the Syriac liturgy they were hearing?

An even bigger question surrounds the word choices and their interpretation in the Dunhuang Christian documents—in particular in *Mysterious Blessedness* and *Origin*. Some have suggested a Manichaean authorship of the former, while others have read both as examples of a wholesale syncretism that eventually caused the disappearance of the Jingjiao. We cannot provide

---

36. Takahashi, "Representation of the Syriac Language," 39.
37. Nicolini-Zani, "Luminous Ministers," 50–53.
38. Takahashi, "Representation of the Syriac Language," 39.

any final answers to these questions, but it would seem highly unlikely for any substantial syncretism to have taken hold within an organization that had such a rigid hierarchy controlling it, and which had such close connections with the church outside China. Remember that the father of the chorepiscopus of Chang'an, Yazdbozid, served as a priest in Balkh. The multiplicity of such connections would have served as a check against any overly enthusiastic en-culturation of Jingjiao teachings.

At the same time, as Chinese laity entered the church, they undoubtedly brought some religious baggage with them. First-generation converts are often unable to totally disconnect from their previous ideas and experiences. Just as one sees this in the "Christian amulets" found among the Greek and Coptic churches of Egypt and the Middle East, so one would expect to see similar things in the Jingjiao. The Chinese church did indeed reflect the teaching and practice of the Middle Eastern Church of the East, yet adaptation did take place at certain places. As in every church body, the ideas and practices of some adherents were less than fully orthodox. Some of that may have been tolerated, but other forms would have been judged as inappropriate or even heretical. That seems to be exactly what we find in our extant sources.

At the Margins of Society?

Throughout the Tang period, the Jingjiao remained a small foreign religion in China. It is difficult to picture it claiming more than the tiniest market share in the larger religious mosaic. Many of its leaders were foreigners, or men of foreign descent. This would have brought special problems as they sought to influence the Han majority, stubbornly ethnocentric and justly proud of a millennia-long cultural heritage. Yet the Jingjiao were not totally ignored or marginalized.

After the imperial court granted them the formal right to preach in China, the Jingjiao were shown imperial favors on several occasions. In the mid-seventh century, Emperor Gaozong conferred on Alopen the honorary title or titles of Grand Master of Religious Teaching and Protector of the Nation (*Stele* 15.11). In the second quarter of the eighth century, Xuanzong gifted them with imperial portraits and a hundred bales of silk (17.5–18.1) and later asked them to perform a special service of blessing in one of his palaces (18.9–18.11). As a thank-you gift for those prayers, the emperor provided them with some of his own calligraphy to display on their premises (18.12–19.5). Jingjing says that these "bountiful gifts exceeded the height of the Southern Mountains;

this flood of favors was as deep as the Eastern Sea" (19.6–19.7). Later in the century, Suzong helped rebuild Jingjiao temples in the northwest (19.12–20.2) and Daizong gave the Jingjiao food and other gifts (20.8–20.10). Conversely, the Jingjiao were important enough to have both Buddhist and Daoist leaders speak against them at court and seek to derail their ministry during the period of Empress Wu (16.4–16.9). Thus, even though these events were spaced out over almost two centuries, it is clear that the Jingjiao was a religious entity on the imperial radar, even if it was considered a small and mostly foreign player in the larger cultural landscape of China.

This picture is confirmed by what we know of several important members of the Jingjiao community. The most important of these is Yisi. Jingjing speaks of him as still living when he writes the stele, and describes him as a *seng*, 僧, here probably meaning a Jingjiao priest rather than a monk (23.3). Although he himself was a foreigner from the distant city of Balkh, he became, in Jingjing's words, "our great benefactor." In addition, however, he carried four imperial titles. He was awarded the title of Great Master of the Palace with Golden Seal and Purple Ribbon.[39] This was an honorary title that placed him at the 3A rank, near the top of the nine-level pyramid of imperial officials. The title of Deputy Military Commander for the Shuofang region reflected his work as the top assistant to general Guo Ziyi in ending the An Lushan revolt.[40] It is unclear whether his title of Appointed Director of the Palace Administration had formal duties associated with it or not, but the title again clearly gave him high standing in the court and society.[41] The final honor, being the recipient of the Imperially Conferred Purple Gown (22.13–23.3), was awarded period- ically to recognize important religious figures, usually Buddhist monks.[42] It was probably given to Yisi in recognition of his position within the Jingjiao. He had achieved this success because he was viewed as a man of high moral principles and great ability (23.8–23.9), and he was granted these honors and titles during a long and distinguished political and military career at the highest levels (23.10–24.7). The wealth he amassed was then used for a great variety of charitable acts within the church (24.8–26.1). Hence we see that Yisi/Yazdbozid,

---

39. See the translation and discussion of these titles by both Deeg, "A Belligerent Priest," 112–14, and Nicolini-Zani, *The Luminous Way*, 211–12 and nn. 100–103. Both agree that this position is that listed as no. 1159 (p. 168) in the exhaustive study of bureaucratic titulature by Charles Hucker, *A Dictionary of Official Titles in Imperial China* (1985; reprint, Taipei: SMC Publishing, 2001).

40. Nicolini-Zani identifies this title with Hucker no. 777, p. 144.

41. See Hucker no. 6558, p. 502, and the discussion of Deeg, "A Belligerent Priest," 112.

42. See Nicolini-Zani, *The Luminous Way*, 212n103, and Deeg, "A Belligerent Priest," 112.

the chorepiscopus of Chang'an of Sogdian background, was able to rise to an exalted place in the Chinese imperial court and army. His loyalty to the Tang emperors during the An Lushan rebellion was properly rewarded socially and financially. He apparently did not hide the fact that he was a practicing member of the Jingjiao and at some point had become a clergyman. Thus, all his activities won "face" not only for himself but also for his religion, the Jingjiao.

Jingjing ends his description of Yisi by saying that even among Christians, "such excellence is unknown" (26.3). While Yisi was certainly exceptional in many ways, other such Christian men impacted the Chinese community with their good deeds in smaller ways, and in doing so brought honor to the Jingjiao. The Chinese text at the bottom of the stele mentions the chief monk, Yeli, who also held the title of Master of Imperial Rites and also, like Yisi, had been awarded the Imperially Conferred Purple Gown (36–38). The historical note at the end of the Luoyang Pillar mentions several more such men who, like Yisi, rose to high positions in the military. One, whose name is lost due to the break in the inscription, had among his several ranks and appointments the lengthy title of Military Commander of the Mercenary Division of the Right Army of the Celestial Water Bearer at the Eastern Capital (Pillar 38). Another, a relative of the deceased woman in whose memory the pillar was erected, served as Inactive General of the Left Dragon Army at the Capital and as Acting Chief General of the Left Military Guard (Pillar 40).[43] Such men were able to bring "face" as well as wealth and social standing to the small religious group. While the Jingjiao always remained on the margins of Chinese life and culture, it was never totally marginalized. Most Chinese living in this period may never have known that the Jingjiao existed, yet many highly placed government and military officials not only knew of it but appreciated the talents and integrity of some of its adherents.

Decline under the Tang

As Jingjing composed his poem and commentary in 781, he had every reason to be optimistic in his outlook. The Jingjiao had weathered a few brief storms thus far in its nearly 150-year history in China, but it had experienced many more

---

43. Tang, "A Preliminary Study," 112–25, has so far provided the only complete translation of the historical section of the Luoyang pillar. Nicolini-Zani, "Luminous Ministers," 118, provides a partial translation in his study of the clergy mentioned in the note, and I have adapted his renderings here.

periods of unhindered work. Among its adherents were powerful and respected men whose service had reflected well on the minority religion. When the Zoroastrian general of Sogdian heritage, An Lushan, had revolted a quarter of a century earlier (755–763), declaring himself to be an incarnation of the God of Light, Sogdian Christians in the northwest territories rallied behind the throne and were instrumental in helping to defeat him. Thus, Jingjing could be confident that the "great plan" of spreading the gospel was gradually being implemented "step-by-step" (*Stele* 22.2–22.3), and he could end his poem by optimistically noting that "The Way is spread widely, and with great effect. . . . The Lord is able to act, his servants but record . . . his fundamental goodness" (30.8–30.11).

Little did Jingjing realize that this open door would last only another two generations. Although the Tang imperial family would remain on the throne for another century and a half after regaining it from the rebels, the glory days never did return. The economy rebounded and even boomed after a series of fiscal reforms and with less official oversight. Emperor Xianzong (805–820), perhaps the most able ruler of the period, rebuilt the army and regained control of various provinces from governors who had in effect become independent local warlords during the days of An Lushan. Yet the imperial eunuchs were increasingly developing into major power brokers in the palace. The short reigns of Muzong (820–824) and Jingzong (824–827) were given over to decadent living. Their successor, the seventeen-year-old Wenzong (827–840), was hampered by indecision, rebellious provinces, and court intrigues. Wuzong (840–846) was no more successful in reestablishing a firm and prosperous rule for his family. By the end of his reign, the decline of the dynasty had become ever more obvious, even though it would last officially for another half century (until 907).

The openness to outside cultural and religious influences that was a hallmark of the early Tang period fell victim to its insecurities in the ninth century. The toleration that had been enjoyed (with brief exceptions) began to unravel by the time Wuzong took the throne. When a confluence of political, economic, and religious factors was added into the mix, a rather sudden change took place.

The Zoroastrians had already fallen in status in the aftermath of An Lushan's rebellion. Now the same would happen to the Manichaeans. During the seventh century, the expansive steppes to the north and northwest of China had become a vast tribal confederation under the Göktürks. Among its constituent groups were the Uyghurs. About AD 740 the Uyghurs formed their own confederation of nine tribes and successfully rebelled against the Göktürks. Their new empire was ruled by a khagan and lasted a century. In general, they enjoyed good relations with their Tang neighbors, providing troops to fight the usurper An Lushan. About 840, however, their kingdom imploded and was destroyed by Kyrgyz invaders. A large group of survivors crossed into Shaanxi seeking a new home but were defeated in 843 by a Tang army that inflicted massive casualties on them. Although a sizable number of Uyghurs were already Manichaeans, this crisis led even more Uyghurs to adopt that religion. Because the Uyghurs were now seen as enemies, a general crackdown on Manichaeism began across China in the coming years.[44]

A second military campaign created additional stress on China's floundering economy. When an insubordinate governor in eastern Shaanxi unilaterally decided, without imperial approval, to keep that position within his family, quick action was needed. The chief minister Li Deyu called up forces and ended the attempt within a year, but with a significant financial outlay. Emperor Wuzong came to believe that the only solution to his economic problems was to increase the tax base. And the easiest way to do that was to rein in the ever-expanding Buddhist presence.

Wuzong was himself partial to Daoism; his premature death may have been caused, at least in part, by the Daoist potions he regularly ingested in his search for immortality. Yet his initial moves against Buddhism seem to have been motivated more by economic than religious reasons. The Buddhist temples that dotted the landscape had become famous for their icons and accoutrements made from or plated with gold, copper, and silver. Michael Dalby has calculated that this had created "a very great strain upon the currency-starved economy" and was in "direct contravention of the government's anti-hoarding regulations."[45] Second, the temples had become landlords, both purchasing and receiving as gifts huge tracts of tax-exempt land. The estates brought in huge profits when they were sublet for agricultural use and for the harvesting of lumber. Finally, the number of tax-paying citizens was also falling due to the ever-increasing ranks of the Buddhist clergy. All attempts to limit the ordination of new monks and nuns to a reasonable number had failed.

These factors had resulted in a growing anti-Buddhist sentiment at the court, and Wuzong now began to act. In 842, he issued a series of edicts that set strict qualifications for monks and nuns. Clergy and monks were given

---

44. For these events, see now Michael Drompp, *Tang China and the Collapse of the Uighur Empire: A Documentary History*, Brill's Inner Asian Library 13 (Leiden: Brill, 2005).

45. Michael Dalby, "Court Politics in Late T'ang Times," in *The Sui and T'ang China, 589-906, Part 1*, vol. 3 of *The Cambridge History of China*, ed. D. Twitchett (Cambridge: Cambridge University Press, 1979), 667.

the choice of continuing their monastic lives but in poverty (donating their possessions to the government), or of returning to lay life as tax-paying citizens. Two years later he ordered severe limitations on the number of temples and monasteries, confiscating many together with their lands. He then forced even more clergy to return to lay life—and the tax rolls. While there had been power struggles between Confucianists and both Daoists and Buddhists in the past, Emperor Wuzong's persecution of Buddhism, as Lin Wushu has pointed out, "signaled a qualitative change in the balance between Daoism and Buddhism."[46] By 845, Wuzong's extensive persecution of the Buddhists was well under way, and the Jingjiao and the Manichaeans were unavoidably caught up in the religious purge. A sweeping edict of that year describes the progress already made but specifically includes some new victims:

> The [Buddhist] temples of the empire which have been demolished number over 4,600; 26,500 monks and nuns have been returned to lay life and enrolled as subject to the twice yearly tax. More than 40,000 privately established temples have been destroyed, releasing 30 or 40 million *qing* of fertile, topgrade land [ca. 600 million acres] as well as 150,000 male and female servants who will become subject to the twice yearly tax. Monks and nuns have been placed under the jurisdiction of the Director of Aliens to make it perfectly clear that this [Buddhism] is a foreign religion. Finally, we have ordered more than 2,000 men of the Da Qin [Christian] and Zoroastrian religions to return to lay life and to cease polluting the customs of China.
>
> Alas, what had not been carried out in the past seemed to have been waiting for this opportunity. If Buddhism is completely abolished now, who will say that the action is not timely? Already more than 100,000 idle and unproductive Buddhist followers have been expelled, and countless of their gaudy, useless buildings destroyed. Henceforth we may guide the people in stillness and purity, cherish the [Daoist] principle of nonaction, order our government with simplicity and ease, and achieve a unification of customs so that the multitudes of all realms will find their destination in our august rule. Since this eradication of evil began, it has daily and in unknown ways worked its effect. Now we send down this edict to the provincial officials that they may further carry out our will. (*Old Book of Tang*, 18A:15a)[47]

---

46. Lin Wushu, "A General Discussion of the Tang Policy towards Three Persian Religions: Manichaeism, Nestorianism and Zoroastrianism," *China Archaeology and Art Digest* 4, no. 1 (2000): 103–16, at 112.

47. I have slightly adapted the translation found in William Theodore De Bary, Wing-tsit

While the surviving versions of the edict disagree on whether two thousand or three thousand Da Qin and Zoroastrian clergy were ordered to end their religious activities, the result was equally devastating.

Wuzong died the following year (846). His successor, Emperor Xuanzong (846–849), soon began pulling back on the harshest anti-Buddhist provisions. In 847 he allowed the rebuilding of some Buddhist temples, and other restrictions were relaxed. He himself also sponsored and participated in Buddhist services. Many institutional checks and controls, however, remained in place, and it took centuries before Buddhism had totally regained its status.

The "three foreign religions" were not so lucky. The bans against them remained in place. We have little evidence for what happened to their adherents. The Manichaeans gradually were absorbed into the Chinese and Buddhist religions. The Zoroastrians disappeared almost totally, although a few temples may have survived into the Song period. To all outward appearances, the Jingjiao that had gradually matured for over two centuries was also wiped from the Chinese landscape in the space of just a few years.

Looking back, it is remarkable that the demise does not seem to be the result of long-standing animosities and persecution. Rather, it seems that the Christian church was merely caught up in the imperial crossfire directed against the Buddhists and, to a lesser extent, against the Manichaeans and Zoroastrians.[48] Unfortunately, we have no details about the church during those fateful years. We don't know what happened to either the Jingjiao clergy or the laity. Some may have continued to worship privately or in secret. Was this the beginning of the long tradition of underground worship that continues in the Middle Kingdom right up until the present? Others may have moved to rural areas, or completely out of the country, seeking a place where they could continue to practice their faith. Still others may have apostatized. All we can say is that shortly after 845 the Jingjiao disappeared from the Chinese literary sources and from the archaeological record—or did they?

Chan, and Burton Watson, eds., *Sources of Chinese Tradition*, vol. 1, Records of Civilization: Sources and Studies (New York: Columbia University Press, 1964), 381–82.

48. The parallel to the situation of twentieth-century Syriac-speaking Christians is remarkable. After surviving for more than a millennium and a half, Syriac-speaking Christianity now has a vastly reduced presence in the Middle East, as its adherents increasingly became "collateral damage" amid Wahabi-Suni-Shia religious and political infighting. Many Christians moved to safety in the West, where their communities often are larger than those in the homeland.

The Yelikewenjiao Revival
under the Yuan

Already several centuries before 845, when Wuzong issued his stunning edict against Buddhism and the three barbarian religions, momentous changes had begun altering the population of the vast steppe areas that bordered China to the north and west. Turkic and Mongolian tribes made and broke alliances in what seemed to be a constantly changing power struggle. Many of the leaders took the title of khan or khagan, and their confederations are remembered in history as khanates or khaganates. The Chinese trade along the silk routes was at times interrupted by the wars that accompanied these rivalries, affecting to some extent the Chinese economy. Some khanates paid tribute to the Tang; China had to open its imperial purse to maintain the support of and peace with other groups. As the dynasty and its economy grew more fragile, the border problems grew in number and in importance.

Starting about 550, a confederation of nomadic tribes known as the Blue Turks or Göktürks gradually took over much of Central Asia and Mongolia. Within a few generations they were coming into conflict with the expanding Tang Empire, beginning a century of periodic clashes that ended with a decisive Tang victory in 744. The Chinese were assisted in this by their Uyghur allies, who soon established their own Uyghur Khaganate (744–840). In 751 the westward expansion of the Tang came to a permanent halt when its army was defeated by an Islamic Abbasid army at the Battle of the Talas River. As a result, much of Central Asia, the homeland of the Sogdian people, came firmly under Muslim rule for the coming centuries. This, however, did not mean that everyone living there became Muslim. During this period, the Uyghurs continued to have a good trading relationship with the Sogdians and had been influenced by the religions coming down the Silk Road. While some had become Christians, Manichaeism seems to have been more successful.

When the Uyghur Empire collapsed a few years before Wuzong's decree, the Manichaean religion became an even more defining part of Uyghur culture. This lasted until they converted to Islam in the fifteenth century. Most of the other steppe tribes farther north, however, might have been expected to retain their traditional shamanistic religions.

The Mission Continues

Despite the advances of Islam, however, the Church of the East continued to send out clergy to the cities along the Silk Road. Some were sent to reinforce the work already being done. The stele mentions Luohan and Jilie, who came to China shortly after the time of trouble under Wu Zetian (ca. 715). In 745 the newly arrived bishop or metropolitan Jihe likewise presented himself to the imperial court. Writing about 850, the Syriac bishop Thomas of Marga mentions that a certain Persian monk named David was appointed and sent out to serve as metropolitan of China in the early ninth century. Similar events played out periodically all along the Silk Road, where the metropolitans and bishops at Merv, Rai, Samarkand, and elsewhere were regularly replenished with clergy from Syria.[1]

Other men of lesser rank were sent out as well to strengthen the Christian presence in the East. In some areas these missionaries founded Christian communities, and in other areas they reestablished a Church of the East presence. The unsettled political situation resulted in some Christian groups fleeing while others were slaughtered by enemy armies. While one should not overstate the latter, it did happen. It is not without justice that David Wilmshurst entitled his history of the Church of the East *The Martyred Church*. Persecution took place in the heartland, but also in the external provinces. Yet the missionaries kept coming, and so the gospel slowly spread to cities on the network of roads that radiated out from the Silk Road as well as among the nomadic tribes that interacted with the settled peoples. Writing in the last years of the eighth century, Timothy I, the catholicos of the Church of the East from 780 to 823, chastised Middle Eastern monks for living in comparative luxury while many of their brother monks "go to China, carrying only a staff and a knapsack."[2]

---

1. On these events, see David Wilmshurst, *The Martyred Church: A History of the Church of the East* (London: East & West Publishing, 2011), 167–71.

2. From Timothy I's Letter 13 to Sergius, the metropolitan of Elam, as cited by Wilmshurst,

Political Upheavals and Alliances:
The Tenth to Thirteenth Centuries

The world of Central Asia and China from the ninth to the thirteenth century was a time of frequent upheavals interspersed with periods of economic stability and prosperity. In China itself, the Tang dynasty continued in a weakened state until its collapse early in the tenth century. This was followed by a seventy-two-year period known as the "Five Dynasties and Ten Kingdoms" (907–979). As the name indicates, the story of tenth-century China is one of division and power struggle, with five short-lived and overlapping groups struggling to control the north-central plain, and at least ten others struggling for primacy in the south.

The Song dynasty (960–1279) eventually emerged from this chaos and was able to reunite the south and central areas. But the Khitan people kept control of northern China and Manchuria, taking the name of the Liao dynasty (907–1125). A few decades into the eleventh century, the Tangut people, known in China as the Western Xia dynasty (1038–1227), took control of the northwestern provinces. While centered in what is now Ningxia and Gansu Provinces, at various times they also controlled parts of Qinghai, Xinjiang, Shaanxi, and Inner and Outer Mongolia. The map of China was divided between these three groups for a century.

This ended, however, when some Jurchen people came from the northeast, ending Liao rule and taking control of the north as the Jin dynasty (1115–1234). Early in the thirteenth century an even greater change took place when Genghis Khan and his Mongol army ended all three kingdoms (Song, Jin, and Western Xia) in quick succession, making China part of the larger Mongol Empire. However, the Chinese region was soon partitioned off under the rule of one of the Mongol khans. Later, one of the grandsons of Genghis, Kublai Khan, declared the founding of a new Chinese dynasty, the Yuan (1271–1368). When the last vestiges of the Song were defeated a few years later, the Yuan monarch controlled virtually all of China, and Mongolia as well.

Meanwhile, along the Silk Road, the Muslim Umayyads (661–750) had gradually spread their rule as far as Samarkand. The Kara (i.e., Black) Khanids (840–1212), a confederation of Turkic tribes in western China and modern Kyrgyzstan, gradually strengthened and expanded their rule over the Silk Road from Samarkand to Kashgar. To their west, another group of Turkic peoples took over much of Iran and Afghanistan. Known as the Ghaznavid dynasty

---

The Martyred Church, 176. The Syriac text edited by O. Braun is in Corpus Scriptorum Christianorum Orientalium 74, Scriptores Syri 30: 106–9, with Latin translation in 74/Syri 31: 69–72.

(977–1186), they became highly Persianized in culture. They were gradually replaced by yet another Turkic group, the Khwarazmian dynasty (1077–1231). During this entire time the indigenous Sogdian population continued to function as traders, much as they had for centuries. Their rulers, although Islamic, were generally tolerant of all religions as long as the residents were paying taxes and the travelers were paying duties on their wares.

A traveler penetrating farther north from the Silk Road would enter the steppe with its more nomadic cultures stretching eastward all the way to the Pacific Ocean. The Uyghurs, after fighting alongside the Chinese army to help the Tang emperor regain his throne from An Lushan, fell from grace in the early ninth century. A somewhat similar group were the Ongut (or Öngüt), a Turko-Mongol tribe living along the Great Wall in Inner Mongolia. In the seventh century they extended their territory into modern Xinjiang Province as allies of the Tang. Like the Uyghurs, they contributed troops in the fight against An Lushan and his rebels. To their northeast lived a federation of three tribes who came to be known as the Merkit, centered southeast of Lake Baikal (today on the Russia-Mongolia border). To their west lived the Mongol tribal confederation known as the Oirat. To the west and southwest, where today the borders of China, Russia, and Kazakhstan meet and where the Altai Mountains dominate the landscape, another group of Turko-Mongolian tribes settled and became known as the Naiman. When the remnants of the Liao dynasty settled just to their southwest in circa 1125, becoming known as the Kara (or Black) Khitai, the Naiman became a vassal state to them. Another tribal group in this area were the Kerait. They dominated much of Mongolia during parts of the eleventh and twelfth centuries before settling in this area.[3]

This partial list of seminomadic Turkic and Mongol tribes and coalitions of tribes shows the complexity of the habitation patterns of the Mongolian steppe region before its unification by Genghis Khan. Yet there was also a shared underlying stratum of cultural, religious, and linguistic identity. Trade and war were the source of periodic if not continual interactions among these groups, and between them and the khanates along the Silk Road farther to the south and west: the Kara Khanids, Ghaznavids, and Khwarazmians. While some trade also existed between the steppe tribes and the Chinese, the latter had much less interest in cultural exchanges of any kind, as the traditional Chinese xenophobia quickly reasserted itself after the Tang period.

---

3. For the intersection of these tribal groups with the Church of the East, see Christoph Baumer, *The Church of the East: An Illustrated History of Assyrian Christianity*, new ed. (London: I. B. Taurus, 2016), 197–211.

Christianity Comes to the Steppes

The Church of the East had gradually created a Christian presence in the cities along the silk routes from the fourth to the seventh centuries, culminating with Alopen's arrival in Chang'an in 635. By 845, when Wuzong's decree banned the Jingjiao from China, the Church of the East had a presence in virtually all the major settlements throughout what is now Afghanistan, Tajikistan, Kyrgyzstan, and Xinjiang Province in China, as well as in numerous major cities within China. In the ninth to twelfth centuries, with China again closed to Christian activity, the gospel message somehow flowed around the northern borders of the Song and penetrated the tribes of the steppes all across Mongolia. We know few details of how this happened. Patriarch Timothy I, writing about 800, asserted that "The king of the Turks with nearly all his territory, has left his ancient godless error, for he has become acquainted with Christianity by the operation of the great power of the Messiah." The catholicos goes on to state that this king "has written to him requesting that a metropolitan be appointed and sent out for his subjects."[4] Timothy later confirms that "the Spirit has anointed in these days a metropolitan" for the Turks.[5] We do not know of which ruler or tribe he was speaking, but a significant number of Turkic tribal leaders and their people turned to Christianity in these centuries.

How was it that such a major mission advance took place? It certainly was due in large part to mission reinforcements sent out from the Church of the East heartland. It seems just as likely, however, that Jingjiao Christians deserve some of the credit. After the decree of 845, faithful monks and priests had the choice of either trying to keep their faith alive via illegal and secretive gatherings or moving to locations where they could worship more freely. Those who chose the latter might have moved to rural areas or cities farther from the capital, where there was less scrutiny; or they could have emigrated out of China. With the Muslim presence strengthening along the Silk Road and in the countries to the west, moving northward might have been the most viable alternative. The cultural change would have been dramatic for any who tried this, but it would have also presented a new mission field. The positive advance of the gospel in greater Mongolia during this period leads me to conclude that, despite the lack of substantial concrete evidence, members of

4. From Timothy's Letter 41 in the translation of Mark Dickens in "Patriarch Timothy I and the Metropolitan of the Turks," *Journal of the Royal Asiatic Society*, 3rd ser., 20, no. 2 (2010): 119.

5. Timothy's Letter 47 in Dickens, "Patriarch Timothy I," 119.

the Jingjiao laity and clergy were at least partially responsible.[6] The fact that some of the crosses on thirteenth- and fourteenth-century tombstones are of the *crux Vaticana* type, like the cross atop the Chang'an stele, is evidence that those buried were connected with the Church of the East and possibly with the earlier Jingjiao.[7]

One of the few events to which we can give an approximate date is a mass conversion in AD 1007. The story is told most fully by the Jacobite Syriac historian Bar Hebraeus, whose *Ecclesiastical History* extended to 1285, the year before his own death. In it he mentions an exchange of letters between the Church of the East patriarch Yohannan V (1000–1011) and Abdisho, a metropolitan of Merv (in modern Turkmenistan). Abdisho's letter said that the khan of the Turkic Kerait tribe had become lost in a snowstorm. After he had given up all hope of survival, Saint Sergius appeared to him in a vision and led him safely back to his camp. The khan immediately summoned some Christian merchants who were residing there and asked them to explain the Christian faith. They did so, gave him a copy of a gospel, and told him of the necessity for baptism. The khan then requested that Abdisho or another priest come and baptize him. It seems that in the letter Abdisho was seeking approval for the baptism from the patriarch. The patriarch responded that Abdisho should indeed send priests and deacons as well as the accoutrements for an altar so that they "could baptize those who have believed and teach them Christian customs." This led not only to the baptism of the khan but to the conversion of two thousand of his subjects.[8]

However, some doubt whether this conversion actually involved the Kerait. Erica Hunter has pointed out that a twelfth-century Nestorian writer, Mari ibn Suleiman, tells a similar story in his *Book of the Tower* without mentioning that

6. Samuel Lieu cautiously argues for a survival of the Jingjiao in the southeastern port of Quanzhou as well. See Lieu et al., *Medieval Christian and Manichaean Remains from Quanzhou (Zayton)*, Corpus Fontium Manichaeorum, Series Archaeologica et Iconographica 2 (Turnhout: Brepols, 2012), 31–34. See also Wang Yuanyuan, "Doubt on the Viewpoint of the Extinction of *Jingjiao* in China after the Tang Dynasty," in *From the Oxus River to the Chinese Shores*, ed. Li Tang and Dietmar W. Winkler, Orientalia-Patristica-Oecumenica 5 (Vienna: LIT Verlag, 2013), 279–96.

7. See the photos of gravestones provided by Dickens in "Gravestones in the Tashkent History Museum," in *Hidden Treasures and Intercultural Encounters*, ed. Dietmar Winkler and Li Tang, Orientalia-Patristica-Oecumenica 1 (Vienna: LIT Verlag, 2009), 29, 37, and 40.

8. The story is recounted by the Syriac Christian historian Bar Hebraeus. It is in part 2, sections 279–281 in David Wilmshurst, *Bar Hebraeus the Ecclesiastical Chronicle: An English Translation*, Gorgias Eastern Christian Studies 40 (Piscataway, NJ: Gorgias, 2016), 398 (with Syriac on the facing page).

the converted king was a Kerait. She postulates that the story may reflect an early conversion among the Oghuz tribe.[9] More recently, Christopher Atwood has argued that the story actually is about the conversion of the Ongut.[10]

Whether the snowstorm involved them or another tribe, it was still the Kerait, a coalition of eight ethnically diverse clans that emerged as a khanate about 1000 and as one of the earliest seminomadic groups to contain a significant number of Christians. In the second quarter of the twelfth century, the Kerait khan Saraq (also known as Buiruq khan) had the Christian name Marcus. Captured in a clash with the Tatars, he was handed over to the Chinese Jin dynasty, which executed him by publicly nailing him to a wooden donkey, indicating that the Jin already had some knowledge of Christianity as well. After the brief rule of Marcus's son, Cyriacus, the latter's son Toghrul (given the name Wang Khan by the Chinese) ruled the last half of the century near modern Ulan Bator. He became closely allied with Genghis Khan's father, and the young Genghis was raised at the Kerait court, where, by the end of the twelfth century, we hear that members of the court worshiped with elaborately robed priests conducting the service in a culturally appropriate way—in a circular tent constructed like a Mongolian-style *yurt* or *ger*.[11] While the actions of the rulers call into question the depth of their Christian knowledge and practice, it is clear from the sources that the Kerait had to a large degree self-identified as Christians in the Church of the East tradition.

We know much less about the Christianization within the other tribes of the steppes and very few details about the overall development of Christianity in the region before the early thirteenth century. However, the biographical details about Genghis Khan found in the *Secret History of the Mongols* provide us with many references to the widespread presence of Christianity among the surrounding tribes, at least among their ruling families. Genghis's mother was a Merkit, and his father was the blood brother of a leading Kerait. Genghis de-

9. See the analysis of Erica Hunter, "The Conversion of the Kerait to Christianity in AD 1007," *Zentralasiatische Studien* 22 (1989–1991): 142–63.

10. Christopher Atwood, "Historiography and Transformation of Ethnic Identity in the Mongol Empire: The Öng'üt Case," *Asian Ethnicity* 15, no. 4 (September 2014): 514–34. The Persian Jewish courtier and historian Rashid-al-Din Hamadani (1247–1318) mentions the conversion of the Kerait to Christianity but gives no further details. See Rashīd al-Dīn and W. M. Thackston, *Jami't-Tawarikh: Compendium of Chronicles; A History of the Mongols* (Cambridge MA: Harvard University Press, 1998–1999), part 1, 61.

11. On the Kerait, see İsenbike Togan, *Flexibility and Limitation in Steppe Formations: The Kerait Khanate and Chinggis Khan*, Ottoman Empire and Its Heritage 15 (Leiden: Brill, 1998), esp. 60–76. Also Mark Dickens, "Syriac Christianity in Central Asia," in *The Syriac World*, ed. Daniel King (London: Routledge, 2019), 605.

feated the Merkit in a series of battles between 1200 and 1205. He took a Merkit noble named Khulan as a wife, and gave Töregene, the wife of the Merkit khan's son, as a wife for his own son Ögedei. After defeating the Kerait in 1203–1204, he took the khan's niece Ibaka-Beki as another wife and gave in marriage two of her younger sisters, Bektumish-Beki and Sorghaghtani, to his sons Jöchi and Tolui. Genghis's own daughter Alakhai-Beki wed an Ongut leader and later served as regent for several underage princes.[12] Similar marriage alliances brought still other women from previously rival tribes into positions of influence among the Mongols. Many of these women were Christians. When forty years later the Franciscan priest John of Plano Carpini visited the court of the Great Khan Güyük in Karakorum, he reported that he was "surrounded by Nestorians." Since Genghis Khan insisted that all religions could be freely practiced in his realm, Christians of the Church of the East were found across Mongolia during the thirteenth century. Christoph Baumer, however, most likely overstates the situation when he estimates that "some 30–40 per cent of the Turko-Mongols" in this area were Nestorian Christians.[13]

The Mongol Expansion into China

By 1206 the Mongol leader Temüjin, known to us as Genghis Khan, had achieved rule over all his surrounding rivals, including the Merkit, Naiman, Kerait, Uyghurs, and other Mongols. This put him in position to hold a great tribal council, or *kurultai*, at which he took for himself the title Genghis Khan. This, however, was just the beginning of his plans. In the years following, his armies of Mongol cavalry continued to expand his influence toward the west. After adding territory at the expense of the Western Xia (1038–1227), Genghis brokered an alliance with them. Together they turned their attention to the Jin dynasty (1115–1234) in northern China. After an initial victory in 1211, they continued to harass the Jin, finally capturing the central Jin capital near modern Beijing in 1215. The Jin were then forced to give up the vast majority of their territory and retrench their forces in Kaifeng.

Turning again to the west in 1219, the Mongols invaded Khwarezmia (1077–1231), gaining its submission by 1221. Since the Western Xia had refused to par-

---

12. For these events, see the translation (vol. 1) and notes (vol. 2) of Igor de Rachewiltz, *The Secret History of the Mongols: A Mongolian Epic Chronicle of the Thirteenth Century*, new ed., 2 vols. (Leiden: Brill, 2006).

13. Baumer, *The Church of the East*, 198.

ticipate in those campaigns, Genghis then turned on them, destroying them in a series of campaigns between 1225 and 1227, the year of Genghis's own death. It was left to Genghis's son and successor, Ögedei, to attack Kaifeng in 1233, causing the ultimate collapse of the Jin a year later. Now controlling all of northern China, the Mongols were brought face-to-face with the Song dynasty, or the Southern Song (1127–1279), as it is referred to following its loss of northern China to the Jin. The Song had cooperated with the Mongols in dismantling the Jin, but in the aftermath they had tried to retain Kaifeng and other areas they had previously lost, and this provided the Mongols with an excuse to consider their alliance at an end. In 1259 the Mongols began a series of simultaneous attacks against the Song from the north and west, but these were only partially successful. It was only in the late 1260s that the Song defenses began crumbling significantly. By 1271, the new khan, Kublai, had secured enough territory to declare the beginning of a new dynasty. Song forces continued fighting as they retreated, until the late 1270s, when the thirteen-year-old Song emperor gave up all hope and committed suicide.

Kublai Khan tried in many ways to adapt Mongol rule to Chinese culture. He claimed the mandate of heaven for his Yuan dynasty, that is, he proclaimed that the heavens supported the accession of his rule and would continue to do so until he stopped ruling in a just and equitable manner. He adopted many Confucian rituals, portrayed himself as a sage-emperor, and showed his filial piety by inaugurating family and imperial worship for his grandfather Genghis. While leaving much of the previous bureaucracy in place, he adopted the economic and monetary reforms suggested by his Chinese advisors. Yet, while on the one hand introducing some more egalitarian ideas, he divided the population into four social classes, with the Han in the lowest.

Kublai's later years were marred by military failures that sapped the treasury, and, after his death in 1294, his successors struggled to maintain the status quo. When Buyantu Khan took the throne as Emperor Renzong (1311–1320), he tried to integrate the dynasty more thoroughly into Chinese culture by reinstating the Confucian-inspired civil service and examination system. The dynasty was weakened, however, by clan infighting and court intrigues among his successors. Tugh Temür, known as Emperor Wenzong (1328–1332), sought to further Sinicize the dynasty by founding the Academy of the Pavilion of the Star of Literature to promote the Chinese cultural heritage among the Mongol aristocracy, and he himself became the first Yuan emperor to lead the traditional annual rituals and offerings at the Temple of Heaven.

With the Mongols now controlling the entire eastern half of the Silk Road, trade flourished and China was again opened to the West. Foreign cultural influences and visitors became common at the khan's capital of Khanbaliq (modern Beijing). As we have seen, the Mongol aristocracy soon became a mix of Mongol and Turkic men and women, and some of these were Christians from the Kerait, Naiman, and other tribes. The Mongol ideal of freedom of religion allowed religious affiliations to be passed down from generation to generation within the tribal clans. Even though the Yuan rulers attempted to become more Chinese, Christians were to be found in the Yuan aristocracy as well. At the same time, a new wave of Christian traders and missionaries appeared—both via the land routes of the Silk Road and via the sea routes that had opened up during the Song to connect the Middle East and India with China's southern and southeastern coasts. Four centuries after the Tang had outlawed the Jingjiao and it had disappeared from public life, it reappeared in an even more visible and protected way in China during the rule of the Mongols.

One outpost on the northwest edge of China has left us a remarkable record of the ethnic diversity within the Christian community of the steppes. The modern oasis town of Turfan (or Turpan) in Xinjiang Province is located along the silk route that skirts the northern side of the Taklamakan Desert. Within a few miles on either side of the present city, the cities of Jaohe (100 BC to AD 700) and Gaochang (100 BC on) had flourished for centuries. The latter became the center of the Uyghur kingdom of Qocho from 860 to 1284, with its inhabitants being mostly Buddhist, but also with some Manichaeans and Christians. Early in the twentieth century, fragments of Christian texts were discovered in the ruins of a Christian monastery a few miles north of Turfan as well as at several other nearby locations. The manuscripts date from the ninth to the thirteen centuries, with texts in Syriac, Sogdian, and Uyghur, as well as two Persian dialects, and they are written in a variety of scripts.[14] There are portions of Scripture, liturgical fragments, prayer books, stories of saints, and other devotional writings. Unlike the Jingjiao texts from Dunhuang, however, we don't find locally composed texts, but rather, nearly all are translations of older works. Scholars such as Hidemi Takahashi, Nicholas Sims-Williams, Erica Hunter, and Pier Giorgio Borbone all agree that Turfan and surrounding areas had multiethnic and multilingual Christian communities that were part of the Church of the East. As a result, Syriac, the language

---

14. The multicultural breadth of this small oasis is demonstrated by a chart found on the German "Turfanforschung" website that shows that extant writings from the area have been identified in some twenty different languages and twenty different scripts! See http://turfan.bbaw.de/bilder/sprachenschriften_gr.gif.

all Christian monks had at least a smattering of, continued to be used in the liturgy, even though other local vernaculars soon found a place alongside it. Outside of the monasteries, and as one went farther from the Silk Road, the Turkic languages became more dominant, for example, among tribes like the Ongut. There, many faithful Christians probably knew little Syriac beyond the formulas of the liturgy. One exception may have been the Ongut monk Mark, who traveled from China to Mesopotamia in the 1270s and impressed the clergy there so much that he was soon elected patriarch of the whole church. While he professed that he was unfit for such a position because of his ignorance of Syriac, his protestations were probably meant more as an expression of his humility.[15]

We also have a few accounts of Christian worship on the steppes. Early European travelers described round tent churches modeled on the portable habitations of that region known as *yurts* or *gers*. The Christian wife of the khan Hülegü had a church at the entrance to the royal enclosure. William of Rubruck mentions altars, icons, a baptistry, and ovens dedicated to baking bread for the sacrament; bells were rung, and wooden *semantrons* (suspended slabs of wood that were struck with a mallet as a call to worship) and liturgical crosses (but not crucifixes) were displayed. Marco Polo describes an Easter service that was conducted in the presence of Kublai Khan: "Learning that this was one of our principal feasts he made all the Christians come to him, and desired them to bring the book in which are the four Gospels, which he had censed many times with great ceremony, kissed it devoutly, and desired that all his barons and lords who were present should do the same. And he always observes this custom at the chief feasts of the Christians, as is Easter and the Nativity."[16] This, however, was not a sign of Kublai's own beliefs but rather his policy of encouraging all religious practices, for Polo adds, "he did this also on the special days of the Muslims, Jews and heathens [i.e., Buddhists]."

15. See Hidemi Takahashi, "Representation of the Syriac Language in Jingjiao and Yelikewen Documents," in *The Church of the East in Central Asia and China*, ed. Samuel N. C. Lieu and Glen L. Thompson, China and the Mediterranean World 1 (Turnhout: Brepols, 2020), 57–58. Takahashi concludes his exhaustive study of the evidence by saying that "the Syriac language and script evidently always had a special symbolic value for the Christian community" in China, but little more (63).

16. The compositional history of Marco Polo's great book is extremely complex, and its many manuscripts vary widely from one another. I have cited from book 1, §81 in the translation of A. C. Moule and Paul Pelliot, *Marco Polo: The Description of the World*, vol. 1 (London: Routledge, 1938), 201.

The Yelikewenjiao

This Christian presence is evident both in archaeological remains from the period and in references by Chinese documents dating to the Yuan era. It is also clear that the vast majority of the Yuan-era Christians among the steppe tribes and in Yuan China were products of the mission work of the Church of the East, just as the Jingjiao had been. That makes it even more surprising that the documentary references no longer call these Christians *Bosi* (Persians), or *Da Qin* (Roman or Byzantine), or *Jingjiao*, but instead uniformly refer to them as the *Yelikewen*, 也里可溫. Modern scholars do not agree on the origin or meaning of the term, but one conjecture is that it came from the Mongol word *ärkä'ün*, which was a rendering of the Syriac transcription of a Greek term for leader—ἀρχηγός or ἄρχων.[17]

The preservation of an official register of buildings and people from the area of Zhenjiang gives us our best snapshot of the Yelikewen presence in the early fourteenth century. Located on the south side of the Yangtze River between the modern cities of Nanjing and Shanghai, the district comprised some 13,500 inhabitants, according to the census register from about 1330. Some 3,000 people lived alone, and the rest lived in 3,845 families. These are further subdivided by location (those living in the city of Zhenjiang, and those in each of the three rural districts), and by ethnicity and religion (Yelikewen, Mongols, Uyghurs [i.e., Manichaeans], Muslims, Tanguts, Khitai, Tatars, Chinese). Twenty-three families (19 within the city) and 109 "solitaries" are listed as Yelikewen, making a total of about 200 Christians. This is much less than 1 percent of the total, and only about 9 percent of the foreign population.[18]

The same document lists high government officials who had served in the region over the previous half century, starting about 1275. Numerous men are identified as Yelikewen. Perhaps most prominent is Mar Sargis (*Ma Xielijisi*). His family seems to have originated in Samarkand, and his grandfather George; his father, Mieli; and his maternal grandfather, Sabi, had all become physicians at the Mongol court. Sabi was credited with curing Genghis Khan's son, Prince Tolui, using a concoction of boiled fruit and honey (called *sheliba*

17. On the meaning of the term *yelikewen*, see Li Tang, *East Syriac Christianity in Mongol-Yuan China*, Orientalia Biblica et Christiana 18 (Wiesbaden: Harrassowitz, 2011), 53–57. See also Yin Xiaoping, "On the Christians in Jiangnan during the Yuan Dynasty according to 'The Gazetteer of Zhenjiang of the Zhishun Period' 1329–1332," in Winkler and Tang, *Hidden Treasures and Intercultural Encounters*, 305n2.

18. The Chinese text and an English translation are provided by Yin Xiaoping, "On the Christians in Jiangnan," 306–9.

in the sources, translated "sherbet"). This led to the family being granted a royal patent and monopoly on the medicine. Later, Mar Sargis provided this special medicine to Kublai Khan on several occasions, and in 1278 he was appointed an assistant governor for Zhenjiang. About the same time, he began building a series of seven "Cross Monasteries" in the region, even converting his own house into one of them. An imperial grant endowed the monasteries with five hundred acres of farmland, and Mar Sargis purchased an additional six hundred for their ongoing maintenance. A bishop or metropolitan, Mar Shili, came to dedicate the buildings.[19] A register from the early 1330s shows that at least four of the monasteries were still functioning at that time. Despite the imperial standing of the monasteries' patrons, however, two of them had been converted into Buddhist establishments.

Mar Sargis was merely the most illustrious of the small Yelikewen community in Zhenjiang. The register names other men of note: An Zhenhang, Mar Aolahan, Kuolijisi and his son Luho, An Malihusi and his son Yeliya, Tahai, Taiping, and Woluosi—all these held regional government positions in the half century leading up to 1330. Thus, a significant percentage of the two-hundred-plus Yelikewen in the district were members of the government elite. And judging from their names, they were almost all of foreign origin. This would lead to the conclusion that the census may have listed only foreign Christians in the category of Yelikewen. Any locals who had converted would have been counted among the "Chinese" (Buddhists and Daoists were also not listed as separate categories). While this register, known as *The Annals of Zhenjiang of Zhishun Period*, gives us a rare insight into the Yelikewen in a provincial center, it is of little help in determining how many local Chinese were impacted by the message of the gospel.

An even more influential Yelikewen was Aixue (愛薛) or Isa (1227–1308), a Christian of the Church of the East who came originally from Syria.[20] In 1246, upon the recommendation of Rabban Ata, a Church of the East official highly respected among the Mongols, the nineteen-year-old Aixue began serving at Güyük's court. There he met and married a Kerait woman named Sala (Sarah). Beginning as an interpreter, he eventually worked his way up to the director-

19. On Mar Sargis and his family, see Yin Xiaoping, "On the Christians in Jiangnan," 309–10 and 313–17.

20. On Aixue, see Yin Xiaoping, "The Institution of Chongfu Si of the Yuan Dynasty," in *Winds of Jingjiao*, ed. Li Tang and Dietmar W. Winkler, Orientalia-Patristica-Oecumenica 9 (Vienna: LIT Verlag, 2016), 316–19; also extracts about him and his family from the official Yuan history (元史, *Yuan shi*) are given by A. C. Moule, *Christians in China before the Year 1550* (London: SPCK, 1930), 228–33.

ship of the offices of astronomy and medicine. His efficiency and energy were recognized, and he was appointed the first director of the Bureau of Medicine, newly organized in 1273. He was prominent enough that the Persian writer Rashid al-Din blamed him for some of Kublai Khan's anti-Muslim policies in the late 1270s. Then, from 1283 to 1285, he was a member of a politically sensitive delegation sent by Kublai to Arghun, the Mongol leader trying to retain control in the Middle East. This included negotiations with Westerners as the Mongols sought to arrange an alliance with Pope Honorius IV.

Although the latter idea never bore fruit, that mission must have further demonstrated Aixue's loyalty and abilities, for when he returned to the Mongol court he received one promotion or honor after another—director of the Palace Library (1287), director of the new Office of Chongfu (1289), minister of state (1297), and finally duke of the Kingdom of Qin (1298). In true aristocratic fashion, he was able to establish a family dynasty, with several of his sons inheriting their father's positions. His eldest, Yeliya (Elijah), later became duke of Qin, headed the Office of Chongfu, and also became director of the Imperial Hospital and Medical Academy as well as of the Imperial Astronomical Observatory. His son Luhe (Luke) later became the director of both the Bureau of Medicine and the Office of Chongfu.[21]

Aixue and his family were also grouped into the religious and ethnic minority known to the Mongols and Chinese as Yelikewen. In 1289 a single government office was established to oversee the Yelikewen across China. This was what the Office of Chongfu was, and it was yet another indication that this group had been afforded official recognition, bringing them in line with the Buddhists and Daoists who had been overseen and regulated by separate government bureaus for almost a millennium. An entry in the official *History of the Yuan Dynasty* (元史, *Yuan shi*) described the newly established office as follows:

> The director of the Office of Chongfu (崇福司) will be given a fixed salary at the grade of the lower second court. The bureau will have jurisdiction over bishops, priests, and all *yelikewen*, and over the temples, worship, and other affairs in the Cross Monasteries.
>
> It will have four directors who rank in grade at the lower second court;
> two associate directors who rank in grade at the lower third court;

21. See Yin Xiaoping, "The Institution of Chongfu Si," 311–31.

two subordinate directors who rank in grade at
 the lower fourth court;
two deputies who rank in grade at the lower fifth court;
one chief secretary who ranks in grade at the lower sixth court;
one assistant secretary who ranks in grade at
 the lower seventh court;
one commissary of records who ranks in grade at
 the upper eighth court;
plus two historians, one translator, one interpreter, one seal-keeper
 and two couriers.

The Bureau was founded in the 26th year of the *Zhiyuan* period [1289]; in the 2nd year of the *Yanyou* period [1315] it was upgraded and expanded to become the Department for Christian Affairs (崇福院) with one President over it to direct all its affairs. To this Department all affairs of *yelikewen* were transferred after the 72 Offices for Local Christian Affairs across the Empire were abolished, which had previously overseen the affairs of the *yelikewen*. Seven years afterwards, however, the department was made into a bureau again, and the above-mentioned officials were attached to it.[22]

This sort of government oversight and coordination would not have seemed out of place either to the Chinese or to the Yelikewen themselves. The Sasanian government had formally overseen the mother church in Persia almost since its inception. With the arrival of Islam, the patriarch had become the officially recognized spokesman for the church, often serving in an advisory capacity for the caliph. He was expected to keep his clergy and churches informed about and obedient to government policy. In China, this had been done in the early years of the Yuan dynasty by the seventy-two local and regional offices mentioned in the official notice quoted above. But unlike in Persia, the Yelikewen men who served as directors of the Office of Chongfu do not appear to have been clergy or monks, but rather influential aristocratic laymen. It is even possible that several of the directors were not Yelikewen at all. The new arrangement seems to have worked well from the government's point of view, since a quarter of a century later the *office* (*si*) was upgraded to a *department* (*yuan*), even though it reverted in status a few years later.

22. From the *Yuan shi*, book 89, translation by Yin Xiaoping, "The Institution of Chongfu Si," 312–13.

We are unaware whether the church itself was uncomfortable with the arrangement. A notice of 1311 confirms that all religious professionals—Buddhist monks, Daoists, Yelikewen, and Muslims—were required to pray that the emperor have long life, and in return did not have to participate in the periodic forced labor on government projects expected of everyone else.[23] Normally, prayer for the head of state would be natural for Christians even without a special injunction for it. On another occasion, a command was given for special prayers by the Yelikewen at the imperial shrine for Empress Xianyi Zhuangsheng. To bring themselves in line with Chinese culture, the Mongols had instituted ancestor worship in the mid-thirteenth century and had built ancestral temples on the Chinese model. Conducting Christian rituals for the non-Christian dead may well have been a bridge too far for the Yelikewen. However, Xianyi Zhuangsheng was the posthumous title of Empress Sorghaghtani Beki. She was not only the mother of three great khans—Kublai, Möngke, and Hülagu—but she was also a Yelikewen herself. Honoring this most famous of Christian women would have been much more acceptable, even if it was done in the surroundings of an imperial temple.[24] A second notice from 1336 mentions that a similar ritual was to be conducted in her honor "in the cross monastery of Gansu Circuit, in Gansu Province." Such duties were totally in line with the remembrances given to the Christian saints in the Syriac liturgy.

Complications and Competitors from the West

In 1241 Genghis's son Ögedei and a Mongol army rode deep into Europe and decisively defeated a European army in western Poland. Still smarting from the crusaders' defeats at the hands of Muslim armies in the Holy Land, the Christian West was now confronted by a ruthless new threat, known to them as the Tatars. Rumors of the strength and savagery of the Mongols had been circulating there for years. It was also during the Crusades that Westerners traveling in Palestine and Syria had met priests and monks from the Church of the East, people they immediately labeled "Nestorians." From them the first

23. The notice is also found in *Yuan shi*. The text and English translation are given in Yin Xiaoping, "The Institution of Chongfu Si," 320.

24. On this remarkable woman, see Li Tang, "Sorkaktani Beki: A Prominent Nestorian Woman at the Mongol Court," in *Jingjiao: The Church of the East in China and Central Asia*, ed. Roman Malek, Collectanea Serica (Sankt Augustin, Germany: Instituta Monumenta Serica, 2006), 349–55.

reports of Christians in India and the Far East began to filter in. By 1145 the German churchman Otto of Freising was writing that somewhere "beyond Persia and Armenia in the uttermost East" there was a Christian kingdom with a "Nestorian" priest who also served as king, Prester John.[25] Arising from garbled accounts of various Turkic rulers, the legend would continue to grow, as Christian generals were among the Mongol troops overrunning parts of the Middle East.

These reports of Mongol armies and eastern Christian rulers and generals provided the impetus for Pope Innocent IV (1243–1254) to send several embassies eastward in 1245. They carried letters for the Mongol rulers, seeking their submission to the Roman pontiff and assurances of peace for Europe. The Dominican priest Andrew of Longjumeau was able to deliver his letter to a Mongol general near Tabriz. At the Mongol camp, Andrew met Rabban Ata, the Church of the East monk who had helped the young Aixue find a position at the Mongol court; he had been put in charge of protecting local Christians as much as possible during the Mongol campaign. Two other Dominicans, Simon of St. Quentin and Ascelin of Lombardy, reached the camp of the chief general, Baiju Noyan, in Armenia. In 1248, they returned to Innocent with two Mongol envoys bearing a dismissive reply from the Mongol leader.[26]

Meanwhile, in April of 1246, the Franciscan John of Plano Carpini arrived at the Mongol camp of the top Western commander, Batu, on the Volga River. Batu sent the Westerners on to the camp of the supreme khan near Karakorum, where they arrived just in time to witness the election of a new khan, Güyük. After an audience with him, John received a letter to carry back to the pope. Since God had favored the Mongols with such vast conquests, the letter called for the pontiff's submission to them. A year or two later, Andrew of Longjumeau made a second journey, this time finding his way also to the Mongol capital at Karakorum. He arrived shortly after the death of Güyük and was received quite kindly by his wife, Oghul Qaimish, who was serving as regent. She sent him back to Europe with gifts but bearing yet another letter demanding submission. Although none of Innocent's embassies had their desired effect, John's travel accounts, published as *A History of the Mongols*, and an excerpt from Andrew's

25. See book 7, section 33 in the translation of Charles C. Mierow, *The Two Cities: A Chronicle of Universal History to the Year 1146 A.D. by Otto, Bishop of Freising* (New York: Columbia University Press, 1928), 443–44. On the larger legend, see Robert Silverberg, *The Realm of Prester John* (Athens: Ohio University Press, 1996).

26. For more detail on these early journeys, see the introduction in Christopher Dawson, *Mission to Asia: Narratives and Letters of the Franciscan Missionaries in Mongolia and China in the Thirteenth and Fourteenth Centuries* (New York: Harper & Row, 1966), vii–xxi.

journals preserved in Vincent of Beauvais's *Mirror of History*, provided confirmation that "Nestorian" Christians were indeed part of the Mongol court.[27]

An even more detailed account would be provided a decade later, after the Franciscan William of Rubruck returned from a visit to several important Mongol officials, including the great khan Möngke (1251–1259). The *Itinerary of Brother William* is one of the masterpieces of early travel literature, although it would soon be eclipsed in popularity by that of Marco Polo.[28] While Rubruck was certainly skeptical of the quality of doctrine and practice among the Christians he met along the way, he did not show the utter disdain that some monastic travelers did. He describes the wonder with which Christians viewed his crucifix, for "Nestorians and Armenians never put the figure of Christ on their crosses which gives the impression that they have a wrong idea about the Passion or are ashamed of it" (15.7). He observes that they call the believers to prayer by striking a board, and that they then chant their liturgy (18.2). In one of his longer descriptions, he is less sympathetic.

> The Nestorians there know nothing. They say their [liturgical] offices and have their sacred books in Syriac, a language of which they are ignorant, and so they sing like our monks who know no grammar, and this accounts for the fact that they are completely corrupt. In the first place they are usurers and drunkards, and some of them who are with the Tartars [Mongols] even have several wives like them. When they enter a church, they wash their lower members [feet] like the Saracens [Muslims]; they eat meat on Fridays and have feasting on that day after the Saracen custom.
>
> The bishop puts off coming into these regions; he comes perhaps scarcely once in fifty years. When he does come, they have all the little male children, even those still in their cradles, ordained priests, consequently almost all their men are priests, and after this they marry, which is clearly contrary to the decrees of the Fathers, and they are bigamists, for when their first wife dies these priests take another. They are also all of them simonyical [i.e., they practice simony] administering no sacrament without payment.[29]

27. The Latin text of John of Plano Carpini can be found in Anastasius van den Wyngaert, *Itinera et Relationes Fratrum Minorum Saeculi XIII et XIV*, Sinica Franciscana 1 (Ad Claras Aquas [Quaracchi-Firenze]: apud Collegium s. Bonaventurae, 1929), 27–132; Dawson, *Mission to Asia*, 3–72.

28. Rubruck's Latin text can be found in Wyngaert, *Itinera et Relationes*, 147–332; English translation in Dawson, *Mission to Asia*, 89–220.

29. Section 26.12–13; Latin text in Wyngaert, *Itinera et Relationes*, 238; English translation in Dawson, *Mission to Asia*, 144–45.

While there are certainly some elements of truth in William's critique, it is easy to see both his own misunderstanding of some of the local customs and his conviction that Roman Catholic customs were the only proper way to do things. He was a bit more charitable after observing a service at Epiphany time:

> All the Nestorian priests assembled before daybreak at the chapel and beat the board. And they sang solemn Matins, and put on their vestments and prepared a thurible and incense. . . . The chief wife, by name Cotota Caten . . . entered the chapel with a number of other ladies and her eldest son Baltu and her other little children; and they prostrated, placing their foreheads on the ground after the Nestorian custom, and then they touched all the statues with their right hand, always kissing the hand afterwards; and then they proffered their right hand to all present in the church, for this is the custom of Nestorians on entering church. The priests then sang many things and gave incense into the lady's hand, and she put it onto the coals and then they censed her. . . . I do know that they do not celebrate Mass in a tent but only in a permanent church. At Easter I saw them baptize and bless [baptismal] fonts with great solemnity, a thing they did not do on this occasion.[30]

While William's account added much to Western knowledge of the Mongols and the "Nestorian" Christians in Asia, he obviously emphasized the differences rather than the similarities. His description of Easter, however, once again brought out some compassion in him. It also shows us that both Catholics and "Nestorians" were unsure whether the Christian rites of the other side were completely orthodox and acceptable or not:

> Maundy Thursday and Easter Sunday were approaching, and I had not got our vestments; I was watching closely the way the Nestorians celebrated and was much distressed as to what I should do, whether I should receive the Sacrament from them or celebrate in their vestments with their chalice and on their altar, or whether I should abstain entirely from the Sacrament. At that time there was a large crowd of Christians there—Hungarians, Alans, Russians, Georgians, Armenians—all of whom had not set eyes on the sacrament from the time they had been taken prisoner, for the Nestorians were unwilling to admit them into their church unless they were re-baptized

---

30. Section 29.19; Latin text in Wyngaert, *Itinera et Relationes*, 258–59; English translation in Dawson, *Mission to Asia*, 161–62.

by them, so they said. However, to us they made no mention of this, on the contrary they acknowledged to us that the Roman Church was the head of all the churches, and that they would receive a Patriarch from the Pope, if only the way [road] were open. They freely offered us their Sacrament, and made me stand at the door of the choir so that I could see how they celebrated, and also on Easter Eve, I stood near the font so that I could see their way of baptising.[31]

William also took part in a religious debate in the presence of Möngke. The religious openness of the khan was on full display as Buddhists, Muslims, and Christians were told to argue the case for their own religion with civility and gravity.

A decade and a half after William's visit, the young Marco Polo arrived in China as part of a trading expedition; he would remain for seventeen years. Möngke had died in 1259 and had been succeeded by the famous Kublai Khan, who soon established the Yuan dynasty, incorporating ever more Chinese culture and traditions into his court. There remain many problems to be sorted out concerning Polo's travels and the various surviving manuscripts that describe them, but as one scholar recently wrote, Marco Polo did indeed travel extensively in China.[32] Even taking a conservative view of some of the material that may not be original, Polo met with Christians all along the Silk Road and almost everywhere he went in China—and most of them were "Nestorians." Along the Silk Road he mentions Christians or churches in Samarkand and Kashgar, among the Uyghurs of Yarkand, and in several towns and provinces of Tangut. He finds them at the capital of Khanbaliq (now Beijing), and in the old capital of Chang'an as well. In northern China they wore beards and celebrated with special prayers on the Chinese emperor's birthday. In Zhenjiang (near modern Nanjing), "where there had been no Christians previously," he saw two of the churches recently built by Mar Sargis. One manuscript mentions a large contingent of "ancient" Christians in Fuzhou. These are but some of the intriguing comments that he makes about the church in China.[33]

31. Section 30.10; Latin text in Wyngaert, *Itinera et Relationes*, 280; English translation in Dawson, *Mission to Asia*, 178–79.

32. See most recently Hans Ulrich Vogel, *Marco Polo Was in China: New Evidence from Currencies, Salts, and Revenues* (Leiden: Brill, 2013). For editions, see also n. 16 above.

33. Moule and Pelliot, *Marco Polo*. Book 1 has descriptions of Samarkand, Kashgar, and Yarkand (§51-3, pp. 143–46), of the Tangut provinces (§60-2, pp. 156–60), of Khabaliq (§98, pp. 242–47) and Xi'an (§111, pp. 263–64). On the identification of the places mentioned by Polo, see the still-useful book of P. Pelliot, *Notes on Marco Polo*, 2 vols., Ouvrage Posthume (Paris: A. Maisonneuve [Imprimerie Nationale], 1959, 1963).

In 1287 Pope Nicholas IV (1288–1292) received a letter from Arghun, the khan who ruled Persia for the Mongols from 1284 to 1291. Arghun, a devout Buddhist whose mother was a Yelikewen Christian and whose two sons would convert to Islam, had been trying to broker an alliance between the Mongols and Western powers for some time. This had led him to send Aixue to the papal court in 1285, and the Chinese Christian monk Rabban Sauma in 1287 (see below). In his letter of 1287, Arghun asked that papal envoys be sent to the court of Kublai Khan, and Nicholas responded by selecting an Italian Franciscan named John of Montecorvino for the job. Since 1275, John had been in the Middle East and had already been focusing his mission efforts on "Asians."[34]

In 1289 he set out, first traveling to Persia, then by sea to India. By the time he arrived at Khanbaliq in 1294, Kublai had died and his grandson Temür had taken the throne as Emperor Chengzong (1294–1307). Unlike previous Western monks, John saw himself as a missionary, not simply an envoy. He threw himself into the work. Soon he had dismissed the local Yelikewen as little more than heathen, thus alienating most of them. Building a church near Khanbaliq, he began holding Catholic services and soon assembled a small following—partly by purchasing young boys whom he then trained to be his choir and liturgical assistants! Whenever possible, he spent his time explaining the differences between Catholicism and the Church of the East to any Yelikewen who would listen.

His most famous convert from among the local "Nestorians" was an Ongut prince named George. He was one of the sons of the Ongut king Aibuga, who had been killed while fighting in the Mongol army. Temür had given George the title Prince of Gaotang and appointed him a military commander as well. Within John's first year in Khanbaliq, he traveled north to visit the Ongut court and struck up a friendship with the well-educated prince. George soon converted to Catholicism, built a church, and began assisting John in his services, even wearing vestments himself. Soon many other Ongut Yelikewen had joined the "Roman Church," further antagonizing the local Yelikewen. George was captured and executed while on campaign in 1298, and soon after his sons and many other Yelikewen reverted to their former church allegiance.[35]

---

34. On John, see Dawson, *Mission to China*, xxxii–xxxv.

35. On Prince or King George, see Maurizio Paolillo, "In Search of King George," in Winkler and Tang, *Hidden Treasures and Intercultural Encounters*, 241–55; Pierre Marsone, "Two Portraits for One Man: George King of the Önggüt," and Li Tang, "Rediscovering the Ongut King George: Remarks on a Newly Excavated Archaeological Site," both in Tang and Winkler, *From the Oxus River to the Chinese Shores*, 241–55 and 255–66, respectively.

Besides reinvigorating the legends about Prester John, George had given John of Montecorvino enough credibility to continue his work. In 1299 he overcame the objections of the local Yelikewen and gained permission to build a church in Khanbaliq itself. In 1305, in one of his few surviving letters, he calculates that he had been blessed with six thousand converts. A letter of the following year told of the construction of a second church building and of a school.[36] When this news was passed on to the new pope, Clement V (1305–1314), he immediately sent out seven newly appointed bishops to China. In 1313, the three who survived the trip ordained John as archbishop of Khanbaliq and metropolitan of China. The new archbishop served fifteen years in that capacity before his death, leaving a small but thriving Catholic mission in China.

The Syriac Church in China's Southeastern Ports

It was not just from the Silk Road and from the steppes that Christianity came into China during the Yuan period. It also came by sea. There is some evidence that already during the Tang period the Church of the East had an outpost on the southern coast at Guangzhou, called Panyu at the time. According to the Islamic traveler Aboul Zeyd al Hassan, the city was sacked in 878 by an army of rebels under Huang Chao. Zeyd wrote that the destruction targeted foreign businessmen, and that 120,000 Muslims, Jews, Christians, and Persians "who were living in the city and doing business there" were killed.[37] During the Song period, sea trade with the West continued to increase, and besides the ports of Guangzhou in the south and Yangzhou in the north (near modern Nanjing), a third port city for international trade grew up in the center of the east coast on the site of modern Quanzhou (in Fujian Province). In Western sources of the time, it was known by its Arabic name, Zayton.[38]

During the Yuan dynasty, Zayton's importance in the world of trade grew until it rivaled that of the land routes from the west. It became the Chinese starting and ending point for a "maritime silk road." The city itself became the home to a wide variety of international traders and businessmen. Without ever leaving Zayton, Zhao Rukuo, an early thirteenth-century customs inspector,

---

36. Three letters of John's have survived, dating to 1292/1293, 1305, and 1306. The Latin texts can be found in Wyngaert, *Itinera et Relationes*, 340–55; an introduction and translation of the second and third letters are provided by Dawson, *Mission to Asia*, 222–31.

37. Moule, *Christians in China*, p. 76, no. 16.

38. On the rise of Zayton as a port, see Lieu et al., *Medieval Christian and Manichaean Remains*, 1–10.

wrote a lengthy book entitled *Description of Barbarian Nations*. His first volume describes forty-six geographically distinct trading partners; his second, forty-three important trade items.[39] During this period, Zayton's population mushroomed from 200,000 to almost a half million, making it China's largest seaport. Marco Polo set off on his return to Italy from this "splendid city," which he said could rival Alexandria.

By then the city contained not only famous Buddhist and Daoist temples but also impressive mosques, Hindu temples, and Christian churches. Already centuries earlier the Church of the East had developed a strong presence on the west coast of India. It is not surprising that it also planted churches along sea routes, just as it had along the overland trade routes. We cannot trace how or when that happened, but in the past century archaeological evidence of its presence in Zayton/Quanzhou has grown, mostly in the form of funerary inscriptions. Several of these short texts use terminology that was common among the Jingjiao of the Tang period but not used by the Yelikewen—*da de* (bishop) and *Qin jiao* (as in the Da Qin religion). This has led Samuel Lieu to conclude that "the Chinese-speaking members of the Church of the East in Quanzhou . . . had survived the persecution of foreign religions in the 9th C. and had continued a subliminal existence in the port-city."[40]

If a small indigenous Jingjiao community did survive for several centuries, they were certainly strengthened significantly with the arrival of foreign Christians by the thirteenth century. Lieu and others have catalogued almost eighty Christian gravestones and other decorative elements dating to the Yuan period. The Yelikewen inscriptions are in Syriac, Chinese, Phagspa (a Mongolian attempt to create an Esperanto-type common language and script), and one in Uyghur. Most, however, are in the Turkic tribal languages of the steppes, although written in Syriac script. This would indicate a multiethnic membership in the local Christian community, at least among the wealthier members (those who could afford a grand tombstone). The preponderance of those people were of Turkic descent, perhaps part of the Mongol bureaucracy. Lieu hypothesizes that in Zayton the Yelikewen church used Turkic as their liturgical language, and that use of these foreign scripts by locals might also have been a way for them to identify with those in political power.[41]

---

39. See the now-dated English translation of Friedrich Hirth and W. W. Rockhill, *Chau Ju-kua: His Work on the Chinese and Arab Trade in the Twelfth and Thirteenth Centuries, Entitled Chu-fan-chï* (St. Petersburg, Russia: Imperial Academy of Sciences, 1911).

40. Lieu et al., *Medieval Christian and Manichaean Remains*, 33.

41. The inscriptions are catalogued by Lieu et al. in *Medieval Christian and Manichaean*

A unique Latin tombstone, also discovered at Quanzhou, was that of the Franciscan missionary Andrew of Perugia. Other records confirm that Zayton had a small Catholic community during this period. John of Montecorvino had entered China by sea through Zayton in 1293. At that time Gerard of Albuini was also appointed as the first catholic bishop of Zayton, which must have had numerous Roman Catholics among its many foreign traders and inhabitants. A wealthy Armenian woman financed the building and upkeep of a cathedral for the new diocese. Andrew of Perugia served as the third bishop there, until his death in 1332. Yet clearly, as elsewhere in China, the Catholic community in Zayton was small compared to the Yelikewen church.[42]

Bar Sauma and Mark Visit Mother Church

About the year 1325, a Persian monk wrote a biography of the recently deceased catholicos of the Church of the East, Mar Yaballaha III (r. 1281–1317); another monk then translated it into Syriac. He begins his introduction as follows:

> God Omnipotent, gracious, and merciful in the abundance of His grace brought everything into existence. . . . He then cast the net of life-giving evangelization in every place and region, scattering the good seed of His message over the whole Earth through the activity of His disciples. After them, their own disciples brought light to the four ends of the world, which, illuminated by true faith and by the glory of the august Trinity have begun to shine in their excellent perfect customs. . . . The words superseded by facts, until the lawless became God's children: the Indian, the Chinese, and other Eastern peoples were ensnared; they received the discipline of the fear of God, and their senses and consciences were anointed by the Spirit.[43]

Remains, 83–214; on Lieu's evaluation of the use of Turkic as a liturgical language and foreign scripts, see 39 and 44, respectively.

42. Andrew's tombstone has been edited by Lieu et al., *Medieval Christian and Manichaean Remains*, 129–30. Much of our knowledge of Andrew and his congregation in Zayton comes from his 1326 letter, translated by Dawson, *Mission to Asia*, 235–37 (Latin text in Wyngaert, *Itinera et Relationes*, 373–77). Additional information on Zayton is supplied in a 1318 letter from the earlier bishop, Peregrine of Castello (text in Wyngaert, 365–68; translation in Dawson, 232–34).

43. Cited from L. Parodi's new English translation of Pierre Giorgio Borbone, *History of Mar Yahballaha and Rabban Sauma*, edited, translated, and annotated by Pier Giorgio Borbone, English trans. Laura E. Parodi (Hamburg: Verlag tradition, 2021), 91. The Syriac text is on 90.

These words indicate that by the latter years of the Yuan dynasty, Christians in the Middle East (and even farther westward, as we shall see) knew about the Yelikewen and about the Christian church among the Turkic tribes of the steppes. While this knowledge had gradually spread to the West, the lives of Mar Yaballaha III and his teacher brought it all into focus. For Mar Yaballaha III himself came from China!

The future catholicos was born into a Christian Ongut family in the center of Inner Mongolia about 1245 and was named Mark. His father was an archdeacon in the church, and when he was eighteen, Mark took the vows of a celibate monk. He joined a "Cross Monastery" in the countryside of Fangshan district south of Khanbaliq where a famous Ongut monk named Rabban ("Teacher") Bar Sauma resided. A decade or so after his arrival (ca. 1275–1278), Bar Sauma and Mark set out on a pilgrimage to visit the sacred sites of the Holy Land. They must have received permission for this trip from their metropolitan in Khanbaliq, and they carried letters of introduction and safe conduct from him and from the Mongol khan. Bar Sauma seems to have kept a diary of the journey, which the Persian biographer used.

Their first stop was Mark's Ongut hometown, where they were received with great honor by both the local Christians and the rulers and were given gifts to help them on their way. From there they crossed the territory of the Tangut (modern Ningxia), where again they were eagerly welcomed by "men and women, old and young, for the Tangut people were ardent believers and their minds were pure." Following the Silk Road through Kashgar, they found the city almost deserted, having been recently sacked by a rebel band. From there they passed through Talas and Khorassan and finally arrived in the northern Persian city of Maragheh, where the patriarch Denha II (1265–1281) had been forced to move his headquarters. After paying their respects, they continued on to tour famous Christian sites in Persia. Along the way they delivered letters from the patriarch to the khan Abaqa, who, finding out their destination was the Holy Land, entrusted them with letters to deliver. But due to ongoing war in the area, they had to turn back without ever making it to Palestine. As they prepared for their return to China, Denha consecrated Mark to be the new metropolitan for northern China, appointing Rabban Sauma as his assistant or "visitor general." Before they could leave on their return journey, however, Denha died, and the new Chinese metropolitan took part in the convocation to elect a new catholicos. The Ongut Mark must have been totally surprised when he himself was elected to be the new leader of the entire Church of the East!

His election actually made good sense. Coming from China, he had not become embroiled in the local church politics that frequently caused problems in the Persian church. He also had family connections and positive relationships with the ruling Mongols. This was demonstrated when the leading Mongol in Persia, Abaqa, confirmed his election in the name of the supreme khan Möngke. Elevated to his new position in 1281 with the name Yaballaha III, he continued to serve in that position until his death more than thirty-five years later.

The other Chinese monk, Rabban Sauma, also never made it back to China. He remained in Persia to assist his former student, now patriarch. In 1287, Arghun, the khan overseeing Persia, tried again to broker an alliance with Western rulers in order to jointly wrest Jerusalem from Muslim control. Rabban Sauma was selected to lead a delegation to Europe. After meeting with the Byzantine emperor Andronicus II (r. 1282–1328) in Constantinople, he sailed to Naples and then on to Rome, arriving while the cardinals were in convocation to elect a new pope. He was warmly received by them, and when asked why a Christian like himself was serving as an ambassador for the Mongol king, he replied:

> My dear fathers, be aware that many of our fathers went to the lands of the Mongols, the Turks and the Chinese to instruct them, so that today there are many Christians among the Mongols. There are even sons of kings and queens who have been baptized and profess Christ's religion, and there are churches in their encampment. Christians are greatly honoured, and many of the Mongols are believers. Therefore, the king, who is bound by affection to the catholicos and wishes to conquer Palestine and the lands of Syria, requests your assistance regarding the capture of Jerusalem. This is why I was chosen as an envoy: since I am Christian, my word will be believed by you.[44]

Later, conversations with Bar Sauma about the state of Christianity in the Far East sparked the interest of the newly elected pope, Nicholas IV. This in turn led to the commissioning of John of Montecorvino as a missionary to the Chinese court, as we heard earlier. During his time in Rome, Bar Sauma also engaged in doctrinal discussions, presenting an eastern creed that included the following christological statement:

> I believe that one of the hypostases (*qnōmē*) of the regal Trinity, the Son, at the end of time garbed Himself in a perfect man, Jesus Christ, from the Holy Virgin Mary, was united to Him personally (*parṣōpāit*) and in Him saved the world; in His divinity he is eternally generated by the Father and in His humanity, temporally, by Mary. This unity is undivided and unbroken for eternity; the unity is without mixture, confusion, or composition. This Son

---

44. Borbone, *History of Mar Yahballaha and Rabban Sauma*, 155 (Syriac on 154).

of unity is a perfect god and a perfect man, two natures and two hypostases (qnōmē), one person (parṣōpā).[45]

When asked about the Byzantine debate with the Roman Catholic Church over the addition of *filioque* in the Nicene Creed, however, the monk declined to comment, citing his role as a mere letter carrier for the khan and the catholicos.

After touring the sites of Rome, Bar Sauma continued west all the way to Paris, where he met with King Philip the Fair, and then on to Bordeaux, where he met King Edward I of England. He was warmly received by both kings, although he failed to arouse any interest in an alliance (which would have meant another crusade). On his return trip, he spent Holy Week of 1288 in Rome, where he participated in Catholic services and was permitted to celebrate the Church of the East liturgy in Syriac.[46] Remaining in Persia, Rabban Sauma died in 1294 in Baghdad.

The story of these two thirteenth-century Ongut monks—walking from China to the Middle East, Mark becoming patriarch of the Church of the East, and Bar Sauma meeting the pope and several European kings—is remarkable in itself. But it also has several important implications for the larger story of early Chinese Christianity. First of all, it demonstrates the increasing contact between East and West in this period, and the increasing knowledge about the Mongols and China that must have been transmitted. Second, it also confirms that the Yelikewen church in China maintained contact with the mother church and its headquarters in Persia and had not become an independent "renegade" church body. Finally, the reception Bar Sauma received in Constantinople and Rome shows that while Westerners may still have referred to the Church of the East as "Nestorian," this did not prevent them from being viewed as fellow Christians. At a time when Albigensians and other heretics were being hunted down and executed across Europe, Bar Sauma was allowed to conduct his liturgy in Syriac in a Roman Catholic church in Rome. The Church of the East was not officially viewed as heretical.

Tombstones and Crosses

This chapter has demonstrated from a wide variety of documentary and literary sources that, even though it did not gain widespread adherence within

45. Borbone, *History of Mar Yahballaha and Rabban Sauma*, 155 (Syriac on 154).
46. Borbone, *History of Mar Yahballaha and Rabban Sauma*, 175 (Syriac on 174).

China, the Church of the East became a firmly established minority religion between the twelfth and fourteenth centuries, especially among the non-Han population. We will conclude this chapter by providing additional archaeological evidence for this. While we have no equivalent to the great Jingjiao stele, we do have a much more extensive collection of smaller artifacts that are useful in driving home some key points about the Yelikewen church.

Tombstones and funerary inscriptions are the most important physical witnesses we have for the Yelikewen Christianity of this period. From the eastern ends of the Silk Road and across the steppe regions, a large number of inscribed and decorated Christian tombstones have come to light over the past two centuries. Beginning in the 1880s, in the Semirechye or "Seven Rivers" region of what is now southeastern Kazakhstan, over six hundred Christian tombstones have been discovered, many of which contain Syriac inscriptions. Those that contain dates are mainly from the thirteenth and fourteenth centuries. Most feature a large central cross, some very crudely drawn, others more elegantly. The accompanying inscription is almost always in Syriac script, although the language is often Turkic. Dates are given in both the traditional method of the Church of the East (according to the Seleucid era) and using the twelve-year cycle of animal names used in Turkic and Chinese cultures. About 120 of the 300 males who were commemorated by such inscriptions held offices within the church. A typical inscription might read as follows:

In the year 1618 [AD 1307], the [Chinese] year of the sheep, and the Turkic year of the sheep. This is the tomb of Julia, beloved young woman, the bride of chorepiscopus John.[47]

An unusually elaborate one reads

In the year 1627 [AD 1316], the year of the eclipses, and the Turkic year of the dragon. This is the tomb of Shelicha, the famous exegete and preacher who enlightened all the monasteries with light; the son of the exegete Peter. He was famous for his wisdom, and when preaching his voice rang out like a trumpet. May our Lord unite his enlightened soul with those of the righteous and of the forefathers so that he may be worthy of participating in all glories.[48]

---

47. Yoshirō Saeki, *The Nestorian Documents and Relics in China*, 2nd ed. (Tokyo: Toho Bunkwa Gakuin/Academy of Oriental Culture, Tokyo Institute, 1951), 412–13.

48. Saeki, *The Nestorian Documents*, 414–15.

Two more short texts come from those recently published by Mark Dickens from the History Museum in Tashkent:

In the year 1605 [AD 1294], the year of the horse. This is the grave of Isaiah the priest, son of the church visitor Qutluq.

In the year of the dragon. This is the grave of the believer Sauma, son of Isho, the head of charity.[49]

In the past century many additional Christian tombstones, some with inscriptions, have come to light in the wider areas of Kazakhstan and Kyrgyzstan.

Two other substantial corpora have been added to this one. One we have mentioned earlier: the nearly eighty tombstones, most with funerary inscriptions, that have been found at Zayton/Quanzhou. As noted, these exhibit an even wider variety of language and cultural influences, with texts in Chinese, Phagspa, Syriac, and Turkic. A good example of this mixture is seen in the following trilingual inscription:

[Chinese] This is the tomb of Elizabeth, wife of Hindoo from Dadu [Khanbaliq/Beijing]. She died in her 33rd year and was buried on the 16th day of the 5th month [25th July]. She died on the 9th day of the 3rd month [20th May] of the Dingsi Yanyou year [AD 1317].
[Syriac] In the name of our Lord Jesus Christ.
[Turkic] In the year 1628 of the reckoning of King Alexander [the Great; AD 1317], in the Turkic year of the snake, in the 3rd month, on the 9th day [20th May], the lady Elizabeth, wife of John Sam-Sha of Dadu [Beijing], in her 33rd year carried out the command of God and laid aside her life. Her body was hidden inside this tomb. May her soul take up residence and a place with the pure princesses—Sarah, Rebecca and Rachel. May she be remembered in posterity and may her name remain forever . . .
[Syriac] Amen, yes and Amen.[50]

While the poor condition of the stones, and the difficulty of interpreting some of the Syro-Turkic, has made evaluation difficult, one message of the stones is clear. The Church of the East community on China's southeast coast was very interconnected with that of northern China and the steppes.

---

49. Mark Dickens, "Syriac Gravestones in the Tashkent History Museum," in Winkler and Tang, *Hidden Treasures and Intercultural Encounters*, 36–40.
50. Lieu et al., *Medieval Christian and Manichaean Remains*, 172–74.

The final corpus of tombstones comes from the Ongut regions of Inner Mongolia. These come in a variety of forms and styles, including a large number of decorated horizontal stone slabs. Again, they almost all prominently feature a cross. Some also have inscriptions in Syriac or Uyghur script. These are found scattered across the countryside and have recently been extensively studied and documented by Tjalling Halbertsma.[51] They clearly document the presence of Ongut Christians in the region (see figure 8).

In addition to these funerary remains and other miscellaneous objects,[52] we also have several thousand small bronze objects that have traditionally been referred to as "Nestorian crosses" or "Ordos crosses." These first came to the attention of Western collectors browsing the antique markets of Beijing in the early twentieth century. The F. A. Nixon collection, now in the University of Hong Kong Museum and Art Gallery, numbers just under one thousand. Another thousand have been documented in other museums and private collections. Cast in bronze, each is about 1.5 inches in height and width (4–6 cm), and each one is unique. Some are flat on the back, but others have vertical loops (as on a button); it is still unclear how they were used. Many have one or more crosses embedded within their overall design, while others are shaped like birds or have other geometrical shapes. There is also a wide variety of smaller designs within the larger shape, including swastikas. Several recent studies have surveyed the interpretation of these crosses and have sought to explain their historical and cultural significance.[53] Some have suggested that the mix of Christian and non-Christian elements is an indication that they came from a Christian community that had syncretized its beliefs with shamanistic and Buddhist elements (see figure 9).

It does seem clear that these "crosses" emanated from the Ongut community, which, as we have seen, had many Christians within it. But not all Onguts were Christian. In fact, the Ordos crosses provide a useful caution since there is a tendency to speak of a tribe "converting" to Christianity. Whether

---

51. Tjalling H. F. Halbertsma, *Early Christian Remains of Inner Mongolia: Discovery, Reconstruction, and Appropriation*, 2nd ed., revised, updated, and expanded (Leiden: Brill, 2015).

52. Among the miscellaneous objects are mirrors, bricks, and liturgical objects. See, for example, Niu Ruji, "History Is a Mirror: On the Spread of Nestorianism in China from the Newly Discovered Bronze Mirror with Cross-Lotus and Syriac Inscriptions," in Lieu and Thompson, *The Church of the East in Central Asia and China*, 177–88.

53. See the concise overview by Patrick Taveirne, "The Study of the Ordos 'Nestorian Bronze Crosses': Status Quaestionis," in Lieu and Thompson, *The Church of the East in Central Asia and China*, 213–33.

Kerait, Naiman, or Ongut, the conversion to Christianity of prominent tribal members or leaders of clans often did lead to a significant segment of the population changing its religious identity. What this meant in reality, however, was something quite different. As has been the case wherever Christianity has spread, it takes many generations for the tenets and practices of the faith to affect all aspects of the new culture it has entered. Symbols and concepts of the previous religion(s) are never instantly obliterated. As a result, we should not expect to see a complete change in the religious material culture either.

On the other hand, not everyone within a tribe converts when the leader does. Neither logic nor our sources would lead us to believe that the members of a tribe were always in lockstep in their religious beliefs. When they came into contact with outside cultures and religions, as happened again and again during this period, different members of the tribe reacted in different ways. Whether the influence was from Manichaeism, Buddhism, Islam, or Christianity, some were influenced to adopt some or all of the new ideas, and others were not. As the tribes became ever more integrated during the period of Genghis Khan and his successors, the mix must have only increased. Thus, the multifaceted aspect of these bronze objects, with only some being truly crosses and others having a mix of symbols, is in fact exactly what we should expect from the situation as we have described it. Those that are crosses should be interpreted as further evidence for a Christian community within the Ongut of the period; those that are not should remind us that the entire tribe was never Christian.

The Second Decline

During the thirteenth century, the Church of the East planted churches or expanded its earlier presence all along the eastern reaches of the Silk Road, across the steppes, and throughout the major cities of China. By the beginning of the fourteenth century, it seemed poised to put down even deeper roots into the local cultures. But that was not to be. Just as with the Jingjiao in the ninth century, a most promising situation changed very quickly. By 1400 there were few signs of Christianity left in China.

The Christian expansion had been fueled by the ease of communication established under the Mongolian Peace (*Pax Mongolica*), a name given to the safe and efficient trading environment made possible by Mongol control of the Silk Road from Persia all the way to China. Christianity had also benefited from the practice of religious tolerance that the Mongol rulers implemented. Both factors produced a period of accelerated expansion by the Church of the East.

This all began to fall apart in the early fourteenth century as the already partitioned Mongol Empire further disintegrated. The northwestern section that had become known as the Golden Horde adopted Islam in the 1310s and allied itself with the Mamluks in raids upon both the Christian West and Mongol Persia. The Yuan rulers in China descended into internecine rivalries. By the 1330s the Black Plague had begun in the steppes of northern China and in the following years spread throughout the region. A large number of the Christian graves from the Seven Rivers region of Kazakhstan date to 1338 and 1339 and were a result of the plague. The disease then traveled by sea and along the silk routes, reaching Constantinople in 1347. Millions across Europe and Asia died, and in China the suffering was increased by famine and drought. The foreign Mongol government became the focus of complaint, and the disasters were interpreted as a clear sign that the Yuan dynasty had lost its mandate of heaven. Chinese nationalists formed the White Lotus Society to work for the overthrow of the Yuan, and by the 1250s they formed the Red Turban Army. The Yuan rulers were too divided and incompetent to mount a coordinated resistance. By 1368, the rebels had captured Khanbaliq and had forced the Yuan rulers back into the steppes. In 1387 a new Ming dynasty was founded.

Meanwhile in Central Asia, throughout the 1260s a new Mongol leader named Timur had been gradually extending his power over the remnants of the Mongol Empire. Remembered today as Tamerlane, he claimed to continue the rule of Genghis Khan. Yet, as a Muslim, he called himself the "Sword of Islam." He ravaged and pillaged from India to Syria and Turkey, and, in the aftermath, many Central Asian tribes adopted Islam.

As had been the case with the Jingjiao in the ninth century, most of the Christians in China and the steppes were mere bystanders to these events. As we have seen, however, the Yelikewen presence in China had seemingly originated with and been strengthened by foreigners. In this case they were largely from the steppe tribes, and they could be found throughout the Yuan bureaucracy. The Christians in government undoubtedly remained loyal to the Yuan, and this would have been noted by the nationalist rebels. Once the Yuan were swept from power, the Yelikewen and the Christian religion in general would have been looked on with distaste, even if not formally outlawed, as had happened in the ninth century. The Christian base among the Mongol tribes was also effectively brought to an end by the Islamization that took place under Timur.

So it was that the second period of Syriac mission activity in China came to an end. The Church of the East came under renewed pressures in its Persian heartland, making it nearly impossible to send out new missionaries or bishops to the East. Communications were totally cut off between the mother church and any surviving groups within China or on the steppes. The Catholic presence in China suffered a similar fate. It would not be until the late sixteenth century that Catholic missionaries again entered China. When they did so, they searched but found almost no sign of the earlier Christian presence. Only a few tombstones and some widely scattered references in Chinese historical sources remained behind to be eventually rediscovered and thus to preserve the memory of both the Jingjiao and the Yelikewenjiao.

Epilogue

SO WHAT?

By the end of the fourteenth century, the Yelikewen Christians in China, as well as the churches among the steppe tribes and along the eastern half of the Silk Road, disappear from the Syriac records of the Church of the East. Timur and his Islamic horde had overrun the Silk Road countries and Mesopotamia, bringing renewed upheaval for Christians across the Middle East. The lack of any documentary or archaeological evidence must lead us to believe that Christianity again all but died out in Central Asia or China for a century or more. When about AD 1600 Jesuit missionaries slowly gained access to China, they searched for a Christian remnant but found none. The Yelikewen Christians they had heard about in the travelogues of Marco Polo, William of Rubruck, and others had by then seemingly disappeared without a trace. That is why they were overjoyed when one of their own converts, Li Zhizao, relayed to them the news of the discovery of the Chang'an Christian stele (as described in chap. 2). The impact of the discovery, however, was minimal in China for another three centuries. Western scholars debated the stele's authenticity, and Christian missionaries dismissed any earlier work that had been done as the product of heretical Nestorians. Doubters still claim that Marco Polo was exaggerating the presence of Christians in Yuan China.

The information presented in the preceding chapters should dispel all such doubts. The church did exist in China during both the Tang and the Yuan periods. Although it remained a small minority religion in both periods, its members could be found in the highest levels of government and its teachings had official recognition. The church did indeed exist in China during these periods; and where the Word was preached, it did bear fruit. We will close our story with some of the more important implications of that fact and with some relevant conclusions about the Jingjiao and Yelikewenjiao in China.

The Jingjiao and Yelikewenjiao as "Orthodox" Churches

Interest in early Chinese Christianity has been hindered by the perception that it was heretical and therefore of little interest to orthodox Christians. This idea has resulted from two main misconceptions or oversimplifications: that the Chinese church was "Nestorian," and that it had syncretized its belief with the other Chinese religions and worldviews, in particular Confucianism, Daoism, and Buddhism. This compromise not only caused an importation of non-Christian ideas but also led the church to minimize some of its own key teachings such as the crucifixion of Christ. An improper relationship between the Jingjiao and the imperial government was either a further cause or a result of these problems. This view concludes that the Jingjiao allowed itself to be improperly regulated by the emperor.

Our study does not claim to exhaustively evaluate all the teachings of the Church of the East nor to give a detailed analysis of its Christology. As Sebastian Brock and others have argued, however, most variations in its theological expressions from those of the Greek and Latin church have grown out of its different historical and linguistic circumstances.[1] These have caused suspicions and at times prevented the full practice of fellowship between the Syriac churches and their Western counterparts right up to the present. Yet we have noted several situations where leaders and clergy of Western churches, both Roman Catholic and Byzantine, had friendly interactions with and fellowshiped with leaders from the Church of the East in the fifth century and following—that is, even *after* the condemnation of Nestorius. On such occasions the Lord's Supper was often observed. Rabban Sauma was allowed both to participate in Catholic services during his trip to Europe and to perform the Syriac liturgy in a Roman Catholic church in Rome. These examples provide a convincing indication that the differences in christological formulations were often not considered heretical at the time.

While the Church of the East did respect Nestorius as a bold confessor who stood fast in his faith and endured imperial exile, there is little evidence that it taught the radical view that Christ had two separated natures, the accusation

---

1. The classic studies are those of Sebastian Brock, "The 'Nestorian' Church: A Lamentable Misnomer," *Bulletin of the John Rylands Library* 78, no. 3 (Autumn 1996): 23–35, and "The Christology of the Church of the East," in *Traditions and Heritage of the Christian East*, ed. D. Afinogenov and A. Muraviev (Moscow: Izdatelstvo "Indrik," 1966), 159–79. Both are reprinted with original pagination in Sebastian Brock, *Fire from Heaven: Studies in Syriac Theology and Liturgy*, Variorum Collected Studies Series (Aldershot, UK: Ashgate, 2006).

at the heart of Nestorius's condemnation. The Syriac church certainly thought that the Alexandrian christological terminology and emphases created their own problems, but normally they were much more concerned with countering the Monophysite position rather than the theology approved at Chalcedon. Political and turf wars between the Syriac-speaking Jacobite churches of the Middle East and the "Nestorian" Church of the East do loom rather large in the contemporary accounts of church history preserved in Syriac. Yet this is probably not a reflection of normal congregational concerns and parish life in the church. Nor was it the main motivation for the mission endeavors that led the Church of the East to India and along the Silk Road to China. Thus, while the Jingjiao and Yelikewenjiao were clearly arms of the Church of the East, this does not provide a reason for dismissing them as not being truly Christian churches.

Since the Western churches had become accustomed to uniformly use the designation "Nestorian" for the Church of the East, that name was automatically passed on to the Jingjiao and Yelikewenjiao, even if neither deserved it.[2] This has encouraged some scholars to seek evidence of Nestorian theology in the text of the Chang'an stele and other Jingjiao texts. Several claimed to have succeeded, most particularly in the stele's description of the Messiah's incarnation. The poem says in one line "dividing his being he came to earth" (26.13), and the commentary explains: "Therefore, our Three-One divided being, the luminous and honorable Messiah, concealing his true majesty, appeared as a human being" (6.4–6.7).

However, because this description is so concise, it is also ambiguous, typical of the classical Chinese of the stele text. We should thus be cautious in making any definitive conclusions about what is being taught about the relationship between the Messiah's two natures. Similarly, several of the Dunhuang documents speak of the Messiah as God's Son becoming man through a human birth. The concrete details of the incarnation are emphasized—that the Holy Spirit impregnated a virgin named Mary, who gave birth "without a man" (*Lord Messiah* 115–118). There is no attempt, however, to describe in detail the relationship between the divinity and the humanity of the Messiah. Much more attention is devoted to the fact that God sent a Messiah and to his innocent suffering, death, and resurrection. These documents, as mentioned earlier, are not extensive enough to allow us to write a complete Jingjiao Christology.

---

2. See Glen L. Thompson, "How the Jingjiao Became Nestorian," in *From the Oxus River to the Chinese Shores*, ed. Li Tang and Dietmar W. Winkler, Orientalia-Patristica-Oecumenica 5 (Vienna: LIT Verlag, 2013), 417–39.

Therefore, any conclusions about the teachings of the Jingjiao or Yelikewen-jiao on the relationship between Christ's natures must be treated as highly speculative.

More consistent and troubling have been the interpretations of some Jing-jiao documents as indicating a religious syncretism. Perhaps the most widely known version of this position is found in Martin Palmer's 2001 book *The Jesus Sutras: Rediscovering the Lost Scrolls of Taoist Christianity*. This inspired similar works with titles such as *The Lost Sutras of Jesus: Unlocking the Ancient Wisdom of the Xian Monks*.[3] Scholars agree that Confucian, Daoist, and Buddhist terminology and concepts are to be found in both the stele text and the Dunhuang documents.[4] But that is exactly what one would expect in texts produced in a missionary situation in China during the Tang dynasty. The church would undoubtedly have attempted to explain its teachings using the terminology and concepts of the dominant religious groups. This does not, however, explain away numerous problematic texts in which it is difficult to follow how Christian teaching is being distinguished from the Daoist or Buddhist concepts. This is especially true in *Origin* and *Mysterious Blessedness*, which seem especially Chinese in their approach as well as their lexical choices. However, the latter points to an evidently distinct body of "truthful and luminous teaching" (37) and, in a triple reiteration that concludes the text, proclaims that "only this supreme transcendent doctrine" of the Jingjiao can protect, provide for, and direct all creatures toward a life of truth and wisdom and eliminate sin and suffering (137–145). Thus, even *Mysterious Blessedness* is clearly claiming for the Jingjiao an independent and superior truth to that of other teachings. This leaves us with the question whether this distinct Jingjiao

---

3. Martin Palmer, *The Jesus Sutras: Rediscovering the Lost Scrolls of Taoist Christianity* (New York: Ballantine Books, 2001), and Ray Riegert and Thomas Moore, *The Lost Sutras of Jesus: Unlocking the Ancient Wisdom of the Xian Monks* (Berkeley, CA: Seastone, 2003).

4. For some more judicious discussions, see Stephen Eskildsen, "Parallel Themes in Chinese Nestorianism and Medieval Daoist Religion," and Chen Huiayu, "The Connection between Jingjiao and Buddhist Texts in Late Tang China," both in *Jingjiao: The Church of the East in China and Central Asia*, ed. Roman Malek, Collectanea Serica (Sankt Augustin, Germany: Institut Monumenta Serica, 2006), 57–91 and 93–113, respectively; Max Deeg, "Ways to Go and Not to Go in the Contextualisation of the Jingjiao Documents of the Tang Period," in *Hidden Treasures and Intercultural Encounters*, ed. Dietmar W. Winkler and Li Tang, Orientalia-Patristica-Oecumenica 1 (Vienna: LIT Verlag, 2009), 135–52; and Samuel N. C. Lieu, "Lost in Transcription? The Theological Vocabulary of Christian Texts in Central Asia and China," in *Winds of Jingjiao*, ed. Li Tang and Dietmar W. Winkler, Orientalia-Patristica-Oecumenica 9 (Vienna: LIT Verlag, 2016), 349–66.

teaching is that of traditional Christianity or is a new amalgam that was arrived at over the two centuries the church existed in Tang China.

One important piece of often-overlooked evidence is found in the ongoing relationship that the Jingjiao and Yelikewenjiao had with the "mother church," the Church of the East, headquartered in Persia. The Jingjiao began as a formal mission led by Alopen, an official representative of the Church of the East in Persia, and this led to its official recognition by the imperial court in Chang'an (*Stele* 11.3–13.5). The publicly displayed stele text mentions that on several occasions further reinforcements and replacements arrived from the far-off mother church (16.10–16.15; 18.6–18.8). Syriac sources also mention the appointment of bishops and metropolitans for the church in China. Thus, it is clear that the Jingjiao did not function on its own initiative but was clearly an arm of the Church of the East. There is also no evidence from either Chinese or Syriac sources that the Jingjiao was looked at with suspicion or was in any way taking its own course either in its doctrine or in its administration and loyalty. It began as a part of the Church of the East, and it remained so.

We have provided even clearer demonstrations of this for the Yelikewenjiao. Syriac church sources described the appointment in Persia of church leaders for the Chinese church. Members of the Church of the East traveled to China and became imperial officials and advisors. Most impressively, two Christian monks, born and bred in China, traveled across Central Asia, receiving honor and welcome from churches all along the way. When they arrived in Persia, one of them was elected to replace the recently deceased patriarch and became a longtime and revered catholicos of the Church of the East. The other was chosen to represent the Church of the East on an important diplomatic mission to the primates of the Greek and Latin churches and to the kings and courts of several major European countries. Nowhere in any of these stories do we find these travelers being surprised by new doctrines or hierarchies. The Yelikewenjiao church was merely a local configuration of the Church of the East. Lay Christians and clergy moved freely and comfortably between the Middle East and China and were received completely as brothers in the faith wherever they went.

Thus, while we continue to struggle to interpret the theological message intended in some of the Dunhuang texts, we must do so from the presupposition that the Chinese church of both the Tang and Yuan periods was an integral member of the Church of the East, and that the Church of the East taught the same basic message as all other Christian churches. If the orthodoxy and Christian teaching of the Jingjiao and Yelikemenjiao were not questioned by their contemporaries, we must also be careful not to question them. What has been said about the Turfan Yelikewen community is equally valid for the rest of the Jingjiao and Yelikewen church:

> The Sogdian and Turkish language of Turfan's small Christian community is very much in the tradition of its East Syrian–Nestorian mother church, whose spiritual center Baghdad is far away, but which is present in its Syrian church and liturgical language. Regardless of the overwhelming preponderance of other religions, the texts translated into the vernacular do not reveal any syncretism to the detriment of its normal tradition: they are orthodox in the sense of Nestorian Christianity.[5]

Evaluating Relationships with the Tang and Yuan Governments

Some studies of the Jingjiao have pointed to its official relationship with the imperial government as an inappropriate policy decision and one of the causes of its own demise. The stele text makes it very clear that the initial establishment of the Jingjiao was approved by the Tang court bureaucracy. The commentary section of the stele not only cites Taizong's imperial decree to that effect (11.9–13.5) but further highlights numerous occasions when that relationship was confirmed by interactions between the government and the church. Taizong had provided imperial portraits for display within the Jingjiao complex (13.10–14.2). Gaozong gave honorary titles to Alopen (15.11). Xuanzong in particular seems to have made that relationship clear. He ordered a delegation of princes to attend the rededication of Jingjiao buildings (17.1–4) and sent along imperial gifts of silk and portraits (17.6–18.5). He further commanded Jingjiao priests to perform prayers for him in one of his palaces (18.9–18.11) and in return composed a special poem and presented this to them in his own calligraphy (18.12–19.7). The rebuilding of churches under the patronage of Suzong (19.12–20.2) and Daizong's granting of special gifts to the church on his birthday (20.8–20.10) are also noted. By providing this detailed list of interactions with the imperial court and favors granted to it by the emperors, the author is going out of his way to emphasize this harmonious relationship between church and state. Therefore, one can see that this might be viewed as

---

5. Wolfgang Hage, "Das Christentum in der Turfan-Oase: Zur Begegnung der Religionen in Zentralasien," in *Synkretismus in den Religionen Zentralasiens*, ed. Walther Heissig and Hans-Joachim Klimkeit, Studies in Oriental Religions 13 (Wiesbaden: Otto Harrassowitz, 1987), 55 (my translation).

problematic by modern Western scholars, imbued with the ideals of a separation between church and state.

Such a comparison, however, is unfair. When the Jingjiao was officially recognized by the Tang court, it was not an innovation. Government oversight of religions within China stretches back at least to the Han dynasty (206 BC to AD 220). Not only adherents to "foreign" religions like Manichaeans and Zoroastrians but also the more mainstream local groups such as Buddhists and Daoists were put under the supervision of a state office. This practice was continued by the Tang and later by the Yuan governments. The latter, as we have seen in the previous chapter, created a special office just for the Yelikewen Christians, and usually a Christian was put in charge of it. Thus, there was no reason for the Church of the East to expect to be exempt from government approval and, to some extent, regulation. When in the mid-twentieth century the Chinese Communist government created a Religious Affairs Bureau to oversee the current religions of China, they were in fact continuing a long-established precedent.

This would not have appeared as something new to the Church of the East either. They could easily cite Romans 13:1–7 to show that it was the duty of Christians, and therefore the church, to be subject to the God-ordained government. In the highly enculturated excursus on the Ten Commandments in *Lord Messiah*, obedience to the emperor is emphatically taught (62–77 and 81–85). The Church of the East had been living under the same reality in Persia for as long as could be remembered. Already in the mid-fourth century, when the Christians of Persia were first establishing a hierarchical structure and the numerous bishops were seeing the need for a larger organization, the Sasanian ruler began using the bishop of Seleucia as a spokesman and intermediary between himself and his Christian subjects. When in the early fifth century the bishop of Seleucia became recognized as the leader of the entire church, with the title of catholicos or patriarch, he naturally continued to serve as intermediary between the church and the Sasanian government. Although the government officially allowed Christians freedom of worship, frequent persecutions took place in the following centuries, and so the patriarch often had to approach the government for redress or protection. The same situation prevailed after the Muslim conquest of Persia in the seventh century. Jews and Christians each had the legal status of a permitted religious minority (*dhimmi*), and the patriarch of the Church of the East was recognized by the government as the leader and spokesman for the Christians. As a result, it soon became necessary for the Islamic ruler to approve the choice of a new catholicos. While this relationship was far from smooth, over the long run it "worked" in Persia, and the church made the best of a less-than-ideal situation. This must be seen as the background for the Church of the East's cooperation with the imperial court of China as well. While it may not have been the relationship the church would have chosen, they had learned to function under such relationships, preserving as much independence as possible. Chinese Christians today will find some apt comparisons with their own situation.

Christianity Did Come from the West, But . . .

In the nineteenth and twentieth centuries, Christianity came to China again, and now it appears to have established itself more permanently. Its adherents may number as many as 100 million when one includes both Protestants and Catholics, and both registered and unregistered groups. It has continued to spread despite xenophobic attempts to keep it out, militant attacks during the Boxer Rebellion, antagonism from nationalists in the first half of the twentieth century, the expulsion of all foreign Christian workers, the severing of all contacts with Christians outside China, violent attempts to suppress it entirely during the Cultural Revolution, and a seventy-five-year period of intense government regulation that continues yet today. During this period of growth, one of the objections that has been continuously raised by its Chinese opponents is that Christianity is a "Western religion." By this they not only mean that Christianity came from the outside but also that it was part and parcel of European colonial expansion and a tool of capitalist Western nations seeking to dominate or at least enfeeble China. They regard it as yet another attempt to marginalize traditional Chinese culture and destroy its rich heritage.

As we have seen, the Jingjiao and Yelikewenjiao did come from the "West," but not from the capitalist European or North American "West." It was not brought by colonialists along with opium and tea, although it did come with international traders and some new science and technology. It came directly from the Middle East, the place where Christianity and its founder had both been born. It was brought by traders and missionaries who helped fuel one of China's greatest periods of economic and cultural strength and prosperity, the Tang dynasty. It flowered a second time during the Yuan period, a time during which Genghis and Kublai Khan (and the Mongolian Peace they created) renewed the connection between China and the Middle East and Europe. Christianity first came to China along the Silk Road and not on European gunboats or via unequal treaties.

The Christianity that returned with the Catholic and Protestant missionaries in the past several centuries was the same Christianity and has the same worldview as the Jingjiao and Yelikewenjiao. There is no need for the Chinese authorities to view it as "a Western threat." Its adherents are loyal to their country and to much of their Chinese heritage. Just as earlier Christians, they too do not see a need to make a choice between their Christian beliefs and their Chinese identity. It is misguided to see the situation as an either/or choice. Jingjiao Christians like Yisi fought loyally to preserve the throne for the Tang. Jingjiao clergy offered up their prayers for the emperor. Yelikewen members held high governmental positions; some were princes and the wives of khans, and others served in the lower levels of the imperial administration. They functioned as astronomers like the later Jesuits, and as physicians like many later Protestant missionaries. They worked as translators and educators just as later missionaries did. Neither the Tang nor the Yuan dynasties lost the mandate of heaven due to the impact of their Christian subjects, and there is no reason to think that modern China will be any different. China's current "One Belt and One Road" initiative is modeled on the ancient Silk Road, and it provides an opportunity for reversing the modern xenophobic trends as well. Chinese Christians wish to serve their country and to help it establish the rule of law and provide all the benefits of a peaceful civil society. Its message is only a threat to the evil of this world. The Jingjiao could be used as a model that service to Christ can coexist with patriotism.

What about My Ancestors?

When Christianity enters a new culture or people group, one of the questions often asked by new converts is, "What about my ancestors who did not have a chance to hear the Christian message?" This is both an emotionally charged question and one that is difficult to answer in a satisfying way. The Scripture that provides the church with its teaching is very clear that there is one way to God—through trust in the atoning sacrifice of his son, Jesus Christ. And what about those who never heard this message? All that we can do is point to the fact that our Creator God, the Lord of the Universe, is also a just God, and whatever he does will be just. It will not be our decision. Yet at the same time, God has given us a role to play. Jesus has left us with his "Great Commission" to make sure no one fails to hear the message. Every Christian is charged to share the gospel at every opportunity, so that everyone will hear the wonderful message of God's grace and Christ's righteousness that covers our sin.

The Jingjiao and Yelikewenjiao stories are two lesser-known parts of that story, and we hope that our readers can now see that the Word that was sown along the Silk Road, across the steppes and all the way to the capital cities of ancient China, did indeed bear fruit. Indeed, Christian laypeople and missionaries from Persia and Central Asia helped Chinese men and women come to the faith over numerous centuries even though the Western church was (and still is) almost totally unaware of this! If that is the case, then we can pray that similar stories took place in many other regions of the world, and that the Word has reached far beyond the places that we know about.

But for today's Chinese Christians, this story is equally important. Although they may not have the equivalent of the traditional ancestor tablets to prove it, it is certainly possible that some of their ancestors did indeed hear the gospel message, whether in Syriac, Uyghur, Turkic, or Chinese. As we have seen, our surviving sources only allow us to trace the merest outlines of the church's presence in China during the Tang and Yuan periods. There is little hope that we will ever be able to fill in the details of the story completely. But we do know that the Word achieves the goal for which our God sends it out (Isa. 55:11). And that is a message that, together with the story of the Jingjiao and Yelikewenjiao, should offer some comfort to contemporary Chinese Christians.

Can Christianity Become Truly Chinese?

Some have claimed that the Jingjiao and Yelikewenjiao failed to take root more deeply because they never truly became Chinese. Others have come to the opposite conclusion—that these churches became too Chinese and lost their distinctive Christian teaching, and that this led to their demise. In the final decades of the twentieth century, Bishop K. H. Ting (d. 2012), the head of the Three Self Patriotic Movement (the legal Protestant church in China), began calling for a "reconstruction of theological thinking" to make Christianity and other Chinese religions even more Chinese. His voice has been co-opted by the government. The Chinese church must undergo a total "Sinification" if it is to be allowed to continue to function. But how exactly can the Christian church become more Chinese in an authentic way while remaining thoroughly Christian?[6]

6. An unofficial English translation of the China Christian Council's five-year plan for Sinicizing the Chinese church (2018–2022) can be found at https://www.ucanews.com /news/protestant-five-year-plan-for-chinese-christianity/ 82107, accessed December 6, 2022. That document cites approvingly a 2017 publication of Bishop Ting's works on Sinicization.

The indigenization of the church has taken on greater urgency and greater importance in China than in many other countries because of the millennia-old traditions of Chinese culture. While the dominant Han Chinese ethnic stock is certainly not pure and has been interwoven genetically with many of the numerous ethnic minorities found within its borders, many of the basic cultural norms—an emphasis on filial piety, correct behavior, social harmony, and family cohesion—have continued to be identity markers for centuries. The Confucian goal of harmonious relationships here on earth has outlived dynastic changes and communist propaganda. The pride in Chinese traditional medicine, classical wisdom, and the arts has stood the test of time. The slow infiltration of Daoism and Buddhism into the fabric of traditional religion and mythology has created a unique amalgam that continues to live even in the vast majority of Chinese who are religiously nonpracticing. A balance between an inbred commercial competitiveness and a tremendous sense of family honor results in a remarkable energy but also deep-seated inner anxieties. And now this has all been challenged and reevaluated by an atheistic government that swears to uphold its socialist values while encouraging rapid economic growth through capitalist enterprises. This is the enigmatic reality of modern China.

So how can the church become more Chinese? During the Tang period, the foreign Syriac element of the Jingjiao remained on display. People of foreign descent continued to dominate the higher positions within the church, and the Syriac language remained somewhat prominent. This was less so during the Yelikewen period, as Syriac was joined by Sogdian and various Turkic languages within the church. Whether Chinese ever became the dominant language of either of these early churches is questionable. The Chinese church today no longer has this problem. It is today clearly Chinese in leadership and in language.

The Jingjiao did make use of both the terminology and conceptual categories of Daoism, Buddhism, and Confucianism in its attempts to explain its own teaching among the Chinese. As we have argued, however, there is no reason to believe that this led to a surrendering of its Christian tenets. The original teachings and practices of Buddhism, on the other hand, were malleable enough to adapt to and adopt aspects of Chinese religions. Elements of traditional Chinese beliefs and of Daoism were incorporated into what became a number of distinctive Chinese forms of Buddhism. Christianity did not have that option. From the beginning it equated a distinct body of teaching with the only way to salvation. Although that teaching was refined and its terminology became more specialized over the centuries, its basic "rule of faith" had to remain intact. Any group that departed from it was quickly excluded from the "fellowship" of the larger church. As we have seen, that did not happen to either the Jingjiao or the Yelikewenjiao.

On the one hand, both the Jingjiao and Yelikewenjiao retained the central liturgical and sacramental practices of the Church of the East. On the other hand, the Jingjiao did make use of many other Chinese cultural distinctives. The poem composed for the Chang'an stele was a typical classical Chinese "ode," 頌 (*song*), and the poem with commentary format was also similar to other such public texts. The Dunhuang documents make use of many of the literary and stylistic features found in other Tang texts. The monks were able to take part in some palace rituals, and yet they retained other outward distinctives (beards and tonsures), while Christians stood out from their peers for their emphasis on equality, chastity, feeding the hungry, clothing the poor, and tending the sick (*Stele* 9.1–9.8; 25.10–26.12). Jingjiao and Yelikewen Christians could serve as priests while also holding government positions or serving in the army. In other words, they functioned as responsible Chinese citizens in their daily life while simultaneously practicing their Christian faith.

This is what Chinese Christians attempt to do today as well. Yet too many Chinese Christians view modern evangelicalism, with its blend of Arminian and Pentecostal theology and American-style Free Church ecclesiology and practice, as almost equivalent in its essence to the Bible and its theology. The Jingjiao can remind us that this is not true. A nondemocratic approach to doctrine, a commitment to liturgy and sacraments, a connection to the primitive mother church and its doctrinal creeds—all these are options that the modern Chinese church should seriously consider. These attributes also, after being appropriately enculturated, will be instrumental in helping to produce a godly and Christian Chinese church.

We do not know how Jingjiao Christians dealt with some of the problems that later Christians faced—how to show respect for ancestors without crossing the line into ancestor worship; how they could continue to value traditional Chinese wisdom and classics without doing obeisance to Confucius. Universally accepted solutions to these and similar problems would elude Chinese Christians right up to the twentieth century. Yet, when solutions were found, they most likely did not come from the outside but were the product of mature Christian thinking and prayer by devout Chinese Christians. At the same time, we recognize that the writings of great Christian thinkers from a variety of ages and cultures can be of assistance in thinking through such issues. Any attempt to forcibly cut off the Chinese church from outside Christian contacts is therefore regrettable and, if anything, will only hinder Chinese Christian leaders in their attempt to formulate God-pleasing answers to the theological and practical problems faced by their Chinese flocks; that is, it will only hinder them from making the church in China more Chinese.

A total Sinicization of the Chinese church will never be fully accomplished, nor should it be. The Chinese church is part of the larger worldwide fellowship of believers, and that larger church will profit from its contacts with the Chinese church just as much as the reverse is true. The church of the Middle Kingdom should be a centerpiece in the worldwide Christian church! As elsewhere, however, enculturation will only grow out of deep reflection on God's Word and its implementation in the local Christian community's life of worship and service. To do that will require first and foremost a fresh look at Scripture itself. One can appreciate the cautions about adopting Western models of interpretation and Western denominationalism. The only true improvements upon such borrowing, however, will come when a generation of Bible scholars arise in China who are thoroughly at home in the ancient texts of Scripture in their original languages. That is the most foundational tool for examining one's own culture from a truly biblical point of view. Only then can Chinese Christians distinguish what is "biblical" from what is the product of Christian traditions within specific cultures.

There is not much evidence that large portions of Scripture were available in Chinese translation during the Tang and Yuan periods.[7] Sections were certainly translated, especially the ones used in liturgical worship, but that our Dunhuang Christian texts contain no direct translations of Scripture may well point to a key weakness in their approach. Modern Chinese churches do not have that problem. However, the ability to read the inspired texts in their

---

7. It should be noted that in the list of writings given in the *Book of the Honored*, the Gospels and books of King David, the apostles, Paul, Zechariah, Moses, and Elijah are all listed among those that had been translated, and many if not all of these may well refer to portions of Scripture. See the various competing interpretations provided by Johan Ferreira, *Early Chinese Christianity: The Tang Christian Monument and Other Documents*, Early Christian Studies 17 (Sydney: St. Paul's Publications, 2014), 270–80; Matteo Nicolini-Zani, *The Luminous Way to the East: Texts and History of the First Encounter of Christianity with China* (Oxford: Oxford University Press, 2022), 228–32; and Li Tang, *A Study of the History of Nestorian Christianity in China and Its Literature in Chinese: Together with a New English Translation of the Dunhuang Nestorian Documents*, 2nd rev. ed. (Frankfurt am Main: Lang, 2004), 185–88. However, extant manuscripts of Chinese translations of Scripture during the Tang period are not found among the Dunhuang documents and the Turfan fragments.

original language and then apply them to Chinese culture will be the only way that the Chinese church can continue to become more Sinicized in a godly way. Only then can the Way taught by the Sage—the Messiah—truly spread as it was intended to.

～

In Jesus's parable of the rich man and Lazarus, the rich man (now in hell) asks Abraham (in heaven) to resurrect Lazarus and send him back to earth to warn his brothers; in that way they will avoid his fate. Abraham answers, "They have Moses and the Prophets; if they do not believe them, they will not believe someone who rises from the dead" (see Luke 16:23–31). We have tried to "resurrect" the story of the Jingjiao and Yelikewenjiao and bring that story back to life. It is a story that holds special interest to Christians, and especially to Chinese Christians. It may even be of some use to believers when talking about Christianity with Chinese unbelievers. Such a story of faith and perseverance cannot itself work miracles, but it is yet another account of the power of the gospel, and that good news is still what is most needed in China and in the rest of the world. Let us pray it will inspire a new generation of heralds.

Appendix 1: The Chang'an Stele

We have included below a fairly literal English translation of the Chang'an stele, together with the Chinese text. It has been laid out by the sense unit system used in my book so as to enable the reader to better grasp the nature of the Chinese literary format.[1] The Syriac portions are given separate line numbers (in brackets, and with an uppercase *S* preceding the line number, as in the system of Eccles and Lieu[2]). In the Chinese text, " [" marks the end/beginning of each new column, and the numbers one or two in parentheses denote the honorific blank spaces in the text. The punctuation in the Chinese text in general follows that of Weng Shao Jun's Hong Kong edition of the text.[3] When the text of Eccles/Lieu and that of Weng disagree on the choice of some characters, I have chosen the option that is closest to that depicted on the stele. The headings that I have added to clarify the text's subdivisions agree in most places with those of Eccles and Lieu.

1. Note that there are several improvements in the marking of the sense units since my initial attempt was published in my article "The Structure of the Stele," in *Artifact, Text, Context*, ed. Li Tang and Dietmar W. Winkler, Orientalia-Patristica-Oecumenica 17 (Vienna: LIT, 2020), 184–93.

2. Lance Eccles and Samuel N. C. Lieu, "Stele on the Diffusion of Christianity (The Luminous Religion) from Rome (Da Qin) into China (The Middle Kingdom), 'The Nestorian Monument,'" March 26, 2022, http://www.unionacademique.org/content/files/1036 2790247079243.pdf.

3. Weng Shao Jun, *Sino-Nestorian Documents: Commentary and Exegesis*, Chinese Academic Library of Christian Thought in History (Hong Kong: Institute of Sino-Christian Studies, 1995), 44-80.

Column and sense unit	Text	Translation
Super-scription	大秦景教流行中國碑	Stele concerning the Luminous Teaching from Da Qin Spreading in the Middle Kingdom
1.1	景教流行中國碑頌並序	Stele concerning the Luminous Teaching's Spreading in the Middle Kingdom; poem with commentary
2.1	大秦寺僧景淨述	Composed by the monk Jingjing of the Da Qin Monastery.
[S1]	ܐܕܡ ܩܫܝܫܐ ܘܟܘܪܐܦܝܣܩܘܦܐ ܘܦܦܫܝ ܕܨܝܢܣܬܢ	Adam, priest and chorepiscopus and *papshi* of China

Part 1. Commentary

1.1 The Eternal God

3.1	粵若	So:
3.2	常然真寂,	The profoundly still and unchanging one,
3.3	先先而无元,	the first of the first without beginning,
3.4	窅然靈虛,	the all-knowing one,
3.5	後後而妙有。	is the last of the last and everlasting one.
3.6	惣玄摳而造化,	The impenetrable core of creation
3.7	妙眾聖以元尊者;	is worthy of utmost reverence among the host of sages.
3.8	其唯 (2) 我三一妙身	Is he not our Three-One wondrous being,
3.9	无元真主	the True Lord who is without beginning,
3.10	阿羅訶歟?	Aluohe [Elohim]?

Column and sense unit	Text	Translation

1.2 Creation of the World and Man

3.11	判十字以定四方,	He created the cross character to establish the four corners of the world;
3.12	鼓元風而生[二氣。	he stirred up the original wind and brought to life the two forces.
4.1	暗空易而天地開,	The dark and void were changed, and heaven and earth came into being;
4.2	日月運而晝夜作。	sun and moon began to move and day and night commenced.
4.3	匠成万物,	Working skillfully, he created 10,000 creatures,
4.4	然立初人。	and then he created the first man.
4.5	別賜良和,	He bestowed goodness and harmony on him,
4.6	令鎮化海。	and commanded him to govern land and sea.
4.7	渾元之性,	The very first human nature
4.8	虛而不盈。	was empty and not full.
4.9	素蕩之心,	It had an opaque naiveté of heart;
4.10	本無希嗜。	at its foundation was an absence of desires.

1.3 Satan and the Fall

4.11	洎乎 娑殫施妄,	However, Satan spread delusions to deceive
4.12	鈿飾純精。	the sinless being with gilt ornaments.
4.13	間平大於 [此是之中,	He planted the idea of equal greatness inside the one man;
5.1	隙冥同於彼非之內。	he fractured the deep unity inside the other creature.
5.2	是以三百六十五種,	Thus 365 offspring arose;

Column and sense unit	Text	Translation
5.3	肩隨結轍。	shoulder to shoulder each followed the path.
5.4	競織法羅,	They vied in weaving a system of teaching;
5.5	或指物以託宗,	Some pointed to inanimate things to help their ancestors;
5.6	或空有以淪二,	some emptied their beings to receive "the two";
5.7	或禱祀以邀福,	some prayed and sacrificed to increase their good fortune;
5.8	或伐善以矯人。	some exaggerated their goodness to deceive men.
5.9	智慮營營,	Their intelligence and concerns are always vacillating;
5.10	恩情役役。	their kindness and emotion are always frivolous.
5.11	茫然[無得,	They are confused and make no moral progress;
6.1	煎迫轉燒,	They are boiled, coerced and toasted on all sides.
6.2	積昧亡途,	They amassed foolishness and lost their way;
6.3	久迷休復。	For ages they are lost and are not restored.

1.4 The Incarnation

6.4	於是	Therefore,
	(2) 我三一分身	our Three-One divided being,
6.5	景尊彌施訶	the luminous and honorable Messiah,
6.6	戢隱真威	concealing his true majesty,
6.7	同人出代。	appeared as a human being.
6.8	神天宣慶,	God in heaven proclaimed a celebration;

Column and sense unit	Text	Translation
6.9	室女誕聖於大秦。	a virgin gave birth to a sage in Da Qin.
6.10	景宿告祥，	A luminous star announced the good news;
6.11	波斯睹耀以來貢。	in Persia they saw it shining and came with tribute.

1.5 The Messiah's Work and Teaching

6.12	圓廿四聖[有說之舊法，	Thus, he fulfilled the ancient word told by the 24 sages,
7.1	理家國於大猷。	regulating both family and nation through his great plan.
7.2	設 (1) 三一淨風無言之新教，	Thus, he established the new teaching unspoken by the Three-One Pure Spirit,
7.3	陶良用於正信。	modeling good practice through proper belief.
7.4	制八境之度，	He created the rules of the eight regions,
7.5	鍊塵成真。	refining the dust into something real.
7.6	啟三常之門，	He opened the door of the three constants,
7.7	開生滅死。	initiating life and extinguishing death.
7.8	懸景日以破暗府，	The Luminous Sun was hung up to dispel the darkness,
7.9	魔妄於是乎悉摧。	and so the devil and the arrogant were totally destroyed.
7.10	棹慈[航以登明宮，	He rowed a voyage of mercy so they could enter the bright palace,
8.1	含靈於是乎既濟。	and thus the people could finish crossing.
8.2	骹事斯畢，	When he had finished his work,
8.3	亭午昇真。	at midday he rose into the air.

Column and sense unit	Text	Translation
	1.6 The Church and Its Life	
8.4	經留廿七部,	He left behind twenty-seven books
8.5	張元化以發靈關。	which proclaim the fundamental change that opens the gate of the soul.
8.6	法浴水風,	In their rites they wash with water and spirit,
8.7	滌浮華而潔虛白。	washing away the superficial and cleansing the artificially pure.
8.8	印持十字,	Their seal contains the cross character
8.9	融四照以合無拘。	combining the four ways of knowing to be suitable for all without restriction.
8.10	擊木震仁惠之音,	Striking the wood, they arouse tones of kindness and benefit;
8.11	東[礼趣生榮之路。	worshiping facing east, they advance the path to life and glory.
9.1	存鬚所以有外行,	To show their identity, they keep their beards;
9.2	削頂所以無內情。	to show the lack of internal desire, they shave their heads.
9.3	不畜臧獲,	They keep neither slaves nor women,
9.4	均貴賤於人。	but treat equally the honorable and lowly.
9.5	不聚貨財,	They do not store up goods or wealth,
9.6	示罄遺於我。	but show they lack possessions by giving away what remains.
9.7	齋以伏識而成,	They abstain from meat to cleanse their minds and develop themselves;
9.8	戒以靜慎為固。	they check their passions, practicing restraint and strengthening themselves.

Column and sense unit	Text	Translation
9.9	七時礼讚,	Seven times a day they worship and pray,
9.10	大庇存亡。	greatly benefiting the living and the dead.
9.11	七日一薦,	Every seven days they make one offering,
10.1	[洗心反素。	to cleanse the heart and make it pure.

1.7 Praise for the Luminous Teaching

10.2	真常之道,	The true and constant way
10.3	妙而難名。	is mysterious and difficult to name.
10.4	功用昭彰,	Its merits are manifest,
10.5	強稱景教。	so we call it the Luminous Teaching.
10.6	惟道非聖不弘,	Without the Sage, the Way could not expand;
10.7	聖非道不大。	without the Way, the Sage could not become great.
10.8	道聖符契,	But the Way is in conformity with the Sage,
10.9	天下文明。	and together they will enlighten the world.

1.8 Taizong and Alopen

10.10	(2)太宗文皇帝	Taizong, a cultured emperor,
10.11	光華啟運,	shone brightly and created new fortune,
10.12	明聖臨人。	a brilliant sage governing his people.
10.13	大秦國有上德	In Da Qin there was a man of excellent virtue,
10.14	曰阿[羅本。	his name was Alopen.
11.1	占青雲而載真經,	He observed the heavens and carried the true scriptures here;
11.2	望風律以馳艱險。	he studied the winds and hurried past great perils.

Column and sense unit	Text	Translation
11.3	貞觀九祀,	In the ninth year of the Zhenguan era,
11.4	至於長安。	he arrived at Chang'an.
11.5	(2)帝使宰臣房公玄齡惣仗西郊,	The emperor sent his minister of state, Duke Fang Xuanling, to receive him in the western suburbs
11.6	賓迎入內。	and to bring him in with a warm welcome.
11.7	翻經書殿,	After his scriptures were translated in the royal library,
11.8	問道禁闈。	the palace officials investigated their teaching.
11.9	深知正真,	After thoroughly understanding it to be suitable and true,
11.10	特令傳授。	special permission was given for its propagation.

1.9 Taizong's Edict Allowing the Propagation of the Luminous Teaching

11.11	貞觀十有二[年秋七月, 詔曰:	Autumn, the seventh month of the twelfth year of the Zhenguan reign; the imperial decree is as follows:
12.1	道無常名,	The way has no single name;
12.2	聖無常體,	the holy takes no single form.
12.3	隨方設教,	When teachings vary from place to place,
12.4	密濟群生。	they give the greatest help to the largest number of people.
12.5	大秦國大德阿羅本。	Alopen is a man of great virtue from Da Qin.
12.6	遠將經像,	He has brought books and images from afar
12.7	來獻上京。	and presented them at the capital.

Column and sense unit	Text	Translation
12.8	詳其教旨,	He thoroughly explained their teachings—
12.9	玄妙無為。	challenging, wonderful and serene in their operation.
12.10	觀其元宗,	When its original teaching is discerned,
12.11	生成立要。	it appears already mature.
12.12	詞無繁說,	Its words have no complicated meaning,
12.13	理有忘筌。	so when understood it is not forgotten.
13.1	[濟物利人,	Since it aids all creatures and profits mankind,
13.2	宜行天下。	it is proper that it be propagated everywhere.
13.3	所司即於京義寧坊	Therefore, in the Yining neighborhood of the capital, officials should immediately
13.4	造大秦寺一所,	construct one Da Qin temple,
13.5	度僧廿一人。	and allow twenty-one men to serve there as monks.

1.10 The Edict is Carried Out

13.6	宗周德喪,	The virtue of the Zhou has departed,
13.7	青駕西昇。	and Laozi's chariot has disappeared into the west.
13.8	巨唐道光,	But now, under the great Tang, the Way is rising,
13.9	景風東扇。	and the Luminous Teaching is blowing into the east.
13.10	旋令有司將 (1)帝寫真 轉摸寺壁。	Quickly officials were ordered to offer the imperial portrait, for copy and display upon the temple walls.

Column and sense unit	Text	Translation
13.11	天姿汎彩,	The heavenly visage radiated color,
13.12	英朗[景門。	it [shone] with bold brightness in the Luminous temple.
14.1	聖跡騰祥,	The sacred image fluttered with good fortune,
14.2	永輝法界。	eternally lustrous in its rule of society.

1.11 Chinese Records Describing Da Qin

14.3	案《西域圖記》及漢魏史策,	According to the *Illustrated Records of the Western Regions* and to the historical records of the Han and Wei dynasties,
14.4	大秦國 南統珊瑚之海,	the land of Da Qin overlooks to its south a coral sea,
14.5	北極眾寶之山,	to its north it abuts mountains of great treasure;
14.6	西望仙境花林,	to its west lie the borders of the immortal realm and dense forests,
14.7	東接長風弱水。	to its east it meets the eternal winds and the mild waters.
14.8	其土出 火綄布 、	Its earth produces asbestos,
14.9	返魂香 、	restorative fragrances,
14.10	明月珠 、	moon pearls,
14.11	夜光璧。	and jade that glows in the dark.
15.1	[俗無寇盜,	There is no thievery there;
15.2	人有樂康。	the people are content.
15.3	法非景不行,	No religion exists but the Luminous Teaching;
15.4	主非德不立。	no ruler is put on the throne unless he is virtuous.

Column and sense unit	Text	Translation
15.5	土宇廣闊，	The land is broad and extensive,
15.6	文物昌明。	and its cultural life prosperous and enlightened.

1.12 Gaozong

15.7	(2)高宗大帝	Gaozong, the great emperor,
15.8	克恭纘祖，	ably and respectfully continued the policy of his predecessor,
15.9	潤色真宗。	and enhanced the true traditions,
15.10	而於諸州各置景寺，	Luminous temples were established in every prefecture;
15.11	仍崇阿羅本為鎮國大法主。	he honored Alopen with the title "Grand Master of Religious Teaching and Protector of the Nation."
15.12	法流十[道，	Religion spread to the ten regions,
16.1	國富元休。	the country prospered, and its foundations flourished.
16.2	寺滿百城，	Temples could be found in one hundred walled cities,
16.3	家殷景福。	and the Luminous Teaching blessed many families.

1.13 Setbacks During the Shengli and Xiantian Periods

16.4	聖曆年	In the Shengli period [AD 698–700],
16.5	釋子用壯	Buddhists used their influence
16.6	騰口於東周。	and raised their voices in the eastern capital [Luoyang].
16.7	先天末	In the Xiantian era [AD 712–713],
16.8	下士大笑	low-ranking scholars stirred up ridicule,
16.9	訕謗於西鎬，	spreading slander in the western capital [Chang'an];

Column and sense unit	Text	Translation
16.10	有若僧首羅含,	then people arose like the head monk Luohan,
16.11	大德及烈,	and the man of great virtue Jilie;
16.12	並金方貴緒,	both were from a noble place and of noble heritage,
16.13	物外高僧,	otherworldly men and senior monks;
16.14	共振玄網,	together they restored the mysterious net.
16.15	俱維[絕紐。	together they tied up the knot that had been cut.

1.14 Xuanzong and the Restoration

17.1	(2)玄宗至道皇帝	Xuanzong, the emperor of perfect understanding,
17.2	令寧國等五王親臨福宇,	ordered the Prince of Ning and other princes (five in all) to personally visit the sacred building,
17.3	建立壇場。	and to restore the altar and sanctuary.
17.4	法棟暫橈而更崇,	The sacred pillars, toppled for a time, rose straight again and to new heights;
17.5	道石時傾而復正。	the stones, displaced for a time, were again realigned.
17.6	天寶初,	At the start of the Tianbao era [AD 742–756],
17.7	令大將軍高力士送(2)五聖寫真寺內安置。	he ordered the great general Gao Lishi be sent with five imperial portraits to be installed inside the temple.
17.8	賜絹百[疋	He also gave one hundred bolts of silk,

Column and sense unit	Text	Translation
18.1	奉慶睿圖。	for the dedication of the portraits of the emperors.
18.2	龍髯雖遠，	Although the beard of the dragon was far away,
18.3	弓劍可攀。	his bow and sword could still be touched.
18.4	日角舒光，	The noble features radiated light,
18.5	天顏咫尺。	and the imperial face was very near to us.

1.15 Arrival of Jihe and New Favors

18.6	三載， 大秦國有僧佶和，	In the third year, the priest Jihe was in the kingdom of Da Qin.
18.7	瞻星向化，	Looking to heaven, he became enlightened;
18.8	望日朝尊。	observing the sun, he came to pay homage at the court.
18.9	詔僧羅含 僧普論等一七人，	The emperor commanded the priests Luohan, Pulun and others (seventeen in all),
18.10	與大德佶和	together with the man of great virtue Jihe,
18.11	於興慶宮修功德。	to perform virtuous and meritorious rites in the Xingqing palace.
18.12	於[是天題寺牓，	Then the emperor composed maxims for display in the temple,
19.1	額戴龍書。	plaques carrying the royal inscriptions.
19.2	寶裝璀翠，	These ornaments sparkled like precious jade,
19.3	灼爍丹霞。	and glowed like the red clouds of sunset.

Column and sense unit	Text	Translation
19.4	睿扎宏空,	The writings of the wise one filled the heavens,
19.5	騰凌激日。	and their rays were like radiant reflections of the sun.
19.6	寵賚比南山峻極,	These bountiful gifts exceeded the height of the Southern Mountains;
19.7	沛澤與東海齊深。	this flood of favors was as deep as the Eastern Sea.
19.8	道無不可,	There is nothing the Way cannot do,
19.9	所可可名。	and what he does can be described.
19.10	聖無不作,	There is nothing beyond the power of the Sage,
19.11	所作可述。	and what he has done can be told.

1.16 Suzong

19.12	(2)肅宗文明皇[帝	Suzong , a cultivated and enlightened emperor,
20.1	於靈武等五郡,	in Lingwu and other commanderies (five in all),
20.2	重立景寺。	rebuilt the Luminous temples.
20.3	元善資而福祚開,	Great benefits were granted, thus the imperial fortune began;
20.4	大慶臨而皇業建。	great rejoicing arrived, thus imperial rule was re-established.

1.17 Daizong

20.5	(2)代宗文武皇帝	Daizong, a cultured and warlike emperor,
20.6	恢張聖運,	broadened and expanded the good fortunes of the empire,
20.7	從事無為。	and served the principle of nonexertion.

Column and sense unit	Text	Translation
20.8	每於降誕之辰,	Yet every year on the morning of his birthday,
20.9	錫天香以告成功,	he offered heavenly incense in thanksgiving for his success;
20.10	頒御饌以光景眾。	he provided royal food for the illustrious Luminous congregation.
20.11	且[乾以美利,	Also, because of the beautiful generosity of the heavenly one,
21.1	故能廣生。	he was able to broaden life.
21.2	聖以體元,	Because he sensed the first principle,
21.3	故能亭毒。	he was able to educate the people.

1.18 Jianzhong Period [AD 780–783]

21.4	(2)我建中聖神文武皇帝,	Our Jianzhong sage is a god-like, cultured and warlike emperor;
21.5	披八政以 黜陟幽明。	implementing the eight governmental activities, he demotes the foolish and promotes the intelligent.
21.6	闡九疇以 惟新景命。	Following the nine categories, he restores the destiny of the Luminous ones.
21.7	化通玄理,	He learns and understands the deepest principles;
21.8	祝無愧心。	he prays in his heart with a clear conscience.

1.19 The Luminous Teaching's Program to Benefit China

21.9	至於方大而虛,	Then, those in high places will yet be humble;
21.10	專靜而恕,	those possessing constancy will yet show mercy;
21.11	廣[慈救眾苦,	broadening mercy will thus rescue many who suffer;

Column and sense unit	Text	Translation
22.1	善貸被群生者,	giving good pardon will thus help many people;
22.2	我修行之大猷,	Thus we put into practice our great plan,
22.3	汲引之階漸也。	implementing it gradually, step-by-step.
22.4	若使風雨時,	Then wind and rain will arrive at the proper time,
22.5	天下靜,	there will be peace in the world,
22.6	人能理,	people will act rationally,
22.7	物能清,	other creatures will be serene,
22.8	存能昌,	the living will prosper,
22.9	歿能樂,	the dead will rest in peace,
22.10	念生響應,	thoughts will create a warm response,
22.11	情發目誠者,	emotions will be made visible and eyes become sincere;
22.12	我景力能事之功用也。	this is what our Luminous religion has the power to achieve.

1.20 Yisi, General and Benefactor

Column and sense unit	Text	Translation
22.13	大施[主 金紫光祿大夫 、	Our great benefactor, the Great Master of the Palace with Golden Seal and Purple Ribbon,
23.1	同朔方節度副使 、	the Deputy Military Commander for the Shuofang region,
23.2	試殿中監 、	the Appointed Director of the Palace Administration,
23.3	賜紫袈裟僧伊斯,	the recipient of the Imperially conferred Purple Gown is the priest Yisi;
23.4	和而好惠,	naturally mild and graciously disposed,

Column and sense unit	Text	Translation
23.5	聞道勤行。	he has learned the Way and follows it diligently.
23.6	遠自王舍之城,	From the distant royal residence city
23.7	聿來中夏,	he came to the Middle Kingdom;
23.8	術高三代,	his moral principles exceed those of the Three Dynasties;
23.9	藝博十全。	his skills are perfect in every respect.
23.10	始效節於丹庭,	At first he served loyally at the Red Court;
23.11	乃策名於王[帳。	later his name was inscribed at the royal tent.
24.1	中書令汾陽郡王郭公子儀	When Duke Guo Ziyi, Secondary Minister of State and Prince of Fanyang,
24.2	初摠戎於朔方也,	first took military command in the Shuofang region,
24.3	(2)肅宗俾之從邁。	Suzong appointed him as [the duke's] attendant on his travels.
24.4	雖見親於臥內,	Although trusted to serve as private chamberlain,
24.5	不自異於行間。	he assumed no distinction on the march.
24.6	為公爪牙,	He was the duke's claws and fangs,
24.7	作軍耳目。	serving as his eyes and ears in the army.
24.8	能散祿賜,	He distributes the gifts conferred on him,
24.9	不積於家。	not accumulating family wealth.
24.10	獻臨恩之頗黎,	He gives away the gifts given him by imperial favor;
24.11	布[辭憩之金罽。	he distributes the golden fabric given as his due.

Column and sense unit	Text	Translation
25.1	或仍其舊寺，	On the one hand, he repairs the old temples;
25.2	或重廣法堂。	on the other hand, he increases the number of religious sites.
25.3	崇飾廊宇，	He honors and decorates the various edifices,
25.4	如翬斯飛。	until they resemble the plumage of a pheasant in full flight.
25.5	更効景門，	He further exerts himself for the Luminous community
25.6	依仁施利。	in the virtuous distribution of his wealth;
25.7	每歲集四寺僧徒，	every year he assembles the monks from four monasteries,
25.8	虔事精供，	for reverent service and divine worship
25.9	備諸五旬。	for fifty days.
25.10	餧者來而飯之，	The hungry come and are fed;
25.11	寒者來而衣之，	the naked come and are clothed;
25.12	病者療而[起之，	the sick are attended to and healed;
26.1	死者葬而安之。	the dead are buried and rest in peace.
26.2	清節達娑，	Even among the pure and moral *Dasuo* [Christians]
26.3	未聞斯美。	such excellence is unknown.
26.4	白衣景士，	But now among the white-robed priests of the Luminous Teaching,
26.5	今見其人。	we see such a man.

1.21 This Stele Is Their Eulogy

26.6	願刻洪碑，	We desire to engrave this magnificent stele
26.7	以揚休烈。	to eulogize such great deeds.

Column and sense unit	Text	Translation

PART 2. POEM ON THE TRUE LORD AND HIS TANG EMPERORS

2.1 The True Lord

26.8	詞曰:	The poem:
26.9	(1)真主无元,	The True Lord is without beginning;
26.10	湛寂常然。	he is profound stillness and is unchanging.
26.11	權輿匠化,	Like a craftsman, he began to create,
26.12	起地立天。	bringing forth the earth and setting the sky in place.
26.13	分身出代,	Dividing his being he came to earth;
26.14	救度無邊。	he saved and expiated without limit.
26.15	日昇暗[滅,	Thus the sun arose and darkness was driven out;
27.1	咸證真玄。	everything proves the true and the deep.

2.2 Taizong

27.2	(2)赫赫文皇,	The most illustrious emperor's
27.3	道冠前王。	way surpassed that of previous rulers.
27.4	乘時撥乱,	He assumed control and dispelled chaos;
27.5	乾廓坤張。	the empire increased and flourished.
27.6	明明景教,	(At that time), the pure, bright Luminous Teaching
27.7	言歸我唐。	was introduced to our Tang kingdom.
27.8	翻經建寺,	Its scriptures were translated and temples built;
27.9	存歿舟航。	the [spiritually] dead revived and boats gave passage [to heaven].

Column and sense unit	Text	Translation
27.10	百福偕作，	One hundred blessings arose together;
27.11	萬邦之康。	ten thousand regions flourished.

2.3 Gaozong

27.12	(2)高宗纂祖，	When Gaozong succeeded his father,
27.13	更築精宇。	he also erected religious buildings.
27.14	和宮敞朗，	Serene buildings, spacious and bright,
27.15	遍[滿中土。	they spread, filling the land.
28.1	真道宣明，	The true Way was proclaimed and it enlightened the people;
28.2	式封法主。	a system of clergy was established.
28.3	人有樂康，	The people were content and happy;
28.4	物無災苦。	they experienced no disasters or hardships.

2.4 Xuanzong

28.5	(2)玄宗啟聖，	When Xuanzong became emperor,
28.6	克修真正。	he recovered and cultivated true rule.
28.7	御牓揚輝，	His imperial tablets were radiant;
28.8	天書蔚映。	his celestial writings were resplendent.
28.9	皇圖璀璨，	The imperial portraits glittered like gems;
28.10	率土高敬。	all the land was most respectful.
28.11	庶績咸熙，	All that was done promoted flourishing;
28.12	人賴其慶。	the people relied on his benevolence.

2.5 Suzong

28.13	(2)肅宗來復，	When Suzong restored rule,

Column and sense unit	Text	Translation
28.14	天威引[駕。	the powers of heaven pulled his carriage.
29.1	聖日 舒晶,	The wise sun unfolded its radiance;
29.2	祥風掃夜。	the winds of good fortune swept away the darkness.
29.3	祚歸皇室,	Blessings returned to the royal house;
29.4	祅氛永謝。	disasters vanished and permanently declined.
29.5	止沸定塵,	Chaos stopped and the dust settled;
29.6	造我區夏。	our Chinese empire was reestablished.

2.6 Daizong

29.7	(2)代宗孝義,	Daizong was filial and just,
29.8	德合天地。	and his good deeds united heaven and earth.
29.9	開貸生成,	He promoted wealth, and produced peace;
29.10	物資美利。	material wealth was beautiful and profitable.
29.11	香以報功,	His incense was the response to merit;
29.12	仁以作施。	his kindness was the response to generosity.
29.13	暘谷來威,	In the valley of dawn there was a fullness of power;
29.14	月窟畢萃.	in the cave of the moon darkness ceased.

2.7 Jianzhong Period

29.15	(2)建[中統極,	Rule reached its zenith in the Jianzhong period,
30.1	聿修明德。	cultivating a brilliant morality.

Column and sense unit	Text	Translation
30.2	武肅四溟，	The emperor's military action has cleared the four seas;
30.3	文清萬域。	his learning has purified ten thousand lands.
30.4	燭臨人隱，	His torch illuminates the secrets of men;
30.5	鏡觀物色。	his mirror reflects the true appearance of things.
30.6	六合昭蘇，	The six directions are glad and prosper;
30.7	百蠻取則。	the one hundred tribes of barbarians profit from his example.

2.8 Praise to the Three-One

30.8	道惟廣兮應惟密，	The Way is spread widely, and with great effect;
30.9	強名言兮演三一。	there is no better name or description [of it] than the Three-One.
30.10	(2)主能作兮臣能述，	The Lord is able to act, his servants but record;
30.11	建豐碑兮頌元吉。	we erect this great stele in praise of his fundamental goodness.

Concluding Information about the Stele

31.1	(1)大唐建中二年歲在作噩太蔟月七日大耀森文日建立	Erected in the great Tang dynasty, in the second year of the Jianzhong period, in the year of the chicken, on the seventh day of the first month, on the Great Sunday.
31.2	(1)時法主僧寧恕知東方之景眾也	In the time when Patriarch Ningshu had oversight over the eastern region of the Luminous people.

Column and sense unit	Text	Translation
[S2]	ܒܝܘܡܝ ܐܒܐ ܕܐܒܗܬܐ ܡܪܝ ܚܢܢܝܫܘܥ ܩܬܘܠܝܩܐ ܦܛܪܝܪܟܝܣ	[S2] In the time of the Father of Fathers, Mar Hananisho, Catholicos-Patriarch
32.1	朝議郎前行台州司士參軍呂秀巖書	The calligraphy is that of Lu Xiuyan, minister and councilor of the court, formerly military commander for Tai Zhou district.

Bottom of the front

Column one shows line numbers (reading from left to right across the bottom); column three gives the the Chinese and Syriac line numbers within the entire stele inscription.

1	ܒܫܢܬ ܐܠܦ ܘܬܫܥܝܢ ܘܬܪܬܝܢ	[S3]	In the year one thousand and ninety and two
2	ܕܝܘܢܝܐ ܡܪܝ ܝܙܕܒܘܙܝܕ ܩܫܝܫܐ	[S4]	of the Greeks, Mar Yazdbuzid, priest
3	ܘܟܘܪܐܦܝܣܩܘܦܐ ܕܟܘܡܕܐܢ	[S5]	and chorepiscopus of Kumdān [Chang'an]
4	ܡܕܝܢܬ ܡܠܟܘܬܐ ܒܪ ܢܝܚ	[S6]	the capital city, son of the
5	ܢܦܫܐ ܡܝܠܝܣ ܩܫܝܫܐ ܕܡܢ	[S7]	late Milis priest, from
6	ܒܠܚ ܡܕܝܢܬܐ ܕܛܚܘܪܣܛܢ	[S8]	Balkh a city of Tokharistan,
7	ܐܩܝܡ ܠܘܚܐ ܗܢܐ ܕܟܐܦܐ	[S9]	erected this stone tablet.
8	ܕܟܬܝܒܢ ܒܗ ܡܕܒܪܢܘܬܗ	[S10]	The things written on it
9	ܕܦܪܘܩܢ ܘܟܪܘܙܘܬܗܘܢ	[S11]	are the teaching of our Savior and the preaching
10	ܕܐܒܗܝܢ ܕܠܘܬ ܡܠܟܐ	[S12]	of our fathers to the emperors
11	ܕܨܝܢܝܐ 僧靈寶	[S13] [33]	of Zinaye [China]. monk Ling Bao

12	ܐܕܡ ܡܫܡܫܢܐ ܒܪ	[S14]	Adam deacon
13	ܝܙܕܒܘܙܝܕ ܟܘܪܐܦܝܣܩܘܦܐ	[S15]	son of the chorepiscopus Yazdbuzid

[major space]

14	ܡܪܣܪܓܝܣ ܩܫܝܫܐ	[S16]	Mar Sargis priest
15	ܘܟܘܪܐܦܝܣܩܘܦܐ	[S17]	and chorepiscopus.

[major space]

17	撿挍建立碑僧	[34]	Supervisor of the stele's erection: the monk
16	行通	[35]	Xingtong,
	ܣܒܪܢܝܫܘܥ ܩܫܝܫܐ	[S18]	The priest Sabranisho.
18	ܓܒܪܐܝܠ ܩܫܝܫܐ ܘܐܪܟܕܝܩܘܢ	[S19]	Gabriel priest and archdeacon
19	ܘܪܫ ܥܕܬܐ ܕܟܘܡܕܢ	[S20]	and head of the church of Kumdān [Chang'an]
20	ܘܕܣܪܓ	[S21]	and of Sarag [Luoyang].
	助撿挍試太常	[36]	Assistant Supervisor: the Master of Imperial Rites,
	卿賜紫袈裟寺	[37]	recipient of the Imperially conferred Purple Gown,
	主僧業利	[38]	the chief monk Yeli.

Left side

First Row

ܡܪܝ ܝܘܚܢܢ ܐܦܝܣܩܘܦܐ	[S22]	My lord Johanan bishop,
大德曜輪	[39]	bishop Yaolun
ܐܝܣܚܩ ܩܫܝܫܐ	[S23]	Isaac priest,
[僧日進	[40]	monk Rijin
ܝܘܐܝܠ ܩܫܝܫܐ	[S24]	Joel priest
僧遙越	[41]	monk Yaoyue

ܩܫܝܫܐ ܡܝܟܐܝܠ	[S25]	Michael priest	
僧廣慶	[42]	monk Guangqing	
ܩܫܝܫܐ ܓܝܘܪܓܝܣ	[S26]	Giwargis (George) priest	
僧和吉	[43]	monk Heji	
ܩܫܝܫܐ ܡܗܕܕ ܓܘܫܢܣܦ	[S27]	Mahdad Gushnasp, priest	
僧惠明	[44]	monk Huiming	
ܩܫܝܫܐ ܡܫܝܚܕܕ	[S28]	Mshihadad priest	
僧寶達	[45]	monk Baoda	
ܩܫܝܫܐ ܐܦܪܝܡ	[S29]	Ephrem priest	
僧拂林	[46]	monk Fulin	
ܩܫܝܫܐ ܐܒܝ	[S30]	Abay priest	
ܩܫܝܫܐ ܕܘܝܕ	[S31]	David priest	
ܩܫܝܫܐ ܡܘܫܐ	[S32]	Moses priest	
僧福壽	[47]	monk Fushou	

Second Row

ܒܟܘܣ ܩܫܝܫܐ ܘܝܚܝܕܝܐ	[S33]	Bacchus priest, solitary monk,	
僧崇敬	[48]	monk Chongjing	
ܐܠܝܐ ܩܫܝܫܐ ܘܝܚܝܕܝܐ	[S34]	Elias priest, solitary monk,	
僧延和	[49]	monk Yanhe	
ܡܘܫܐ ܩܫܝܫܐ ܘܝܚܝܕܝܐ	[S35]	Moses priest and solitary monk	
ܥܒܕܝܫܘ ܩܫܝܫܐ ܘܝܚܝܕܝܐ	[S36]	Abdisho priest and solitary monk	
ܫܡܥܘܢ ܩܫܝܫܐ ܕܒܝܬ ܩܒܘܪܐ	[S37]	Simon priest of the cemetery	
ܝܘܚܢܢ ܡܫܡܫܢܐ ܘܝܚ	[S38]	John deacon and solitary monk	
僧惠通	[50]	monk Huitong	

Third Row

ܐܗܪܘܢ	[S39]	Aaron	
僧乾祐	[51]	monk Qianyou	
ܦܛܪܘܣ	[S40]	Peter	
僧元一	[52]	monk Yuanyi	
ܐܝܘܒ	[S41]	Job	
僧敬德	[53]	monk Jingde	
ܠܘܩܐ	[S42]	Luke	
僧利見	[54]	monk Lijian	

ܡܬܝ	[S43]	Matthew
僧明泰	[55]	monk Mingtai
ܝܘܚܢܢ	[S44]	John
僧玄真	[56]	monk Xuanzhen
ܝܫܘܥܐܡܗ	[S45]	Isho-ammeh
僧仁惠	[57]	monk Renhui
ܝܘܚܢܢ	[S46]	John
僧曜源	[58]	monk Yaoyuan
ܡܫܝܥܒܪ	[S47]	Sabrisho
僧昭德	[59]	monk Zhaode
ܝܫܘܕܕ	[S48]	Ishodad
僧文明	[60]	monk Wenming
ܠܘܩܐ	[S49]	Luke
僧文貞	[61]	monk Wenzhen
ܩܘܣܛܢܛܝܢܘܣ	[S50]	Constantine
僧居信	[62]	monk Juxin
ܢܘܚ	[S51]	Noah
僧來威	[63]	monk Laiwei

Fourth Row

ܐܝܙܕܣܦܣ	[S52]	Izadsafas
僧敬真	[64]	monk Jingzhen
ܝܘܚܢܢ	[S53]	John
僧還淳	[65]	monk Huanchun
ܐܢܘܫ	[S54]	Enos
僧靈壽	[66]	monk Lingshou
ܡܪܝ ܣܪܓܝܣ	[S55]	Mar Sargis
僧靈德	[67]	monk Lingde
ܐܝܣܚܩ	[S56]	Isaac
僧英德	[68]	monk Yingde
ܝܘܚܢܢ	[S57]	John
僧沖和	[69]	monk Chonghe
ܡܪܝ ܣܪܓܝܣ	[S58]	Mar Sargis
僧凝虛	[70]	monk Ningxu
ܦܘܣܝ	[S59]	Pusi
僧普濟	[71]	monk Puji

ܫܡܥܘܢ	[S60]	Simeon
僧聞順	[72]	monk Wenshun
ܐܝܣܚܩ	[S61]	Isaac
ܝܘܚܢ	[S62]	John
僧守一	[74]	monk Shouyi

| 僧光濟 | [73] | monk Guangji |

Right side

First Row

ܝܥܩܘܒ ܩܫܝܫܐ	[S63]	Jacob priest
老宿耶俱摩	[75]	venerable Yejumo
ܡܪܝ ܣܪܓܝܣ ܩܫܝܫܐ	[S64]	Mar Sargis priest and chorepiscopus
ܘܟܘܪܐܦܝܣܩܘܦܐ		of Shangtsua
ܕܫܐܢܓܬܣܘܐ		
僧景通	[76]	monk Jingtong
ܓܝܓܘܝ ܩܫܝܫܐ ܘܐܪܟܝܕܝܩܘܢ	[S65]	Gigoy priest and archdeacon of
ܕܟܘܡܕܢ ܘܩܪܘܝܐ		Kumdan and reader
僧玄覽	[77]	monk Xuanlan
ܦܘܠܘܣ ܩܫܝܫܐ	[S66]	Paul priest
僧寶靈	[78]	monk Baoling
ܫܡܫܘܢ ܩܫܝܫܐ	[S67]	Samson priest
僧審慎	[79]	monk Shenshen
ܐܕܡ ܩܫܝܫܐ	[S68]	Adam priest
僧法源	[80]	monk Fayuan
ܐܠܝܐ ܩܫܝܫܐ	[S69]	Elias priest
僧立本	[81]	monk Liben
ܐܝܣܚܩ ܩܫܝܫܐ	[S70]	Isaac priest
僧和明	[82]	monk Heming
ܝܘܚܢ ܩܫܝܫܐ	[S71]	John priest
僧光正	[83]	monk Guangzheng
ܝܘܚܢ ܩܫܝܫܐ	[S72]	John priest
僧內澄	[84]	monk Neicheng
ܫܡܥܘܢ ܩܫܝܫܐ ܘܩܫܐ	[S73]	Simeon priest and elder

Second Row

ܝܥܩܘܒ ܣܩܘܢܐ	[S74]	Jacob the sacristan
僧崇德	[85]	monk Chongde
ܥܒܕܝܫܘܥ	[S75]	Abdisho
僧太和	[86]	monk Taihe
ܝܫܘܥܕܕ	[S76]	Ishodad
僧景福	[87]	monk Jingfu
ܝܥܩܘܒ	[S77]	Jacob
僧和光	[88]	monk Heguang
ܝܘܚܢܢ	[S78]	John
僧至德	[89]	monk Zhide
ܫܘܒܚܠܡܪܢ	[S79]	Shubhalmaran
僧奉真	[90]	monk Fengzhen
ܡܪܝ ܣܪܓܝܣ	[S80]	Mar Sargis
僧元宗	[91]	monk Yuanzong
ܫܡܥܘܢ	[S81]	Simeon
僧利用	[92]	monk Liyong
ܐܦܪܝܡ	[S82]	Ephrem
僧玄德	[93]	monk Xuande
ܙܟܪܝܐ	[S83]	Zachariah
僧義濟	[94]	monk Yiji
ܩܘܪܝܩܘܣ	[S84]	Cyriacus
僧志堅	[95]	monk Zhijian
ܒܟܘܣ	[S85]	Bacchus
僧保國	[96]	monk Baoguo
ܥܡܢܘܐܝܠ	[S86]	Emmanuel
僧明一	[97]	monk Mingyi

Third Row

ܓܒܪܐܝܠ	[S87]	Gabriel
僧廣德	[98]	monk Guangde
ܝܘܚܢܢ	[S88]	John
ܫܠܝܡܘܢ	[S89]	Solomon
僧去甚	[99]	monk Qushen
ܐܝܣܚܩ	[S90]	Isaac
ܝܘܚܢܢ	[S91]	John
僧德建	[100]	monk Dejian

Appendix 2: Figures and Maps

Figure 1. Photograph of the Chang'an stele in the late 1800s near the Chongren Temple (Xi'an); a rubbing was just made and the paper is still on the stone (courtesy of the Penn Museum, image number 176485)

Figure 2. Top of the stele (rubbing, enhanced)

Figure 3. Syriac text at the bottom of the stele (rubbing)

Figure 4. The ancient text on the left and right sides of the stele

Figure 5. The Luoyang Christian Pillar

Figure 6. The beginning of the *Lord Messiah* scroll (courtesy of Kyo-U Library, Takeda Science Foundation)

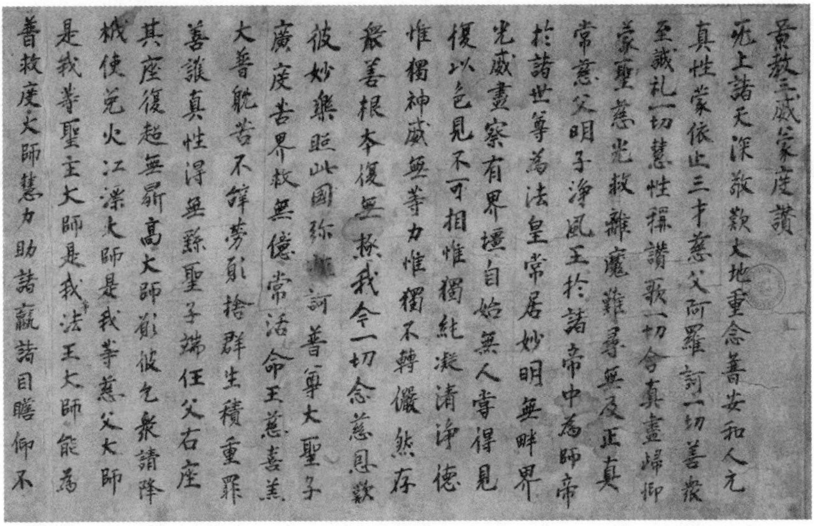

Figure 7. Hymn text in *Pelliot chinois 3847* (courtesy of Bibliothèque nationale de France)

Figure 8. Ongut Christian gravestones (photos copyright Tjalling H. F. Halbertsma)

Figure 9. Ordos or "Nestorian" crosses from the Hong Kong University Museum and Art Gallery; from the top left, nos. 755, 806, 46, 753, 42, 812, 765, 1909, and 1015 (courtesy of the University Museum and Art Gallery, The University of Hong Kong)

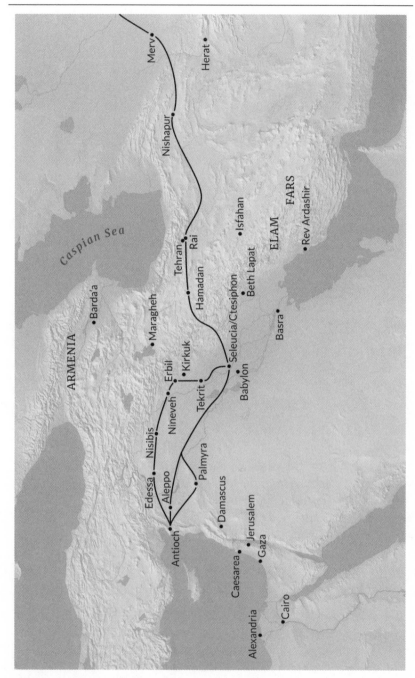

Map 1. The Syriac world

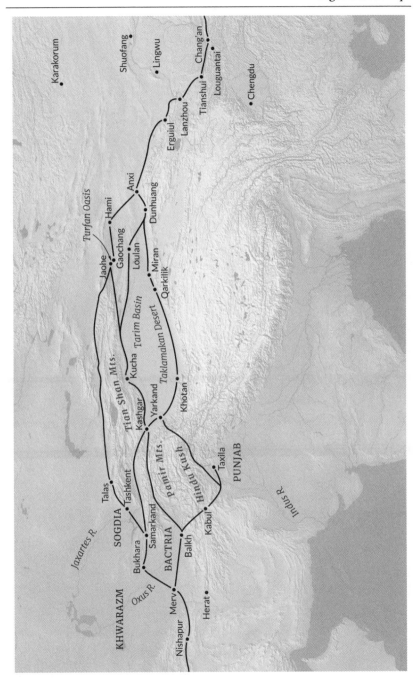

Map 2. Central Asia and the Silk Road

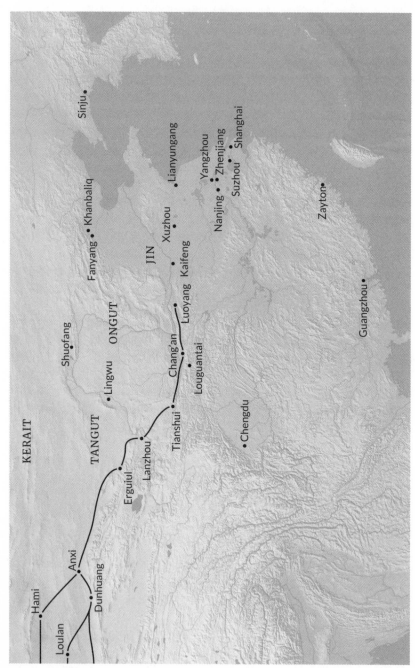

Map 3. China during the Jingjiao period

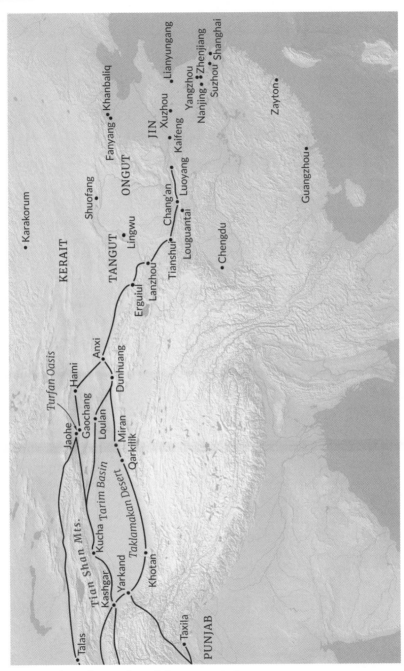

Map 4. China during the Yelekewen period

Select Bibliography

The following list includes those works cited directly in the foregoing text. For the benefit of the intended audience, references were given to works in English as much as possible. The exclusion of excellent studies in Asian and other European languages was necessitated chiefly by the book's intended readership.

Atwood, Christopher. "Historiography and Transformation of Ethnic Identity in the Mongol Empire: The Öng'üt Case." *Asian Ethnicity* 15, no. 4 (September 2014): 514–34.

Barrett, T. H. "Buddhism, Daoism and the Eighth-Century Chinese Term for Christianity." In *Jingjiao: The Church of the East in China and Central Asia*, edited by Roman Malek, 45–53. Collectanea Serica. Sankt Augustin, Germany: Institut Monumenta Serica, 2006.

Baum, Wilhelm. *Shirin: Christian—Queen—Myth of Love; A Woman of Late Antiquity—Historical Reality and Literary Effect*. Piscataway, NJ: Gorgias, 2004.

Baum, Wilhelm, and Dietmar W. Winkler. *The Church of the East: A Concise History*. London: Routledge Curzon, 2003.

Baumer, Christoph. *The Church of the East: An Illustrated History of Assyrian Christianity*. New ed. London: I. B. Tauris, 2016.

Benn, Charles. *China's Golden Age: Everyday Life in the Tang Dynasty*. Oxford: Oxford University Press, 2004.

Birnie, M. J. "The Synod of Mar 'Ishaq (AD 410)." https://www.fourthcentury.com/the-council-of-mar-ishaq-ad-410/.

Borbone, Pier Giorgio. *History of Mar Yahballaha and Rabban Sauma*. Edited, translated, and annotated by Pier Giorgio Borbone. English trans. by Laura E. Parodi. Hamburg: Verlag tredition, 2021.

Braun, Oskar, ed. *Timothei Patriarchae I epistulae*, vol. 1. Corpus Scriptorum

Christianorum Orientalium 74–75, Scriptores Syri 30–31. Paris and Leipzig: Peeters, 1914–1915.

Brock, Sebastian P. "The Christology of the Church of the East." In *Traditions and Heritage of the Christian East*, edited by D. Afinogenov and A. Muraviev, 159–79. Moscow: Izdatelstvo "Indrik," 1966.

———. *Fire from Heaven: Studies in Syriac Theology and Liturgy*. Variorum Collected Studies Series. Aldershot, UK: Ashgate, 2006.

———. "Miaphysite, not Monophysite!" *Cristianesimo nella storia* 37 (2016): 45–52.

———. "The 'Nestorian' Church: A Lamentable Misnomer." *Bulletin of the John Rylands Library* 78, no. 3 (Autumn 1996): 23–35.

Chen Huaiyu. "The Connection between Jingjiao and Buddhist Texts in Late Tang China." In *Jingjiao: The Church of the East in China and Central Asia*, edited by Roman Malek, 93–113. Collectanea Serica. Sankt Augustin. Germany: Institut Monumenta Serica, 2006.

China Christian Council and Three-Self Patriotic Movement of the Protestant Churches in China. *Outline of the Five-Year Working Plan for Promoting the Sinicization of Christianity in Our Country (2018–2022)*. 2018. Accessed December 6, 2022. https://www.ucanews.com/news/protestant-five-year -plan-for-chinese-christianity/82107.

Dalby, Michael. "Court Politics in Late T'ang Times." In *Sui and T'ang China, 589–906, Part 1*, vol. 3 of *The Cambridge History of China*, edited by Denis Twitchett, 561–681. Cambridge: Cambridge University Press, 1979.

Dawson, Christopher. *Mission to Asia: Narratives and Letters of the Franciscan Missionaries in Mongolia and China in the Thirteenth and Fourteenth Centuries*. New York: Harper & Row, 1966.

Deeg, Max. "An Anachronism in the Stele of Xi'an—Why Haenanisho?" In *Winds of Jingjiao*, edited by Dietmar Winkler and Li Tang, 243–51. Orientalia-Patristica-Oecumenica 9. Vienna: LIT Verlag, 2016.

———. "A Belligerent Priest—Yisi and His Political Context." In *From the Oxus River to the Chinese Shores*, edited by Li Tang and Dietmar W. Winkler, 107–21. Orientalia-Patristica-Oecumenica 5. Vienna: LIT Verlag, 2013.

———. "Messiah Rediscovered: Some Philological Notes on the So-called 'Jesus the Messiah Sutra.'" In *The Church of the East in Central Asia and China*, edited by Samuel N. C. Lieu and Glen L. Thompson, 111–20. China and the Mediterranean World 1. Turnhout: Brepols, 2022.

———. "Ways to Go and Not to Go in the Contextualisation of the Jingjiao Documents of the Tang Period." In *Hidden Treasures and Intercultural Encounters*, edited by Dietmar W. Winkler and Li Tang, 135–52. Orientalia-Patristica-Oecumenica 1. Vienna: LIT Verlag, 2009.

Dickens, Mark. "Patriarch Timothy I and the Metropolitan of the Turks." *Journal of the Royal Asiatic Society*, 3rd ser., 20, no. 2 (April 2010): 117–39.

———. "Syriac Christianity in Central Asia." In *The Syriac World*, edited by Daniel King, 583–624. London: Routledge, 2019.

———. "Syriac Gravestones in the Tashkent History Museum." In *Hidden Treasures and Intercultural Encounters*, edited by Dietmar W. Winkler and Li Tang, 13–69. Orientalia-Patristica-Oecumenica 1. Vienna: LIT Verlag, 2009.

Dīn, Rashid al-, and W. M. Thackston. *Jami't-Tawarikh: Compendium of Chronicles; A History of the Mongols*. Cambridge, MA: Harvard University Press, 1998–1999.

Drompp, Michael. *Tang China and the Collapse of the Uighur Empire: A Documentary History*. Brill's Inner Asian Library 13. Leiden: Brill, 2005.

Eccles, Lance, and Samuel N. C. Lieu. "Stele on the Diffusion of Christianity (The Luminous Religion) from Rome (Da Qin) into China (The Middle Kingdom), 'The Nestorian Monument.'" March 26, 2022, http://www.unionaca demique.org/content/files/10362790247079243.pdf.

Eskildsen, Stephen. "Parallel Themes in Chinese Nestorianism and Medieval Daoist Religion." In *Jingjiao: The Church of the East in China and Central Asia*, edited by Roman Malek, 57–91. Collectanea Serica. Sankt Augustin, Germany: Institut Monumenta Serica, 2006.

Ferreira, Johan. *Early Chinese Christianity: The Tang Christian Monument and Other Documents*. Early Christian Studies 17. Sydney: St. Paul's Publications, 2014.

Forte, Antonino. "The Edict of 638 Allowing the Diffusion of Christianity in China." In *L'inscription Nestorienne de Si-Ngan-Fou*, by Paul Pelliot, edited by Antonino Forte, 349–73. Paris: Collège de France, IHEC; Kyoto: Scuola di studi sull'Asia Orientale, 1996.

Godwin, R. Todd. *Persian Christians at the Chinese Court: The Xi'an Stele and the Early Medieval Church of the East*. London: I. B. Tauris, 2018.

Graf, David. "The Silk Road between Syria and China." In *Trade, Commerce, and the State in the Roman World*, edited by Andrew Wilson and Alan Bowman, 443–530. Oxford: Oxford University Press, 2018.

Graham, A. C. *Disputers of the Tao: Philosophical Argument in Ancient China*. La Salle, IL: Open Court, 1989.

Grant, Asahel. *The Nestorians; or, The Lost Tribes: Containing Evidence of Their Identity*. London: John Murray, 1841.

Guidi, Ignazio, trans. *Chronica Minora: Chronicon anonymum de ultimis regibus Persarum*. Corpus Scriptorum Christanorum Orientalium 2, Scriptores Syri 2. Paris: Typographeo Reipublicae, 1903.

Guisso, Richard. "The Reigns of the Empress Wu, Chung-tsung and Jui-tsung (684–712)." In *Sui and T'ang China, 589–906, Part 1*, vol. 3 of *The Cambridge History of China*, edited by Denis Twitchett, 290–332. Cambridge: Cambridge University Press, 1979.

Hage, Wolfgang. "Das Christentum in der Turfan-Oase: Zur Begegnung der Religionen in Zentralasien." In *Synkretismus in den Religionen Zentralasiens*, edited by Walther Heissig and Hans-Joachim Klimkeit, 46–57. Studies in Oriental Religions 13. Wiesbaden: Otto Harrassowitz, 1987.

Halbertsma, Tjalling H. F. *Early Christian Remains of Inner Mongolia: Discovery, Reconstruction, and Appropriation*. 2nd edition, revised, updated, and expanded. Leiden: Brill, 2015.

Havret, Henri. *La Stèle Chrétienne de Si-Ngan-Fou*. 3 vols. Variétés Sinologique 7, 12, 20. Chang-hai: Impr. de la Mission catholique, 1895, 1897, 1902.

Hill, John E. 2015. *Through the Jade Gate China to Rome: A Study of the Silk Routes during the Later Han Dynasty 1st to 2nd Centuries CE: An Annotated Translation from the Hou Hanshu "The Chronicle on the Western Regions."* New updated and expanded ed. CreateSource, 2015.

Hirth, Friedrich, and W. W. Rockhill. *Chau Ju-kua: His Work on the Chinese and Arab Trade in the Twelfth and Thirteenth Centuries, Entitled Chu-fan-chï*. St. Petersburg, Russia: Imperial Academy of Sciences, 1911.

Holm, Frits. *My Nestorian Adventure in China: A Popular Account of the Holm-Nestorian Expedition to Sian-Fu and Its Results*. New York: Revell, 1923.

Hopkirk, Peter. *Foreign Devils on the Silk Road: The Search for the Lost Cities and Treasures of Chinese Central Asia*. Oxford: Oxford University Press, 1984.

Hucker, Charles. *A Dictionary of Official Titles in Imperial China*. Reprint of 1985 edition. Taipei: SMC Publishing, 2001.

Hunter, Erica C. D. "The Church of the East in Central Asia." *Bulletin of the John Rylands Library* 78, no. 3 (1996): 129–42.

———. "The Conversion of the Kerait to Christianity in AD 1007." *Zentralasiatische Studien* 22 (1989–1991): 142–63.

———. "The Persian Contribution to Christianity in China: Reflections in the Xi'an Fu Syriac Inscriptions." In *Hidden Treasures and Intercultural Encounters*, edited by Dietmar W. Winkler and Li Tang, 71–85. Orientalia-Patristica-Oecumenica 1. Vienna: LIT Verlag, 2009.

International Dunhuang Project. http://idp.bl.uk/.

Keevak, M. *The Story of a Stele: China's Nestorian Monument and Its Reception in the West, 1625–1916*. Hong Kong: Hong Kong University Press, 2008.

Kircher, Athanasius. *China Illustrata*. Abridged English translation of the 1667

Amsterdam edition by Charles D. Van Tuyl. Bloomington: Indiana University Research Institute for Inner Asian Studies, 1987.

Kyōu shooku, ed. *Tonkō hikyū: Eihen satsu* [Dunhuang secret collection: Photographic volumes]. 9 vols. Osaka: Takeda kagaku shinkō zaidan, 2009–2013.

Leslie, Donald D. "Persian Temples in T'ang China." *Monumenta Serica* 35 (1981): 275–303.

Lewis, Mark Edward. *China's Cosmopolitan Empire: The Tang Dynasty*. History of Imperial China 3. Cambridge, MA: Belknap Press of Harvard University Press, 2009.

Lieu, Samuel N. C. "From Rome (Da Qin 大秦) to China (Zhongguo 中國): The Xi'an 西安 (Nestorian) Monument as a Bilingual and Transcultural Document." In *The Church of the East in Central Asia and China*, edited by Samuel N. C. Lieu and Glen L. Thompson, 124–41. China and the Mediterranean World 1. Turnhout: Brepols, 2020.

———. "Lost in Transcription? The Theological Vocabulary of Christian Texts in Central Asia and China." In *Winds of Jingjiao*, edited by Li Tang and Dietmar W. Winkler, 349–66. Orientalia-Patristica-Oecumenica 9. Vienna: LIT Verlag, 2016.

———. *Manichaeism in the Later Roman Empire and Medieval China: A Historical Survey*. 2nd ed. Wissenschaftliche Untersuchungen zum Neuen Testament 63. Tübingen: Mohr Siebeck, 1992.

———. "Persons, Titles, and Places in the Xi'an Monument." In *Artifact, Text, Context*, edited by Li Tang and Dietmar W. Winkler, 61–81. Orientalia-Patristica-Oecumenica 17. Vienna: LIT, 2020.

———. "The 'Romanitas' of the Xi'an Inscription." In *From the Oxus River to the Chinese Shores*, edited by Li Tang and Dietmar W. Winkler, 123–40. Orientalia-Patristica-Oecumenica 5. Vienna: LIT Verlag, 2013.

Lieu, Samuel N. C., Lance Eccles, Majella Franzmann, Iain Gardner, and Ken Parry, eds. *Medieval Christian and Manichaean Remains from Quanzhou (Zayton)*. Corpus Fontium Manichaeorum, Series Archaeologica et Iconographica 2. Turnhout: Brepols, 2012.

Lieu, Samuel N. C., and Glen L. Thompson, eds. *The Church of the East in Central Asia and China*. China and the Mediterranean World 1. Turnhout: Brepols, 2020.

Lin Wushu. "Gaonan shi cang jingjiao *Xuting mishisuo jing* zhenwei cunyi 高楠氏藏景教《序聽迷詩所經》真偽存疑" [Doubts concerning the authenticity of the Nestorian *Sūtra of Jesus Messiah* from the Takakusu Collection]. In *Wenshi* 文史 (Letters) 55 (2001): 141–54.

———. "A General Discussion of the Tang Policy towards Three Persian Religions:

Manichaeanism, Nestorianism and Zoroastrianism." *China Archaeology and Art Digest* 4, no. 1 (2000): 103–16.

———. "A Study of Equivalent Names of Manichaeism in Chinese." In *Popular Religion and Shamanism*, edited by Ma Xisha and Meng Huiying, 55–121. Leiden: Brill, 2011.

Malek, Roman, ed. *Jingjiao: The Church of the East in China and Central Asia.* Collectanea Serica. Sankt Augustin, Germany: Institut Monumenta Serica, 2006.

Marsone, Pierre. "Two Portraits for One Man: George King of the Önggüt." In *From the Oxus River to the Chinese Shores*, edited by Li Tang and Dietmar W. Winkler, 225–35. Orientalia-Patristica-Oecumenica 5. Vienna: LIT Verlag, 2013.

Mather, Richard B. "Wang Chin's 'Dhuta Temple Stele Inscription' as an Example of Buddhist Parallel Prose." *Journal of the American Oriental Society* 83, no. 3 (August–September 1963): 338–59.

Mathew, K. S., J. C. Chennattuserry, and A. Bungalowparambil, eds. *St. Thomas and India: Recent Researches*. Minneapolis: Fortress, 2020.

McKechnie, Paul. "How Far Is It from Antioch to Edessa?" In *Aspects of the Roman East*, vol. 2, *Papers in Honour of Professor Sir Fergus Millar FBA*, edited by Samuel N. C. Lieu and Paul McKechnie, 192–211. Turnhout: Brepols, 2015.

Milne, William. *A Retrospect of the First Ten Years of the Protestant Mission to China*. Malacca, Malaysia: Anglo-Chinese Press, 1820.

Mingana, Alphonse. "The Early Spread of Christianity in Central Asia and the Far East: A New Document." *Bulletin of the John Rylands Library* 9, no. 2 (1925): 297–371.

Mirsky, Jeannette. *Sir Aurel Stein: Archaeological Explorer*. Chicago: University of Chicago Press, 1977.

Moule, A. C. *Christians in China before the Year 1550*. London: SPCK, 1930.

Moule, A. C., and Paul Pelliot. *Marco Polo: The Description of the World*. Vol. 1. London: Routledge, 1938.

Nautin, Pierre. "L'Auteur de la 'Chronique Anonyme de Guidi': Élie de Merew." *Revue de l'histoire des religions* 199, no. 3 (1982): 303–14.

Nicolini-Zani, Matteo. "The Dunhuang Jingjiao Documents in Japan: A Report on Their Reappearance." In *Winds of Jingjiao*, edited by Li Tang and Dietmar W. Winkler, 15–26. Orientalia-Patristica-Oecumenica 9. Vienna: LIT Verlag, 2016.

———. *The Interpretation of Tang Christianity in the Late Ming China Mission. Manuel Dias Jr.'s Correct Explanation of the Tang "Stele Eulogy on the Luminous Teaching" (1644)*. Leiden: Brill, forthcoming.

———. *The Luminous Way to the East: Texts and History of the First Encounter of Christianity with China.* Oxford: Oxford University Press, 2022.

———. "A Study of the Christian Clergy Mentioned in the Jingjiao Pillar from Luoyang." In *From the Oxus River to the Chinese Shores*, edited by Li Tang and Dietmar W. Winkler, 141–60. Orientalia-Patristica-Oecumenica 5. Vienna: LIT Verlag, 2013.

———. "The Tang Christian Pillar from Luoyang and Its Jingjiao Inscription: A Preliminary Study." *Monumenta Serica* 57 (2009): 99–140.

Niu Ruji. "History Is a Mirror: On the Spread of Nestorianism in China from the Newly Discovered Bronze Mirror with Cross-Lotus and Syriac Inscriptions." In *The Church of the East in Central Asia and China*, edited by Samuel N. C. Lieu and Glen L. Thompson, 177–88. China and the Mediterranean World 1. Turnhout: Brepols, 2022.

Old Book of Tang (selection). In *Sources of Chinese Tradition*, vol. 1, edited by William Theodore De Bary, Wing-tsit Chan, and Burton Watson, 379–82. Records of Civilization: Sources and Studies. New York: Columbia University Press, 1964,

Olson, Ted. "Did Apostles Go to China?" *Christianity Today* blog, October 7, 2002. https://www. christianitytoday.com/ct/2002/october7/19.14.html.

Otto, Bishop of Freising. *The Two Cities: A Chronicle of Universal History to the Year 1146 A. D.* Translated by Charles C. Mierow. New York: Columbia University Press, 1928.

Palmer, Martin. *The Jesus Sutras: Rediscovering the Lost Scrolls of Taoist Christianity.* New York: Ballantine Books, 2001.

Paolillo, Maurizio. "In Search of King George." In *Hidden Treasures and Intercultural Encounters*, edited by Dietmar W. Winkler and Li Tang, 241–55. Orientalia-Patristica-Oecumenica 1. Vienna: LIT Verlag, 2009.

Pelliot, Paul. *L'inscription Nestorienne de Si-Ngan-Fou.* Edited by Antonino Forte. Kyoto: Scuola di studi sull'Asia orientale; Paris: Collège de France Institut des Hautes Etudes Chinoises, 1996.

———. *Notes on Marco Polo.* 2 vols. Ouvrage Posthume. Paris: A. Maisonneuve (Imprimerie Nationale), 1959, 1963.

Perrier, Pierre, and Xavier Walter. *Thomas Fonde l'Église en Chine (65–68 Ap J.-C.).* Paris: Jubilé, 2008.

Pulleyblank, Edwin. *The Background of the Rebellion of An Lu-Shan.* Oxford: Oxford University Press, 1955.

———. *Middle Chinese: A Study in Historical Phonology.* Vancouver: University of British Columbia Press, 1984.

————. *Outline of Classical Chinese Grammar*. Vancouver: University of British Columbia Press, 1995.

Rachewiltz, Igor de. *The Secret History of the Mongols: A Mongolian Epic Chronicle of the Thirteenth Century*. New ed. 2 vols. Leiden: Brill, 2006.

Renaudot, Eusebius. *Ancient Accounts of India and China by Two Mohammedan Travellers Who Went to Those Parts in the 9th Century*. London: Samuel Harding, 1733. Reprint, New Delhi: Asian Educational Services, 1995.

Riegert, Ray, and Thomas Moore. *The Lost Sutras of Jesus: Unlocking the Ancient Wisdom of the Xian Monks*. Berkeley, CA: Seastone, 2003.

Robinet, Isabelle. *Taoism: Growth of a Religion*. Translated by Phyllis Brooks. Stanford, CA: Stanford University Press, 1997.

Rong Xinjiang. *Eighteen Lectures on Dunhuang*. Translated by Imre Galambos. Leiden: Brill, 2013.

Royel, Bishop Mar Awa. *Mysteries of the Kingdom: The Sacraments of the Assyrian Church of the East*. Modesto, CA: Edessa Publications, 2011.

Ryan, James D. "Christian Wives of Mongol Khans: Tartar Queens and Missionary Expectations in Asia." *Journal of the Royal Asiatic Society* 8, no. 3 (1998): 411–21.

Saeki, Yoshirō. *The Nestorian Documents and Relics in China*. 2nd ed. Tokyo: Toho Bunkwa Gakuin/Academy of Oriental Culture, Tokyo Institute, 1951.

————. *The Nestorian Monument in China*. London: SPCK, 1916.

Shelton, W. Brian. *Quest for the Historical Apostles: Tracing Their Lives and Legacies*. Grand Rapids: Baker Books, 2018.

Silverberg, Robert. *The Realm of Prester John*. Athens: Ohio University Press, 1996.

Spuler, Bertold. *History of the Mongols: Based on Eastern and Western Accounts of the Thirteenth and Fourteenth Centuries*. Translated from the German by Helga and Stuart Drummond. Berkeley: University of California Press, 1972.

Stang, Charles M. "The 'Nestorian' (Jingjiao) Monument and Its Theology of the Cross." In *Syriac in Its Multi-Cultural Context*, edited by Herman G. B. Tuele, 107–18. Leuven: Peeters, 2017.

Stewart, Charles A. "Iconography of Syriac Gravestones in Kyrgyzstan and Kazakhstan." In *Silk Road Traces*, edited by Li Tang and Dietmar W. Winkler, 145–81. Orientalia-Patristica-Oecumenica 21. Vienna: LIT Verlag, 2022.

Sun Jianqiang, "Redating the Seven Early Chinese Christian Manuscripts: Christians in Dunhuang before 1100." PhD diss., Leiden University, 2018.

Swartz, Wendy, Robert Ford, Yang Lu, and Jessey Choo, eds. *Early Medieval China: A Sourcebook*. New York: Columbia University Press, 2014.

Takahashi, Hidemi. "Representation of the Syriac Language in Jingjiao and Yelikewen Documents." In *The Church of the East in Central Asia and China*, edited by Samuel N. C. Lieu and Glen L. Thompson, 23–92. China and the Mediterranean World 1. Turnhout: Brepols, 2020.

Tang Li. *East Syriac Christianity in Mongol-Yuan China*. Orientalia Biblica et Christiana 18. Wiesbaden: Harrassowitz, 2011.

———. "A Preliminary Study on the *Jingjiao* Inscription of Luoyang: Text Analysis, Commentary and English Translation." In *Hidden Treasures and Intercultural Encounters*, edited by Dietmar W. Winkler and Li Tang, 109–32. Orientalia-Patristica-Oecumenica 1. Vienna: LIT Verlag, 2009.

———. "Rediscovering the Ongut King George: Remarks on a Newly Excavated Archaeological Site." In *From the Oxus River to the Chinese Shores*, edited by Li Tang and Dietmar W. Winkler, 255–66. Orientalia-Patristica-Oecumenica 5. Vienna: LIT Verlag, 2013.

———. "Sorkaktani Beki: A Prominent Nestorian Woman at the Mongol Court." In *Jingjiao: The Church of the East in China and Central Asia*, edited by Roman Malek, 349–55. Collectanea Serica. Sankt Augustin, Germany: Instituta Monumenta Serica, 2006.

———. *A Study of the History of Nestorian Christianity in China and Its Literature in Chinese: Together with a New English Translation of the Dunhuang Nestorian Documents*. 2nd rev. ed. Frankfurt am Main: Lang, 2004.

Tang Li and Dietmar W. Winkler, eds. *Artifact, Text, Context*. Orientalia-Patristica-Oecumenica 17. Vienna: LIT, 2020.

———, eds. *From the Oxus River to the Chinese Shores*. Orientalia-Patristica-Oecumenica 5. Vienna: LIT Verlag, 2013.

———, eds. *Silk Road Traces*. Orientalia-Patristica-Oecumenica 21. Vienna: LIT Verlag, 2022.

———, eds. *Winds of Jingjiao*. Orientalia-Patristica-Oecumenica 9. Vienna: LIT Verlag, 2016.

Taveirne, Patrick. "The Study of the Ordos 'Nestorian Bronze Crosses': Status Quaestionis." In *The Church of the East in Central Asia and China*, edited by Samuel N. C. Lieu and Glen L. Thompson, 213–33. China and the Mediterranean World 1. Turnhout: Brepols, 2020.

Thompson, Glen L. "The Cross and Jingjiao Theology." In *Silk Road Traces*, edited by Li Tang and Dietmar W. Winkler, 355–74. Orientalia-Patristica-Oecumenica 21. Vienna: LIT Verlag, 2022.

———. "Did Christianity (or St. Thomas) Come to First-Century China?" In *Byzantium to China: Religion, History, and Culture on the Silk Roads; Studies in Honour of Samuel N. C. Lieu*, edited by K. Parry and G. Mikkelsen, 519–45. Texts and Studies in Eastern Christianity. Leiden: Brill, 2022.

———. "France and the Study of China and Its Religions," In *French Perceptions of Religious and Philosophical Thought in Qing China*, edited by Florian Knothe. Hong Kong: Hong Kong University Press, forthcoming.

———. "How the Jingjiao Became Nestorian." In *From the Oxus River to the Chinese Shores*, edited by Li Tang and Dietmar W. Winkler, 417–39. Orientalia-Patristica-Oecumenica 5. Vienna: LIT Verlag, 2013.

———. "The Structure of the Stele." In *Artifact, Text, Context*, edited by Li Tang and Dietmar W. Winkler, 161–93. Orientalia-Patristica-Oecumenica 17. Vienna: LIT, 2020.

———. "Was Alopen a Missionary?" In *Hidden Treasures and Intercultural Encounters*, edited by Dietmar W. Winkler and Li Tang, 267–78. Orientalia-Patristica-Oecumenica 1. Vienna: LIT Verlag, 2009.

Togan, İsenbike. *Flexibility and Limitation in Steppe Formations: The Kerait Khanate and Chinggis Khan*. Ottoman Empire and Its Heritage 15. Leiden: Brill, 1998.

Twitchett, Denis, ed. *Sui and T'ang China, 589–906, Part 1*. Vol. 3 of *The Cambridge History of China*. Cambridge: Cambridge University Press, 1979.

Vogel, Hans Ulrich. *Marco Polo Was in China: New Evidence from Currencies, Salts, and Revenues*. Leiden: Brill, 2013.

Wang Yuanyuan. "Doubt on the Viewpoint of the Extinction of Jingjiao in China after the Tang Dynasty." In *From the Oxus River to the Chinese Shores*, edited by Li Tang and Dietmar W. Winkler, 279–96. Orientalia-Patristica-Oecumenica 5. Vienna: LIT Verlag, 2013.

Wechsler, Howard. "Tai-tsung (Reign 626–49) the Consolidator." In *Sui and T'ang China, 589–906, Part 1*, vol. 3 of *The Cambridge History of China*, edited by Denis Twitchett, 188–241. Cambridge: Cambridge University Press, 1979.

Weinstein, Stanley. *Buddhism under the T'ang*. Cambridge: Cambridge University Press, 1987.

Weng Shao Jun. *Sino-Nestorian Documents: Commentary and Exegesis*. Chinese Academic Library of Christian Thought in History. Hong Kong: Institute of Sino-Christian Studies, 1995.

Whitby, Michael, and Mary Whitby. *The History of Theophylact Simocatta*. Oxford: Clarendon, 1986.

William of Rubruck. *Itineraria*. In *Itinera et Relationes Fratrum Minorum Saeculi XIII et XIV*, vol. 1, *Sinica Franciscana*, edited by A. Wyngaert. Ad Claras Aquas (Quaracchi-Firenze): apud Collegium s. Bonaventurae, 1929.

Wilmshurst, David. *Bar Hebraeus the Ecclesiastical Chronicle: An English Translation*. Gorgias Eastern Christian Studies 40. Piscataway, NJ: Gorgias, 2016.

———. *The Martyred Church: A History of the Church of the East*. London: East & West Publishing, 2011.

———. "A Monument to the Spread of the Syrian Brilliant Teaching in China." In "Stele on the Diffusion of Christianity (The Luminous Religion) from Rome (Da Qin) into China (The Middle Kingdom), 'The Nestorian Monument,'" by Lance Eccles and Samuel N. C. Lieu, 63–78. March 26, 2022, http://www .unionacademique.org/content/files/10362790247079243.pdf.

Winkler, Dietmar W., and Li Tang, eds. *Hidden Treasures and Intercultural Encounters*. Orientalia-Patristica-Oecumenica 1. Vienna: LIT Verlag, 2009.

Wright, Arthur F. *The Sui Dynasty*. New York: Knopf, 1978.

Wylie, Alexander. "On the Nestorian Tablet of Se-Gan Foo." *Journal of the American Oriental Society* 5 (1855–1856): 275–336.

Wyngaert, Anastasius van den, ed. *Itinera et Relationes Fratrum Minorum Saeculi XIII et XIV*. Vol. 1, *Sinica Franciscana*. Ad Claras Aquas (Quaracchi-Firenze): apud Collegium s. Bonaventurae, 1929.

Yeates, Thomas. *Indian Church History . . . with an Accurate Relation of the First Christian Missions in China*. London: A. Maxwell, 1818.

Yin Xiaoping. "The Institution of Chongfu Si of the Yuan Dynasty." In *Winds of Jingjiao*, edited by Li Tang and Dietmar W. Winkler, 311–31. Orientalia-Patristica-Oecumenica 9. Vienna: LIT Verlag, 2016.

———. "On the Christians in Jiangnan during the Yuan Dynasty according to 'The Gazeteer of Zhenjiang of the Zhishun Period' 1329–1332." In *Hidden Treasures and Intercultural Encounters*, edited by Dietmar W. Winkler and Li Tang, 305–19. Orientalia-Patristica-Oecumenica 1. Vienna: LIT Verlag, 2009.

Zhang Naizhu. "Note on a Nestorian Stone Inscription from the Tang Dynasty Unearthed in Luoyang." In *Precious Nestorian Relic: Studies on the Nestorian Stone Pillar of the Tang Dynasty Recently Discovered in Luoyang*, edited by Ge Chengyong, 17–33. Beijing: Wenwu chubanshe, 2009.

Zhang Xiaogui. "Why Did Chinese Christians Name Their Religion Jingjiao." In *Winds of Jingjiao*, edited by Dietmar Winkler and Li Tang, 283–309. Orientalia-Patristica-Oecumenica 9. Vienna: LIT Verlag, 2016,

Zürcher, Erich. *The Buddhist Conquest of China. The Spread and Adaptation of Buddhism in Early Medieval China*. 2 vols. Reprint with additions and corrections. Sinica Leidensia 11. Leiden: Brill, 1972.

INDEX

Names on the stele are included only if they have additional descriptors beyond such terms as "priest" or "monk."